"Building on their earlier book (*Deliv* Collett join with Fergus McNeill to pro rehabilitation than the narrow correctio...... and much academic research. Rehabilitation and desistance must involve a great deal more than the interventions of criminal justice, but call on the responsibilities of the state and the community. The authors have written a book that combines academic rigour and a compelling political critique to show that, ultimately, questions about punishment and rehabilitation are questions about the kinds of society we want to live in and to strive for."

**Prof. Rob Canton**, *De Montfort University, UK*

"Rehabilitation is buried, then resurrected, with the regularity of a zombie, but what the rehabilitative ideal needs is not another undead awakening but rather a complete reimagination. In this essential new vision, Burke, Collett and McNeill get us closer than ever before to a truly holistic concept of rehabilitation that transcends the individual-blaming of the risk model. We may be closer than ever to realising a vision of justice that is worthy of the name."

**Prof. Shadd Maruna**, *author of* Making Good:
How Ex-Convicts Reform and Rebuild Their Lives

"Despite a significant resurgence of interest in rehabilitation at the policy level in a number of jurisdictions, there have been surprisingly few attempts to outline a vision of what is needed to make this a reality for those caught up in offending and the criminal justice apparatus. This timely book delivers on that with a sophisticated and thoughtful analysis of what an effective rehabilitation strategy might look like. I recommend *Reimagining Rehabilitation* to students, practitioners, scholars and policy makers everywhere."

**Gwen Robinson**, *Reader in Criminal Justice,*
*University of Sheffield, UK*

"Going back to at least the birth of the penitentiary, scholars, policy-makers, and the public have debated the ideal form and functions of punishment. Rehabilitation has been lost, declared dead, and discovered anew. Burke, Collette, and McNeill's *Reimagining Rehabilitation* breathes new life into this enduring debate, providing an imaginative vision for twenty-first-century criminal justice. Rather than a narrow criminology oriented towards reducing risk and reoffending, the authors develop a model of personal, legal, moral, and social rehabilitation that can improve the lives of justice-involved individuals – and, in the process, redeem our democratic ideals."

**Prof. Michelle S. Phelps**, *University of Minnesota, USA*

# REIMAGINING REHABILITATION

This book aims to make the case for and provide some of the resources necessary to reimagine rehabilitation for twenty-first-century criminal justice. Outlining an approach to rehabilitation which takes into account wider democratic processes, political structures and mechanisms of resource allocation, the authors develop a new model of rehabilitation comprising four forms – personal, legal, social and moral.

Personal rehabilitation concerns how individuals make their journeys away from offending and towards reintegration and how they can be supported to do so, whilst legal rehabilitation concerns the role of the criminal courts in the process of restricting and then restoring the rights and status of citizens. Moral rehabilitation is concerned with the ethical basis of the interactions between the individual who has offended and the people and organisations charged with providing rehabilitative services. Social rehabilitation explores the crucial contribution civil society can make to rehabilitation, exploring this through the lens of citizenship, community and social capital.

Drawing on the conceptual insights offered in the late Stan Cohen's seminal work – *Visions of Social Control* – and specifically his insistence that modern social institutions can aspire to doing good and doing justice, the authors argue that these values can underpin a moral pragmatism in designing social interventions that must go beyond achieving simply instrumental ends. Reimagining rehabilitation within the context of social action and social justice, this book is essential reading for students and scholars alike, particularly those engaged with criminal justice policy, probation and offender rehabilitation.

**Lol Burke** is Professor in Criminal Justice at Liverpool John Moores University and specialises in the areas of probation research, policy and practice. He has a particular interest in the way that occupational culture acts out in probation settings and resettlement provision for released prisoners. As a former probation practitioner, he has considerable experience working in both community and custodial settings.

**Steve Collett** worked for three North West probation areas across four decades, retiring from the Cheshire Probation Trust in December 2010 after ten years as its chief officer. He is an Honorary Fellow within the Department of Sociology, Social Policy and Criminology at Liverpool University, an Honorary Reader in Criminology within the School of Law at Manchester University, and an Honorary Fellow of Liverpool John Moores University.

**Fergus McNeill** is Professor of Criminology and Social Work at the University of Glasgow where he works in the Scottish Centre for Crime and Justice Research and in Sociology. Prior to becoming an academic in 1998, Fergus worked for a number of years in residential drug rehabilitation and as a criminal justice social worker.

# REIMAGINING REHABILITATION

## Beyond the Individual

*Lol Burke, Steve Collett and Fergus McNeill*

Routledge
Taylor & Francis Group

LONDON AND NEW YORK

First published 2019
by Routledge
2 Park Square, Milton Park, Abingdon, Oxon OX14 4RN

and by Routledge
711 Third Avenue, New York, NY 10017

*Routledge is an imprint of the Taylor & Francis Group, an informa business*

*British Library Cataloguing-in-Publication Data*
A catalogue record for this book is available from the British Library

*Library of Congress Cataloging-in-Publication Data*
Names: Burke, Lol, author. | Collett, Steve, author. | McNeill,
    Fergus, author.
Title: Reimagining rehabilitation : beyond the individual / Lol Burke,
    Steve Collett and Fergus McNeill.
Description: 1 Edition. | New York : Routledge, 2019. | Includes
    bibliographical references and index.
Identifiers: LCCN 2018022752| ISBN 9781138233171 (hardback) |
    ISBN 9781138233188 (pbk.) | ISBN 9781315310176 (ebook)
Subjects: LCSH: Criminals—Rehabilitation—Great Britain. | Criminal
    justice, Administration of—Great Britain.
Classification: LCC HV9345.A5 B873 2019 | DDC 365/.6610941—dc23
LC record available at https://lccn.loc.gov/2018022752


ISBN: 978-1-138-23317-1 (hbk)
ISBN: 978-1-138-23318-8 (pbk)
ISBN: 978-1-315-31017-6 (ebk)


Typeset in Bembo
by Swales & Willis Ltd, Exeter, Devon, UK

LB: For Sandra, Daniel, Megan and to all those learning together.
SJC: In memory of Colette Feenan and David Feenan and for Mini, 'Arry and Pixie.
FMcN: For John and everyone else who, like me, needs second and third and fourth chances.

# CONTENTS

# FIGURES

# TABLES

# ABOUT THE AUTHORS

**Lol Burke** is Professor in Criminal Justice at Liverpool John Moores University and specialises in the areas of probation research, policy and practice. He has a particular interest in the way that occupational culture acts out in probation settings and resettlement provision for released prisoners. As a former probation practitioner, he has considerable experience working in both community and custodial settings. He has an extensive publication record in probation related matters. These include co-authored monographs *Delivering Rehabilitation: The Politics, Governance and Control of Probation* (Burke and Collett 2015) and *Redemption, Rehabilitation and Risk Management* (Mair and Burke 2011), chapters in seven edited collections, and over 30 published outputs in refereed journals and professional publications. He has nationally/internationally recognised external engagement activities and achievements across a wide range of professional and governmental bodies, including Napo, The Howard League, and the Probation Institute. He was editor of *Probation Journal* from 2007 to 2016 and is on the editorial board of the *European Journal of Probation*. He is a Fellow of the HEA.

**Steve Collett** worked for three North West probation areas across four decades, retiring from the Cheshire Probation Trust in December 2010 after ten years as its chief officer. He also taught social work and social policy in further/higher education in the early 1980s before returning to Probation to take up a joint appointment with Merseyside Probation and Liverpool University (1987–1991). Steve has been an Honorary Fellow within the Department of Sociology, Social Policy and Criminology since then and following his retirement in 2011, he was made an Honorary Reader in Criminology within the School of Law at Manchester University. In 2012, he was made an Honorary Fellow of Liverpool John Moores University. Steve has been a member of the *Probation Journal* Editorial Board for over 20 years. He is a trustee of two Merseyside charities who work with service users including those who are subject to criminal justice sanctions, and he chairs the Rhodes Trust which provides bursaries for probation staff to study features of criminal justice jurisdictions abroad.

**Fergus McNeill** is Professor of Criminology and Social Work at the University of Glasgow where he works in the Scottish Centre for Crime and Justice Research and in Sociology. Prior to becoming an academic in 1998, Fergus worked for a number of years in residential drug rehabilitation and as a criminal justice social worker. His many research projects and publications have examined institutions, cultures and practices of punishment and rehabilitation and their alternatives. Currently, Fergus is working on two major projects: 'Distant Voices: Coming Home' is a major, multi-partner, three-year Economic and Social Research Council/Arts and Humanities Research Council project exploring reintegration after punishment through creative practices and research methods, in particular song-writing and sharing. *Pervasive Punishment* is a British Academy funded Mid-Career Fellowship which critically examines the emergence and contours of 'mass supervision' and how we might best respond to it.

# ACKNOWLEDGEMENTS

The idea for this book came from Tom Sutton, Senior Editor (Criminology) at Routledge and his encouragement to follow up the publication of *Delivering Rehabilitation* (Burke and Collett 2015). He suggested that we should build on but move beyond the critical analysis of recent government policy towards the Probation Service of England and Wales and consider what rehabilitation reimagined might look like broadly within the same jurisdiction. It seemed to us (Lol and Steve) that Fergus's model of *four forms of 'offender' rehabilitation* (McNeill 2012, 2014), provided the perfect structure and potential for a re-conceptualisation of rehabilitation that reflected our knowledge and experience of criminal justice and rehabilitation; one that, crucially, would also allow us to move beyond the individual. So, we invited Fergus to co-author this book with us, developing and applying his model. For Fergus, this meant writing two books in parallel, since he was already embarked on writing *Pervasive Punishment: Making sense of mass supervision* (to be published by Emerald). Whereas this book is consciously rooted in England and Wales and is decidedly prescriptive in its intention to reimagine rehabilitation, *Pervasive Punishment* offers a sociological analysis of how and why 'mass supervision' has emerged in certain jurisdictions and of how and why it might be resisted. The two projects are clearly comple-mentary but distinct, and might best be seen as companion volumes.

As a trio of co-authors, our respective experiences and academic influences have shaped our individual contributions to this work but hopefully not in a way that undermines its overall coherence. We also hope we have done justice to the work of those whose scholarship has clearly influenced us and to whom we owe a debt of gratitude. Our overall approach, however, has been to attempt to reimagine rehabilitation in a way that not only takes account of the lived experience of individuals swept up within the *penal net* but that also reflects the courage and imagination that individuals show in beginning and maintaining their personal journeys towards a better life, often in the most disadvantaged, unjust and discriminatory circumstances.

We know of many individuals struggling against the pernicious and demoralising policies of the State to either remove the right to benefits, housing and health services or to ration access to these services by design or neglect. In both our personal and professional lives, we talk to individuals whose lives (and those of their families) are deeply affected by unnecessary imprisonment. Yet, we see those undermined in this way engaging, for example, in imaginative art and music projects, engaging with university students through shared education projects or attending women's centres to help both themselves and those in similar positions to reimagine their own futures. The personal, legal, moral and social efforts made by individuals to turn their lives round – and by many others to support them – is humbling. To all these people we dedicate this book.

It is our family and friends who withstand the worst of our preoccupations when undertaking a joint project of this sort. We acknowledge and thank them for their forbearance. We also want to think Hannah Catterall, Editorial Assistant at Routledge, for her support and encouragement.

# ABBREVIATIONS

ACSL    Average Custodial Sentence length
BCM     Better Case Management
CCTV    Closed-Circuit Television
CJ Act  Criminal Justice Act
CRC     Community Rehabilitation Company
DWP     Department for Work and Pensions
EBP     Evidence-Based Practice
EM      Electronic Monitoring
GPS     Global Positioning System
HMIP    Her Majesty's Inspectorate of Probation
HMP     Her Majesty's Prison
ICT     Information and Communication Technology
NAO     National Audit Office
Napo    National Association of Probation Officers
NLCJC   North Liverpool Community Justice Centre
NOMS    National Offender Management Service
NPM     New Public Management
NPS     National Probation Service
OBP     Offending Behaviour Programme
ODPM    Office of Deputy Prime Minister
OED     Oxford English Dictionary
PbR     Payment by Results
PCC     Police and Crime Commissioner
PSR     Pre-Sentence Report
RF      Radio Frequency
RNR     Risk, Needs and Responsivity

SEED       Skills for Effective Engagement and Development
STICS      Strategic Training Initiative in Community Supervision
TSJ        Transforming Summary Justice
TUPE       Transfer of Undertakings (Protection of Employment)
VCS        Voluntary and Community Sector

# 1

## INTRODUCTION

### What's wrong with contemporary rehabilitation and why do we want to change it?

This book aims to make a case for and provide some of the resources necessary for reimagining rehabilitation for the twenty-first century. Yet the term *rehabilitation*, at least in its criminal justice related uses, is both ubiquitous and ambiguous, so poorly understood and so vulnerable to misappropriation that, even as we begin, we hesitate. Throughout its history, rehabilitation has been discussed and debated as a process (to rehabilitate, to *do* rehabilitation) and, simultaneously, as a state or an outcome (to *be* or *become* rehabilitated). At different times and in different places, it has been freighted with the baggage of and/or lifted on the wings of theology, ideology and science. It has been concerned with individual *character* or *personality*, as well as with human *rights* and *social justice*. The discourse of rehabilitation has been used to justify everything from political re-programming to castration to aversion therapy to education to family contact to the provision of housing and work.

Later in this chapter and throughout the book, we will have more to say about definitions, forms, models and contexts of rehabilitation, both historically and in the present day. Here, at the outset, we want simply to acknowledge the vagaries of the term and to recognise the need to develop some precision about the different aspects of rehabilitation that this book aims to address and those that it must neglect. We also need to recognise that our illustrations and preoccupations will – to a certain extent – reflect our own histories and our current locations in time and place. The prequel to this book was concerned principally with *Delivering Rehabilitation* in the context of reforming probation services in England and Wales (Burke and Collett 2015). We make no apology for retaining the focus on probation in this volume. If punishment and rehabilitation have been most studied in prisons and jails, we are glad to contribute to redressing the balance. As Robinson *et al.* (2013) point out, most punishment and (we would add) most rehabilitation takes place in the community; in mainland Britain, the number of people undergoing community sentences outnumbers those in custody by more than 3:1. The same is true of the USA (Phelps 2013) and many European jurisdictions (Aebi *et al.* 2015).

Bearing that in mind, although scholars have recently discussed and debated the emergence of *mass supervision* in Europe (McNeill 2012a; McNeill and Beyens 2013) and *mass probation* in the USA (Phelps 2013), we make no apologies for focusing our attention on the jurisdiction that we (or at least two of us: Burke and Collett) know best – England and Wales. Unquestionably, that jurisdiction has wielded disproportionate influence globally in the development of probation practices and services; for example, even today, many jurisdictions are following with great interest (and some alarm) the privatisation of much probation work in England and Wales. Accordingly, we hope that by illustrating our argument primarily with reference to England and Wales (and to a lesser extent, with reference to their very differently constituted and inclined neighbour, Scotland) we will entice rather than alienate readers from further afield. Certainly, we hope that the arguments we offer will resonate in and contribute to debates elsewhere. But let us begin where we are, even if only to move beyond the tyranny of the here and now.

## Here and now

> Most prisoners serving short sentences had multiple and complex needs. Basic custody screenings, completely at the start of sentence, by HM Prison staff, drew only on what the prisoner had said and were a wholly inadequate basis for resettlement planning. The National Offender Management Service guidance for completion of these initial screenings did not promote depth or quality. Resettlement plans, completed by CRC staff within five working days of the screening, did not address the most urgent resettlement needs. In too many cases, resettlement planning consisted of no more than referrals to other agencies, recorded as completed once an email had been sent.
>
> *(Criminal Justice Joint Inspection 2016: 7)*

> She just seemed to have the answers . . . Time was never an issue . . . I mean I carried on seeing her for three months after my probation order ran out . . . I could just talk about things with her that I couldn't talk about with anyone else . . . things that happened during my time in the army. I could be honest with her . . . You know she, yeah I could tell her the truth and she was never, she never judged, which most people do. But no she was brilliant.
>
> *(abridged from Farrall et al. 2014: 129)*

Even outside the confines of the academic community, parliament, government departments and delivery organisations, the appetite for discussing crime, the process of criminal justice and the treatment of those who appear before the courts appears to be insatiable. Whilst much public attention, usually fanned by the news media, is focused on high-profile, shocking or lurid crimes and those who commit them, there is, perhaps, some evidence of a subtle change in the way in which the public is beginning to perceive issues of criminal justice and the challenges of rehabilitation. This reflects a number of trends in wider social and political life but we suspect it also has something to do with a neoliberal ascendancy that seems to have – for the moment at least – won the battle to commodify the rehabilitative resources and structure of the Probation Service in England and Wales, extracting profit for the private sector, at the same time re-shaping practical approaches to the supervision of individual offenders and promising efficiency and effectiveness. What then are the public to make of the quote above, in which a local Community Rehabilitation Company (CRC), in this case Derbyshire, attracts significant criticism (HM Inspectorate of Probation 2016) when, in its previous life as a Probation Trust, Derbyshire was a publicly acknowledged success as were the 34 similar Trusts that made up the National Probation Service before the advent of *Transforming Rehabilitation* (see Ministry of Justice 2013a, 2013b; National Offender Management Service 2013)?

The early signs, just over four years on from the June 2014 introduction of the new arrangements in England and Wales for community supervision and prisoner resettlement, are clearly worrying. Recently, HM Inspectorate of Probation (2017) published a highly critical report about the service provided to sentencers under the new arrangements and in the same year the National Audit Office (2017), when reviewing concerns about the financial arrangements and capacities of the CRCs, also commented that by the end of June 2017 two-thirds of the performance targets set for CRCs by the Ministry of Justice had not been met. In 2018 HM Inspectorate of Probation also highlighted the failure of CRCs to meet the much cherished ambition for greater involvement of the voluntary sector in direct service delivery and the engagement of volunteers as mentors for individuals who have offended. Alongside these and equally dispiriting, as the above quote from the Criminal Justice Joint Inspection highlights, was the poor start to the (Conservative) UK government's flagship *through the gate initiative* based on the re-organisation of the prison estate in November 2014 to designate 89 of the 120 prisons in England and Wales as *resettlement prisons* intended to deliver a seamless service for short-term prisoners. As the quote suggests, there is evidence that (under the *fee for service* arrangements) individuals have become the objects of procedures rather than human subjects of supervision. Compare the *email* determination of an onward referral as a *successful outcome* with the person talking to eminent researcher Stephen Farrall about his experience of probation supervision. Here, the supervising officer responds to this person's needs even when the order had terminated because he still required her help on the journey to desistance from crime. As Ben Crewe has warned, the legitimacy of the system is undermined 'if it appears to operate for its own sake while ignoring real needs, or if it pursues targets as ends in themselves' (2007: 225). One of the questions we will try to tackle in this book will be this: What does an informed public who pay for rehabilitative services through taxation – whether delivered through private or public organisations – want: punishment through *payment by results* (PbR) or reha-bilitation through skilled engagement between worker and the individual who has offended or both or something in between?

This introductory salvo is not intended to preface yet another sociopoliti-cal critique of the commodified approach to delivering rehabilitation that has been gaining momentum under New Labour, Coalition and Tory administra-tions over the past four decades (McCulloch and McNeill 2007). Indeed, from Garland's (2001) masterly analysis of the demise of the *post-war settlement*, the collapse of *penal welfarism* and the advent of a *Culture of Control* through to less ambitious but more recent analyses of British criminal justice policy and politi-cal developments (Mair and Burke 2012; Burke and Collett 2015, 2016), the fragmentation of a unified Probation Service in England and Wales has been critically anticipated for some time. Furthermore, both public and professional attitudes to people who offend and the detailed delivery of rehabilitative ser-vices have changed to both accommodate and reflect continuous shifts in penal politics and policies.

In *Delivering Rehabilitation*, two of us, noting some progress within a deeply critical and pessimistic view of the future of rehabilitation under current neoliberal thinking, reflected the same concerns:

> What we hope our work has demonstrated, nevertheless, [is] that academics and practitioners have joined forces over the past decade or more to reimag-ine rehabilitation as a process that benefits those who offend and those who do not. It now requires our political leaders to do likewise and reimagine a world where social and economic equality brings us all closer together.
>
> *(Burke and Collett 2015:189)*

Our joint focus then and the motivation for undertaking this new work is an attempt to move beyond simply understanding why people offend and how to control crime and towards a better synthesis of the literatures across academic and research disciplines that illuminates the journeys individuals travel to stop offending and find their way towards participation and inclusion in society – and crucially, what is known about how to best support *them* (and *us*) to do so. This book will argue that rights and responsibilities apply to all citizens (not just those who hap-pen to have been successfully prosecuted for offending) and that the State and civil society also need to play their parts in enabling all of us to enjoy our rights and fulfil our shared and mutual obligations. This is not just a matter of individual capacities and motivations; it is about our shared commitments and about the social, eco-nomic and political infrastructure that creates and, conversely, limits opportunities. Therefore, we will consider not just how, why, when and with what sorts of help individuals change, but also wider democratic processes, political structures and mechanisms of resource allocation within which current modes of service delivery are taking place within England and Wales and beyond. In this sense, we take as our starting point the thinking and arguments contained within *Delivering Rehabilitation*

(Burke and Collett 2015) but aim to move beyond a critique of neoliberalism and some basic prescriptions about what is required to deliver rehabilitation to an attempt at *Reimagining Rehabilitation* within the context of broader social change, however hard this may be to achieve. What we are clear about is, first, that the failure of rehabilitation to secure political support can lead to excessive levels of coercion in the community and increased levels of imprisonment and, second, that practical and utopian ideas can and must exist together.

## Unravelling rehabilitation(s)[1]

Textbook discussions of rehabilitation tend to begin with dictionary definitions. Raynor and Robinson's (2009: 2) excellent book, for example, tells us that the Oxford English Dictionary defines rehabilitation as 'the action of restoring something to a previous (proper) condition or status'. So, rehabilitation is (1) an action that (2) restores (3) for the better. Raynor and Robinson (2009: 3) also note that the OED's supplementary definition refers to the 'restoration of a disabled person, a criminal etc., to some degree of normal life by appropriate training etc.'. This version adds the concepts of some (4) 'normal' standard, returning to which requires (5) some form of third-party intervention.

Despite the frequency with which rehabilitation has been discussed in the criminological literature (and, we might add, in policy and practice), the term is rarely 'unpacked' and critically examined. Raynor and Robinson (2009) provide the following example of a problematic criminological description of it:

> [T]aking away the desire to offend, is the aim of reformist or rehabilitative punishment. The objective of reform or rehabilitation is to reintegrate the offender into society after a period of punishment, and to design the content of the punishment so as to achieve this.
>
> *(Hudson 2003: 26)*

As Raynor and Robinson (2009) note, this statement raises a number of issues. First, there seem to be at least two objectives in play here: 'taking away the desire to offend' (that is, somehow changing the 'offender') and reintegration into society (that is, somehow changing his or her relationship with and status in society). But how are these two objectives related? Second, and more directly pertinent to this book, it suggests two different relationships between rehabilitation and punishment; in one rehabilitation comes *after punishment*, in another rehabilitation itself is seen as a distinct *form of punishment*. Considering probation's history, we might also suggest a third relationship, where rehabilitation (particularly in the community) is cast as an *alternative to punishment* (usually in prison).

In an effort to clarify some of these complexities, Raynor and Robinson (2009) go on to offer their own typology of perspectives on offender rehabilitation, examining the meanings and significance of correctional rehabilitation; rehabilitation and reform; reintegration and resettlement; and rehabilitation and the law.

Correctional rehabilitation, they argue, is concerned with effecting positive change in individuals. As such it is the model most commonly associated with treatment programmes or other forms of offence- or offender-focused intervention. At its heart is the notion that many offenders can change for the better, given the right support. The idea of correction implies that the 'offender' can and should be 'normalised' or 'resocialised' in line with commonly accepted (though rarely explicitly articulated) standards of behaviour. Raynor and Robinson make the critical but often neglected point that correctional rehabilitation comes in many forms; the variety of theories and methodologies about how 'correction' is to be achieved is almost as wide as the variety of theories about crime causation itself. That said, correctional rehabilitation, as its name suggests, tends to be preoccupied with fixing or changing 'offenders' themselves, and so is closely associated with theories and methods that explain crime and target intervention at the level of the individual.

Raynor and Robinson's (2009) discussion of rehabilitation and reform notes that some penal theorists and historians draw a distinction between twentieth-century *rehabilitation*, which was mostly concerned with individualistic (psychological) treatment programmes designed to correct the *personality* (or attitudes and behaviour), and *reform* which refers to an earlier preoccupation with offering opportunities for education and contemplation in support of reforming *moral character*. As a form of shorthand, we might say that religion is to reform as the 'psy' disciplines (psychiatry, psychology and social work) are to rehabilitation.

The terms 'reintegration' and 'resettlement' (or in the USA 're-entry') can also be connected with correctional rehabilitation, but they also extend beyond it; in a sense, they imply its objective. If correctional rehabilitation is seen as the journey, reintegration is the implied destination. Raynor and Robinson (2009) draw here on the work of Crow (2001) and others in suggesting that rehabilitation must lead to and involve restoring the ex-offender's status as a citizen and renegotiating his or her access to citizenship's privileges and responsibilities. Whereas correctional rehabilitation dwells on the individual and the psychological, a concern with 'reintegration and resettlement' signals the sociological aspects of rehabilitation; proponents of such an approach tend to have a sharper awareness of the social rather than the individual causes of crime and of the social rather than the individual issues at stake in desistance from crime. Moreover, rather than being a mode of punishment (or a method applied during punishment), this perspective tends to stress the need for rehabilitation to act as an antidote which seeks to address, compensate for or undo the adverse, usually unintended, collateral consequences of punishment itself. Rehabilitation in this vein is sometimes conceived a duty of the State that follows from its obligation to delimit punishment and to bring it to an end (Cullen and Gilbert 1982).

A natural (though again often neglected) corollary of the concern with reintegration and resettlement is a concern with rehabilitation and the law. The earliest use of the term 'rehabilitation' (at least in legal or criminal justice contexts), according to Raynor and Robinson (2009) was in late seventeenth-century France where it referred to the destruction or undoing of a criminal conviction; to the deletion or expunging of the criminal record. A century or so later, Cesare Beccaria (1764/1963) reflected a similar meaning of the term in arguing for the use of punishment as a way of 'requalifying individuals as . . . juridical subjects' (Foucault 1997: 130). In this sense, punishment itself rehabilitates by settling the putative debt that offending created. Rehabilitation was thus the end of punishment in both senses of the word; it was its proper objective and its final conclusion – the restoration of citizenship.

Raynor and Robinson's (2009) taxonomy helps us a great deal with unravelling the complexities of rehabilitation, but there are one or two further strands that we need to identify. First, it is worth stressing that the meanings of rehabilitation are historically, culturally and jurisdictionally conditioned. As we have already argued, the broadly correctional form of rehabilitation has been expressed in very different ways in different times and places. Two decades ago, Edgardo Rotman (1990), in a brilliant and brief introductory chapter to his book *Beyond Punishment*, summarised the history of rehabilitation as being represented in four successive models. The first two of these – the penitentiary model and the treatment model – correspond loosely to our discussion of reform and rehabilitation above. The penitentiary was seen as a place of confinement where the sinner was given the opportunity to reflect soberly on their behaviour, and on how to reform themselves (note 'reform' rather than 'rehabilitate'), perhaps with divine help. But this idea was supplanted progressively by a more scientific or medical model in which rehabilitation was understood as a form of treatment which could correct some flaw in individuals, whether physical or psychological, thus remedying the problem of their behaviour.

However, in the latter half of the twentieth century, this more medical or therapeutic version of rehabilitation was, according to Rotman, itself displaced to some extent, by a shift in emphasis towards a model based on social learning in which behaviours were understood as learned responses that could be unlearned. In this context rehabilitation was recast not as a sort of quasi-medical treatment for criminality but as the re-education of the poorly socialised (see also Garland 1985, 2001). Correctional rehabilitation's interventions may have remained individualised, but they changed to reflect new theories of crime causation and thus new forms of 'treatment'. This distinction between these two versions of correctional rehabilitation (as treatment or as social education) is important, partly because, as we will see in the next section, it was one that was and is often ignored by rehabilitation's critics.

## The fall and rise of rehabilitation

As Bottoms (1980) notes, one cause of rehabilitation's oft-discussed demise in the 1970s was that it came to be seen as being theoretically faulty. In sum, it seemed that rehabilitation had misconstrued the causes of crime as individual when they were coming to be understood as being principally social and structural and it misconstrued the nature of crime, failing to recognise the ways in which crime is itself socially constructed. Moreover, rehabilitative practices had begun to be exposed as being systematically discriminatory, targeting coercive interventions on the most poor and disadvantaged people in society. Rehabilitation was also coming to be seen as inconsistent with justice itself where judgements about liberty were unduly influenced by dubious and subjective professional judgements hidden from or impenetrable to the 'offender'. Through the development of the 'psy' disciplines, experts emerged with the supposed capacity to 'diagnose' what was wrong with the 'offender', who was cast as a victim of his or her lack of insight. By implication, unless and until the 'offender' was corrected by the expert, s/he could not be treated as a subject. It was argued that rehabilitation faced an associated and fundamental moral problem rooted in its attempts to (psychologically) coerce people to change. Finally, at the time when Bottoms was writing, the empirical evidence seemed to suggest that, despite its scientific pretensions, rehabilitation did not seem to work.

Powerful though it is, there are flaws in this critique. Crucially, emerging evidence about 'what works?' (McGuire 1995) played a vital role in challenging the last point; a new evidence base for rehabilitation developed from the 1980s onwards and negative assessments of earlier evidence were questioned and re-examined (McNeill *et al.* 2010). That said, new evidence about 'what works', in and of itself, did not and does not address the other four criticisms discussed above: the problems of crime theory, rehabilitation and injustice, dubious expertise and coerced correction. Contemporary rehabilitation theories perhaps have more in common with a social educational or social psychological than a treatment or medicalised version of correctional rehabilitation (on the distinction, see Johnstone 1996). But, even if rehabilitation is not now based on a strictly medical model, the full force of the criticisms Bottoms (1980) summarises are only partly deflected and, in this short introduction, we can attend to each these criticisms only very briefly.

Whilst contemporary correctional rehabilitation's underlying crime theories avoid the pathologising traps of individualistic positivism, they still have to engage somehow with the problem that crime is (at least in part) a social construct. We do not choose to pursue all interpersonal or social harms through criminalisation; therefore, the explanandum of crime theories is itself socially conditioned. That single insight has profound consequences. It affects and infuses the normative contexts of rehabilitative work (including raising difficult questions about who and what gets selected for penal 'correction' and who and what does not) and it creates a series of complex methodological quandaries about how to judge rehabilitation's effectiveness (see McNeill 2012b).

The problem of rehabilitation and injustice, or of rehabilitation's place in or association with discriminatory practices, remains a challenging one, though it is hardly a criticism that applies only to rehabilitation and not to other criminal justice practices. That said, the problem for rehabilitation is not just systematic (if unintended) biases in terms of who gets selected for 'correction' of which sorts and who gets defined as 'incorrigible', but also a more technical problem of the extent to which rehabilitation's resources (principally assessment tools and intervention approaches) are sufficiently sensitive to, for example, gender differences and cultural diversity (on which see, for example, Raynor 2007; Robinson and Crow 2009: Ch. 6). Significant though these problems are, they are problems about the proper administration of rehabilitation rather than the concept itself.

The problem of dubious expertise is only partly resolved by the development of a more robust evidence base for rehabilitation. Whilst it is true that contemporary approaches, perhaps to varying degrees, tend to formally recognise the need to treat people as active subjects in their own rehabilitation (and not simply as the passive objects of expert intervention), there remains considerable force in critiques both of the professional power of the 'psy' disciplines (e.g. Rose 1989) and, more specifically, of the increasing exercise of that power not in 'treatment' or 'therapeutic' decisions but in influencing decisions about justice itself, specifically in relation to sentencing or release decision-making. We will return to these problems below.

Of course, the enduring problem of coerced correction is closely related to that of dubious expertise; coercion is a problem exacerbated in systems where increasing confidence in rehabilitation's effectiveness has coincided with the development of a *toughening up* of penal policy. As we will see in Chapter 4, one morally problematic consequence of this conjunction in England and Wales was the withdrawal of any requirement for consent to accredited programme conditions within community sentences. These programmes therefore involve rehabilitative treatment without consent; a development that seems to have come to pass without much critique from psychologists or probation staff whose ethical standards it might seem to compromise. Though it might be said that all punishment is coercive, coercion seems to be a particular problem for correctional rehabilitation, since it seeks to change the individual rather than simply to restrain, confine or otherwise punish him or her. That suggests a particular form of intrusion into the inner world, even the identity of the subject, in respect of which coercion raises particular moral problems (Lewis 1953).

Fortunately, Bottoms (1980) also provided some suggestions about how we might best respond to these problems. Reflecting the pessimism of the times, four of his five options imply or require a shift away from rehabilitation, at least as traditionally conceived. However, he also argued that rehabilitation could be rescued through its own correction; that is, by attending more carefully to questions of consent, by committing adequate resources to make it more likely to be effective and by conducting rehabilitative activities in ways which are more respectful of liberty. More specifically, we could ensure that the intrusions that rehabilitation imposes on its subjects are never greater than is merited by their offending behaviour, placing rehabilitative requirements within the envelope of proportionality. These are proposals to which we will return in various chapters of this book.

There is no space here to properly review the renaissance of rehabilitation in the 1980s and 1990s and, in any case, this has become a familiar story at least to readers interested in criminology and probation (see Raynor and Robinson 2009; Robinson 2008). However, leaving aside this well-known tale of the advancement of the evidence base, it is worth recalling that there was also, in the 1980s, a brief flurry of writing about new normative or philosophical approaches to rehabilitation, including Rotman's (1990) work (see also Cullen and Gilbert 1982). The 'new rehabilitationists' (see Lewis 2005), much as Bottoms suggested, proposed four principles to guide rights-based rehabilitation: the assertion of the duty of the State to provide for rehabilitation; the establishment of proportional limits on the intrusions opposed; the principle of maximising choice and voluntarism in the process; and a commitment to using prison as a measure of last resort. Once again, these are important principles with which we agree and to which we will return.

However, as Robinson (2008) has cogently argued, in policy and practice (in England and Wales at least) what emerged at the end of the twentieth century was not a more rights-based but a more profoundly utilitarian and correctional form of rehabilitation increasingly influenced by the preoccupation with public protection and risk reduction. Under this paradigm, probation officers were required to intervene with or treat the offender to reduce reoffending and to protect the public. What is critical about this shift in focus was that the 'client' or intended beneficiary of rehabilitative work was no longer the probationer. Rather both rehabilitation as a practice and probation as an institution were directed at attempts to change 'offenders' in order to protect the law-abiding (see McCulloch and McNeill 2007; Robinson and McNeill 2004). The probationer became less and less an active participant and more and more an object to be assessed through technologies applied by professionals and compulsorily engaged in structured programmes and offender management processes as required elements of legal orders imposed, as we have already noted, irrespective of consent (McNeill 2006).

These developments in the relationship between correctional rehabilitation and those 'offenders' with whom it engages – or, worse, on whom it operates – is a particularly important one. The shift from subject to object of correctional rehabilitation implies a more coercive and utilitarian conception of rehabilitation; one which leaves the individual liberties and rights of the offending citizen much more vulnerable, and one which opens up new prospects of abuses of the 'power to punish', justified in the putative public interest. This form of rehabilitation may still be a process of intervention aimed at some public good, but returning to Raynor and Robinson's (2009) initial definitions, the blunting both of its restorative intent and of its commitment to the 'offender's' interests (always *alongside* others' interests), as well as its willingness to impose (rather than renegotiate) 'norms' on objectified 'offenders' represent major causes for concern.

## Reframing punishment, probation and rehabilitation

An important contribution to the philosophy of punishment perhaps offers us one way to resolve some of these tensions, and of conceiving of punishment *as* rehabilitation. The penal philosopher Antony Duff – whose theory of punishment as communication has been highly influential – has argued convincingly that we can and should distinguish between 'constructive punishment' and 'merely punitive punishment' (Duff 2001, 2003, 2005). Constructive punishment can and does involve the intentional infliction of pains, but only in so far as this is an inevitable (and intended) consequence of 'bringing offenders to face up to the effects and implications of their crimes, to rehabilitate them and to secure . . . reparation and reconciliation' (Duff 2003: 181). Duff (2005) is not arguing for rehabilitation as moral education; to do so would infantilise offending citizens as well as calling into question their culpability for their crimes. Rather than restoring or correcting a deficit in the offending citizen, moral rehabilitation aims to repair a breach in the relationships between the offender, the victim and the community that the offence has created. For Duff, repairing the breach is principally the offender's responsibility; the starting point is a sincere apology which represents the recognition of the wrong done and the relational breach that it has created. But in most criminal cases an oral apology – however sincere – will not be enough:

> [S]omething more is required—something that will make more forceful the apology that I owe . . . something that will show that I am taking seriously the need to avoid such wrongs in future, and to reform myself and my conduct. Two elements of such moral rehabilitation might be, first, undertaking some burdensome task to express my apologetic repentance . . . second, taking steps to address the causes or sources of my wrongdoing, and perhaps seeking help—whether informal or formal—in dealing with them.
>
> *(Duff 2005: 19)*

Duff (2005) admits that he is speaking of criminal justice as it could be, or as it should be, rather than as it is. Nonetheless, he sees in some contemporary practices at least the opportunity for this kind of penal communication and for moral rehabilitation to take place:

> The burden that the offender is required to undertake, as his punishment, can be seen as constituting a formal, and forceful, apology to his victim and to the wider community. The apology has something of the quality of a public ritual rather than of a sincere expression of personal feelings, though we may hope that it will become sincere; but it serves to make clear to the offender the wrong that he has done, and for which he owes and is required to offer this apology, and to make clear to the victim our shared recognition of that wrong. Furthermore, a probation order involves, as probation officers often put it, an attempt to . . . help the offender to confront the character and implications of his crime, and to find ways of avoiding repeating it, partly by programmes that seek to address offending behaviour and its causes: by undertaking such programmes the offender is also making apologetic reparation for his crime.
>
> *(Duff 2005: 19)*

Duff's work also helps us with a second problem, already referred to above, since he recognises that where social injustice is implicated in the genesis of offending, the infliction of punishment (even constructive punishment) by the State is rendered morally problematic. The State itself can be seen as complicit in the offending through having failed in its prior duties to the 'offender', for example, as is so often the case, where the offender was once a child in the care of the State. For this reason, Duff suggests that probation officers or social workers should play a pivotal role in mediating between the offender and the wider polity, holding each one to account on behalf of the other. Here, Raynor and Robinson's (2009) discussion of the relationships between reintegration, resettlement and rehabilitation is relevant – the rehabilitation worker's attempt to advocate for the ex-offender, to secure access (perhaps for the first time) to the full rights of citizenship acts as the counterbalance to direct work with the offender to invite and support their moral rehabilitation. This discomfiting, mediating space is one which many probation and social workers will recognise that they occupy and through which, with or without official or public support, they seek to promote social justice within criminal justice.

Duff's approach may also help us to avoid the dangers of 'authoritarian rehabilitation', which we have mentioned above:

> The authoritarian model of rehabilitation is really only a subtler version of the old repressive model, seeking compliance by means of intimidation and coercion. Rehabilitation in this sense is essentially a technical device to mould the offender and ensure conformity to a predesigned pattern of thought and behaviour . . . The anthropocentric or humanistic model of rehabilitation, on the other hand, grants primacy to the actual human being rather than metaphysical fixations or ideologies, which long served to justify the oppressive intervention of the state. Client centred and basically voluntary, such rehabilitation is conceived more as a right of the citizen than as a privilege of the state. A humanistic public policy regarding crime implies the idea of human perfectibility, which at the level of rehabilitation includes not only the offenders themselves, but also the society that bred them and the institutions and persons involved in their treatment.
>
> *(Rotman 1994: 292)*

For us, Duff's ideas require not just an anthropocentric approach, but also one that is fundamentally dialogical rather than dictatorial in character: the person engaged in rehabilitation must be treated as a moral subject and not as a material object to be manipulated or adjusted in the interests of others. Fundamentally, that dialogue must be about repairing (or even nurturing for the first time) civic and civil relations between people; the links here to reparation or paying back as an important justification of community-based punishment are obvious (Robinson *et al.* 2013). Intriguingly, there is some empirical evidence that 'making good' is important for many of those desisting from crime (Maruna 2001). In a sense, the relevance in this body of evidence of the concept of 'generativity' – referring to the human need to make some positive contribution, often to the next generation – hints at the links between paying back and paying forward, in the sense of making something good out of a damaged and damaging past (see McNeill and Maruna 2007). Bazemore's (1998) work on 'earned redemption' examines more directly the tensions and synergies between reform and reparation, and the broader movements around 'relational justice' (Burnside and Baker 1994/2004) and restorative justice (Johnstone and Van Ness 2007) provide possible normative frameworks within which to further debate and develop these tensions and synergies. But, as we have already noted, in unjust societies, the debts may flow in more than one direction; making reparation therefore is a matter of social justice as well as criminal justice.

## The four forms of rehabilitation

Returning finally to Raynor and Robinson's (2009) discussion of rehabilitation, we can now clearly discern four main forms or meanings of rehabilitation. In recent papers, one of us (McNeill 2012b, 2014) has called these personal (or psychological), judicial (or legal), social and moral rehabilitation. These are the four strands of rehabilitation that must be 'de-fankled' (or untangled) in order for us to analyse their inter-relationships and mutual dependencies.

Personal rehabilitation includes but, as we will see in Chapter 3, extends far beyond what Raynor and Robinson (2009) refer to as correctional rehabilitation. It refers to any effort that seeks to somehow change, develop or restore the person; to develop new skills or abilities, to address and resolve personal limitations or problems.

The second form of rehabilitation concerns the practical expression of Beccaria's concern with the requalification of citizens; this is judicial or legal rehabilitation – which raises questions of when, how and to what extent a person is to be formally restored to full and free citizenship. This includes addressing the issue of criminal records and how the formal stigma that they represent can be set aside, sealed or surpassed. Maruna (2011) has argued cogently that efforts to sponsor rehabilitation and reform must address the collateral consequences of conviction – most notably its stigmatising and exclusionary effects – or be doomed to fail. No amount of correctional or psychological or personal rehabilitation and no amount of supporting people to change themselves can be sufficient to the tasks and challenges of reintegration, resettlement and re-entry, if legal and practical barriers are left in place. We argue in Chapter 4 that we need legal actors – in particular, judges – to play a full and active part in these processes.

Barriers to re/integration are not just legal – they are moral and social too. A solely correctional, psychological or personal conception of rehabilitation is inadequate to the moral and social offence that crime represents. In simple terms, doing something for or to or (better still) with the citizen who has offended, even something that aims at somehow changing them so as to reduce future victimisation, fails to engage with other key aspects of dispensing justice. Perhaps most importantly in moral terms, personal rehabilitation offers no moral redress per se; it operates only on the individual 'offender', not on the conflict itself and not on the victim or the community (Zedner 1994). In Duff's (2005) terms, because it fails to mediate the conflict, it leaves the relational breach unrepaired and that makes re/integration impossible. Critically, reparation – and reparative work in particular – seems capable of fulfilling this function in ways in which personal rehabilitation in and of itself cannot, perhaps principally because reparation allows for both dialogue and redress. Though, as Duff (2005) reminds us, willingly undergoing personal rehabilitation can convey the sincerity of the person's apology and of his or her desire to change, it is more typically a professionalised, private and secretive business, and not one that is explicitly bound into a process of moral rehabilitation. Reparation better speaks to the insistence that moral demands must be satisfied, and moral communication secured, before moral rehabilitation can be recognised (Duff 2001, 2003, 2005). In simple terms, a person who has offended has to 'pay back' or to 'make good' before s/he can 'trade up' to a restored social position as a citizen of good character (McNeill and Maruna 2007). Equally, an unjust society that has permitted criminogenic social inequalities to go unaddressed, creating barriers to the fulfilment of citizenship for people at the hard end of inequalities, will have debts that it must settle in and through the support for re/integration that it makes available.

Ultimately, even where psychological or personal issues are tackled, legal requalification is confirmed and moral debts are settled, the question of 'social rehabilitation' remains. In European jurisprudence, the concept of 'social rehabilitation' entails both the restoration of the citizen's formal social status and the availability of the personal and social means to do so (Van Zyl Smit and Snacken 2009). But here, we mean instead something that is broader, deeper and more subjective; specifically, the informal social recognition and acceptance of the returning citizen. Social rehabilitation is not something that the State itself can order or provide; rather, it is a duty and a function of civil society, but one that the State retains the duty to underwrite and support. In this sense, we argue that rehabilitation is or should be everyone's concern, but no one's business.

## The structure of this book

Much of the structure for this book's reimagining of rehabilitation draws on this model of four forms of rehabilitation but, given our focus here on and interest in probation work, we intend to allow ourselves some latitude in the ways in which we will develop that framework. Our starting point in Chapter 2, *Reimagining social control and support: Current realities, dystopian futures?*, will be a reassessment of the late Stan Cohen's (1985) seminal work – *Visions of Social Control* – which provided a prescient analysis of the dangers inherent in an unregulated expansion of social control in the community; a process that draws an increasing number of individuals into the criminal justice system through the processes of *net widening* and *mesh thinning*. Cautioning us about the risk that rehabilitation feeds penal expansionism, this chapter will include an analysis of what exactly it is that individuals are being drawn into and why this matters. We will then consider how and to what extent the dystopian elements of

Cohen's vision have been realised as more recent technological advancements within a digital world have extended the nature of surveillance and control. This inevitably involves an examination of the potential impact of these developments in terms of both desistance processes and wider notions of community and criminal justice. It also begs the question about how useful the criminal justice system is for controlling crime and rehabilitating people who have offended.

The third chapter – *Reimagining the rehabilitative journey: Personal rehabilitation* – focuses specifically on the personal dimension of rehabilitation. It explores the desistance 'journey', examining how and why people move away from offending and towards an improved social position. Crucially, however, we argue that personal rehabilitation is only one aspect of personal development, and that it cannot be understood or pursued in isolation from the other forms of rehabilitation – legal, moral and social. Ultimately, we argue that processes of personal change cannot and should not be separated from processes of social change. Change at the individual level, however positive, can never be in and of itself enough to deliver social justice but it can be and often must be a part of that project.

Chapter 4 concerns *Reimagining the legal and sentencing framework: Judicial rehabilitation*. As we noted above, the concept of judicial rehabilitation has come to be associated mainly with the issue of criminal records and of whether and how a person can be fully requalified as a citizen. However, in this chapter, we retain the concept's focus on *legal and formal* processes and outcomes but extend the concept in considering an area of policy, law and practice that is often overlooked in the literature on rehabilitation: sentencing. Whilst we would advocate the greatest possible use of diversionary, informal and non-judicial approaches to those who commit crimes, the criminal courts represent key points and key moments in people's experiences of criminal justice, where both civic disqualification and disenfranchisement and the potential for requalification in and through rehabilitation are determined. The *status degradation* involved in sentencing has both material and symbolic qualities and effects (Garfinkel 1956; Maruna 2011). For these reasons, we argue that academic debates about rehabilitation and desistance need to fully engage with both the determination and implementation of court sentences. As well as briefly exploring the philosophy of punishment and, in more detail, elaborating sentencing's purposes and the legal principles that govern it in England and Wales therefore, Chapter 4 also explores debates about therapeutic jurisprudence and problem-solving justice, considering whether courts and judges have a role to play in supporting desistance and, if so, what that might require.

Antony Duff's seminal work on punishment and communication informs the focus on dialogue in both Chapter 4 and Chapter 5, *Reimagining practice cultures and values: Moral rehabilitation*. However, whereas Chapter 4 concerns formal processes through which rehabilitation might be discussed and pursued, Chapter 5 focuses on less formal aspects. As noted above, the concept of moral rehabilitation is inherently dialogical and centres on the renegotiation of shared values and mutual reparation of harms that 'offenders', communities and the State may have done to one another. In this chapter, we focus primarily on the dialogue between the probation officer (as representative of the State and the punishing polity) and the probationer. Drawing on a wide range of literature, we explore the dispositions, values and skills required to support meaningful rehabilitative dialogue and action through professional relationships. But we also argue that these relationships are profoundly affected – for better or worse – by their institutional and organisational contexts. Central to our analysis will be the potential impact of the new delivery and governance arrangements within England and Wales for the supervision of offenders and what this will mean in terms of the ethos, values and organisational culture that has traditionally underpinned service delivery within the public sector. Our analysis will consider whether the knowledge, skills and values of professional and organisational life that are key to supporting desistance will be lost or, alternatively, whether and how new *hybrid* occupational cultures may emerge to replace them. We will also consider whether new models of professional power can be used as the basis of effective advocacy on behalf of people under supervision or whether it will simply be used to reinforce the commodification of 'offenders' and their experience of supervision.

In Chapter 6 – *Reimagining civil society and community engagement: Social rehabilitation* – we aim to look beyond the role of State or State-sponsored providers of rehabilitation to explore the role of community and civil society. This requires a broader discussion of the meaning of rehabilitation within a late-modern State. Our analysis examines the concepts of community, trust and social capital – and of civil society itself. As well as exploring what vision of civil society is compatible both with the pursuit of social rehabilitation and social justice, we also examine the role of devolution and localism and the problems and limits of marketisation.

In the final chapter – *Beyond the personal: Reimagining something better, fairer and more effective?* – we summarise our arguments and draw together the set of prescriptions for change that have emerged in each of the chapters.

## Conclusion

We began this introduction by pointing to the complexities of the term 'rehabilitation', before alluding to the hope that public perceptions about it may be changing. We noted that, as we began this project, a catalogue of reports, highly critical of State-sponsored approaches to social and economic problems are emerging which identify failures in penal-political decision-making and policies. Looking beyond the penal sphere, a study by the Centre for Regional Economic and Social Research at Sheffield Hallam University has estimated that the deindustrialisation of Britain over the past four decades has left not only sustained difficulties for the individuals affected and their communities but a current £30 billion annual cost for the Exchequer (Beatty and Fothergill 2016). More specifically, the then Prime Minister, David Cameron, announced, in the immediate aftermath of the 2011 riots (see Collett 2013), that a *Troubled Families Initiative* would be set up to intervene in the lives of 120,000 families whose 'lives are so chaotic that they cost the Government some £9 billion in the last year alone' (Department for Work and Pensions (DWP) 2012: 1). We might also ask what the failures of government (over decades) have cost these families. Despite spending some £400 million on the *Troubled Families Initiative*, and despite discredited pronouncements that it had been 99 per cent effective, a suppressed report by civil servants found no *discernible impact* on employment, school attendance or offending (see Bawden 2016). Benefits sanctions, another area of contentious social policy, were used against some 70,000 individuals on job seekers allowance during 2015. Notwithstanding the harm and injustice meted out to individuals on the receiving end of this *welfare* regime, the National Audit Office (2016: 5) found that at least half of the estimated £132 million savings in 2015 were swallowed up in administration and hardship payments. The policy of benefit sanctions also has to be located in a contemporary economic context where, in 2014/15, 21 per cent of the United Kingdom's population (13.5 million people) were living in poverty, including 55 per cent who were living in working families (Tinson *et al.* 2016).

These sorts of waste of scarce public resources can be contrasted with the reductions in public expenditure that brings, for example, an already creaking system of incarceration to breaking point. One hundred and two prison suicides occurred from 1 January to 18 November 2016 (Howard League 2016); a young prisoner is not allowed to visit his dying mother because of staff shortages during November 2016 (Crook 2016); and an unannounced inspection of Hindley Prison, an institution containing vulnerable 18–21-year-olds, can state that 'the failings at the prison are so serious as to demand a highly critical report' (HM Inspectorate of Prisons 2016: 5). As we write, two private sector G4S-run prisons – Birmingham and Swaleside – are recovering from riots. These events caused the Chief Inspector of Prisons to recently describe them as 'unacceptably violent and dangerous places' (HM Inspectorate of Prisons 2016: 8). However, as Sim (2016) has noted, the current discord in the prison system is underpinned by a range of factors that pre-date recent policy developments. The inspection into HMP Liverpool, for example, uncovered an institution where years of neglect had led to a situation whereby:

> [m]any cells were not fit to be used and should have been decommissioned. Some had emergency call bells that were not working but were nevertheless still occupied, presenting an obvious danger to prisoners. There were hundreds of unrepaired broken windows, with jagged glass left in the frames. Many lavatories were filthy, blocked or leaking. There were infestations of cockroaches in some areas, broken furniture, graffiti, damp and dirt. In one extreme case, I found a prisoner who had complex mental health needs being held in a cell that had no furniture other than a bed. The windows of both the cell and the toilet recess were broken, the light fitting in his toilet was broken with wires exposed, the lavatory was filthy and appeared to be blocked, his sink was leaking and the cell was dark and damp. Extraordinarily, this man had apparently been held in this condition for some weeks.
>
> *(HM Inspectorate of Prisons 2017: 5)*

Whilst the media response to this inspection demonstrated deep concern about the state of prisons in England and Wales, trying to predict wider public attitudes to crime, punishment and rehabilitation is fraught with difficulties. A pessimist, given the likely stagnation or decline in UK living standards in a post-European Referendum environment, might discern risks of a move to more punitive attitudes to those who offend and other vilified groups and more authoritarian and repressive forms of government. We don't need to look far for examples. More optimistically, greater realisation and understanding of the wastefulness in human and economic terms of penal-political decisions driven by populism may, even within the existing political discourse of austerity and competition, open up the possibility of the public demanding value for money. Hopefully, such a debate might centre as much on the *values* as the *money*. Ultimately, questions about punishment and rehabilitation are questions about the kinds of society we want to live in and to strive for. We offer this book simply as a contribution to that striving.

## Note

1 This section draws on and develops McNeill (2014). We are grateful to the publishers of that paper for permission to use it here.

## References

Aebi, M., Delgrande, N. and Marguet, Y. (2015) Have community sanctions and measures widened the net of the European criminal justice systems?, *Punishment and Society*, 17(5): 575–597.

Bawden, A. (2016) The troubled families scheme has failed – this is the folly of payment by results, www.theguardian.com/commentisfree/2016/aug/09/troubled-families-programme-failed (accessed 4 December 2016).

Bazemore, G. (1998) Restorative justice and earned redemption: communities, victims, and offender reintegration, *American Behavioral Scientist*, 41(6): 768–813.

Beatty, C. and Fothergill, S. (2016) *Jobs, Welfare and Austerity: How the Destruction of Industrial Britain Casts a Shadow over Present-day Public Finances*, Centre for Regional Economic and Social Research: Sheffield Hallam University.

Beccaria, C. (1764/1963) *On Crimes and Punishment* (trans. H. Pallouci), Indianapolis: Bobbs-Merrill.

Bottoms, A. (1980) Introduction to 'The Coming Crisis', in A. Bottoms and R. Preston (eds) *The Coming Penal Crisis*, Edinburgh: Scottish Academic Press.

Burke, L. and Collett, S. (2015) *Delivering Rehabilitation – The politics, Governance and Control of Probation*, London: Routledge.

Burke, L. and Collett, S. (2016) Transforming rehabilitation: Organizational bifurcation and the end of probation as we knew it?, *Probation Journal*, 63(2): 120–135.

Burnside, J. and Baker, N. (eds) (1994/2004) *Relational Justice: Repairing the Breach*, Winchester: Waterside Press.

Cohen, S. (1985) *Visions of Social Control: Crime, Punishment and Classification*, Cambridge: Polity Press.

Collett, S. (2013) Riots, revolution and rehabilitation: The future of probation, *Howard Journal of Criminal Justice*, 52(2): 163–188.

Crewe, B. (2007) Power, adaptation and resistance in a late-modern men's prison, *British Journal of Criminology*, 47(2): 256–275.

Criminal Justice Joint Inspection (2016) *An Inspection of Through the Gate Resettlement Services for Short-Term Prisoners*, Manchester: Her Majesty's Inspectorate of Probation.

Crook, F. (2016) A young person prevented from saying goodbye to his dying mother, http://howardleague.org/blog/sayinggoodbye/ (accessed 6 December 2016).

Crow, I. (2001) *The Treatment and Rehabilitation of Offenders*, London: Sage.

Cullen, F.T. and Gilbert, K.E. (1982/2015) *Reaffirming Rehabilitation* (Second edition 2015), Abingdon: Routledge.

Department for Work and Pensions (2012) *Social Justice: Transforming Lives*, London: DWP.

Duff, R.A. (2001) *Punishment, Communication, and Community*, Oxford: Oxford University Press.

Duff, A. (2003) Probation, punishment and restorative justice: Should altruism be engaged in punishment?, *The Howard Journal*, 42(1): 181–197.

Duff, A. (2005) Punishment and rehabilitation – or rehabilitation *as* punishment, *Criminal Justice Matters*, 60(1): 18–19.

Farrall, S., Hunter, B., Sharpe, G. and Calverley, A. (2014) *Criminal Careers in Transition*, Oxford: Oxford University Press.

Foucault, M. (1997) *Discipline and Punish – the Birth of the Prison*, London: Penguin.

Garfinkel, H. (1956) Conditions of successful degradation ceremonies, *American Journal of Sociology*, 61(5): 420–424.

Garland, D. (1985) *Punishment and Welfare*, Aldershot: Gower.

Garland, D. (2001) *The Culture of Control*, Oxford: Oxford University Press.

HM Inspectorate of Prisons (2016) *Report of an Unannounced Inspection of HMP Hindley: 4–15 July 2016*, London: HMI Prisons.

HM Inspectorate of Prisons (2017) *Report of an Unannounced Inspection of HMP Liverpool by the HM Chief Inspector of Prisons*, London: HMI Prisons.

HM Inspectorate of Probation (2016) *Quality & Impact Inspection: The Effectiveness of Probation Work in Derbyshire*, London: HMIP.

HM Inspectorate of Probation (2017) *The Work of Probation Services in Courts: An Inspection by HM Inspectorate of Probation*, Manchester: HMIP.

HM Inspectorate of Probation (2018) *Probation Supply Chain*, London: HMIP.

Howard League (2016) 2016 becomes worst year ever recorded for suicides in prisons, http://howardleague.org/news/suicidesinprison2016/ (accessed 6 December 2016).

Hudson, B.A. (2003) *Understanding Justice: An introduction to Ideas, Perspectives and Controversies in Modern Penal Theory* (2nd edition), Buckingham: Open University Press.

Johnstone, G. (1996) *Medical Concepts and Penal Policy*, London: Cavendish Publishing.

Johnstone, G. and Van Ness, D. (2007) (eds) *The Handbook of Restorative Justice*, Cullompton: Willan.

Lewis, C.S. (1953) The humanitarian theory of punishment, *Res Judicatae*, 6(230): 224–230.

Lewis, S. (2005) Rehabilitation: Headline or footnote in the new penal policy?, *Probation Journal*, 52(2): 119–135.

Mair, G. and Burke, L. (2012) *Redemption, Rehabilitation and Risk Management: A History of Probation*, London: Routledge.

Maruna, S. (2001) *Making Good*, Washington DC: American Psychological Association.

Maruna, S. (2011) Judicial rehabilitation and the 'clean bill of health' in criminal justice, *European Journal of Probation*, 3: 97–117.

McCulloch, T. and McNeill, F. (2007) Consumer society, commodification and offender management, *Criminology and Criminal Justice*, 7(3): 223–242.

McGuire, J. (ed.) (1995) *What Works? Reducing Reoffending*, Chichester: Wiley.

McNeill, F. (2006) A desistance paradigm for offender management, *Criminology and Criminal Justice*, 6(1): 39–62.

McNeill, F. (2012a) Counterblast: A Copernican correction for community sentences?, *Howard Journal*, 51(1): 94–99.

McNeill, F. (2012b) Four forms of supervision: Towards an interdisciplinary perspective, *Legal and Criminological Psychology*, 17(1): 18–36.

McNeill, (2014) Punishment as Rehabilitation, in Bruinsma, G. and Weisburd, D. (eds) *Encyclopedia of Criminology and Criminal Justice*, New York: Springer Science and Business Media, 4195–4206.

McNeill, F. and Beyens, K. (2013) Introduction: Studying Mass Supervision, in *Offender Supervision in Europe*, Basingstoke: Palgrave Macmillan.

McNeill, F. and Maruna, S. (2007) Giving Up and Giving Back: Desistance, Generativity and Social Work with Offenders, in McIvor, G. and Raynor, P. (eds) *Developments in Social Work with Offenders. Research Highlights in Social Work 48*, London: Jessica Kingsley.

McNeill, F., Raynor, P. and Trotter, C. (2010) (eds) *Offender Supervision: New Directions in Theory, Research and Practice*, Cullompton: Willan.

Ministry of Justice (2013a) *Transforming Justice: A Revolution in the Way We Manage Offenders*, London: Stationery Office.

Ministry of Justice (2013b) *Transforming Justice: A Strategy for Reform*, London: Stationery Office.

National Audit Office (2016) *Benefits Sanctions – Report by the Comptroller and Auditor General*, London: National Audit Office.

National Audit Office (2017) *Investigation into Changes to Community Rehabilitation Company contracts: Report by the Comptroller and Auditor General*, HC 676 Session 2017–2019, London: National Audit Office.

National Offender Management Service (2013) *Probation Trust Annual Performance Ratings 2012/13*, London: NOMS Agency.

Phelps, M. (2013) The Paradox of probation: Community supervision in the age of mass incarceration, *Law & Policy*, 35(1–2): 51–80.

Raynor, P. (2007) Risk and need assessment in British probation: The contribution of LSI-R, *Psychology, Crime and Law*, 13: 121–138.

Raynor, P. and Robinson, G. (2009) *Rehabilitation, Crime and Justice*, Houndmills: Palgrave Macmillan.

Robinson, G. (2008) Late-modern rehabilitation: The evolution of a penal strategy, *Punishment and Society*, 10: 429–445.

Robinson, G. and Crow, I. (2009) *Offender Rehabilitation: Theory, Research and Practice*, London: Sage.

Robinson, G. and McNeill, F. (2004) Purposes Matters: The Ends of Probation, in Mair, G. (ed.) *What Matters in Probation Work*, Cullompton: Willan.

Robinson, G., McNeill, F. and Maruna, S. (2013) Punishment in Society: The Improbable Persistence of Community Sanctions, in Simon, J. and Sparks, R. (eds) *The Sage Handbook of Punishment in Society*, London: Sage.

Rose, N. (1989) *Governing the Soul*, London: Routledge.

Rotman, E. (1990) *Beyond Punishment: A New View of the Rehabilitation of Criminal Offenders*, New York: Greenwood Press.

Rotman, E. (1994) Beyond Punishment, in Duff, A. and Garland, D. (eds) *A reader on punishment*, Oxford: Oxford University Press.

Sim, J. (2016) Letter to *The Guardian, The Guardian*, Monday 19 December 2016.

Tinson, A., Ayrton, C., Barker, K., Barry Born, T., Aldridge, H. and Kenway, P. (2016) *Monitoring Poverty and Social Exclusion 2016*, London: Joseph Rowntree Foundation/ New Policy Institute.

Van Zyl Smit, D. and Snacken, S. (2009) *Principles of European Prison Law and Policy*, Oxford: Oxford University Press.

Zedner, L. (1994) Reparation and retribution: Are they reconcilable?, *The Modern Law Review*, 57: 228–250.

# 2

# REIMAGINING SOCIAL CONTROL AND SUPPORT

## Current realities, dystopian futures?

We build adventure playgrounds because we believe in this, and not because it might reduce vandalism. Similarly (to talk about less measurable matters), if we are against inequality, racism and exploitation, our convictions should not be weakened in the slightest by the demonstration of low correlation coefficients with official crime rates. The choice here is between two quite different political options. One would be the strategic use of social-control resources as an opportunity for welfare improvement – deliberately seeking out, for example, the type of gains from the soft machine that I have just described. The alternative would be to divert scarce resources right away from the system and devote them to policies (family, educational, community, health, fiscal, etc.) which are not justified in control terms at all. To pursue my simple example: the strategy would be to use the excuse of 'vandalism prevention' in order to build adventure playgrounds for kids living in high-rise apartments; the second would be to forget about vandalism and simply build playgrounds as part of a neighbourhood project.

*(Cohen 1985: 264)*

## Charting the waters

The intention of *Delivering Rehabilitation* (Burke and Collett 2015) was to map out and analyse the social and economic policy and the wider political contexts within which the rehabilitative endeavour had developed and been delivered over the past 20 years or so. Specifically, we were concerned to identify the impact of the Coalition and Conservative administrations between 2010 and 2015 on the Probation Service of England and Wales as it reached its critical denouement under the *Transforming Rehabilitation* plans (Ministry of Justice 2103a, 2103b; Burke and Collett 2016). Our starting point for that work was the masterly analysis offered by David Garland in *The Culture of Control* (2001). Notwithstanding the critical attention given to this highly influential work (see Cavadino 2010), it offered appropriate analytical and intellectual insights, and in its all-encompassing approach, Garland's work provided the right pitch for a contemporary analysis of how major social, cultural and political changes were impacting upon social institutions, the market itself and the role and approach of crime agencies and correctional services.

For this chapter, we have turned to another critically acclaimed work published some 16 years before *The Culture of Control* and, interestingly if not entirely surprising, containing *Control* in its title – the late Stan Cohen's *Visions of Social Control* (1985). Whilst there is much in common between these books – particularly around the contradictions, unintended consequences, professional power, sources of resistance and outcomes of penal and rehabilitative initiatives – Cohen's work offers a series of cautionary tales, pragmatic approaches and moral responses to the realities of crime and control that assist us in our journey to *reimagine rehabilitation*.

Cohen's work covers a period when the sands of control were being blown by both a mixture of political/ideological winds and professional responses to what were considered major problems in the supervision and sentencing of individuals. He captures, in the broadest sense, the battle raging in what became known as *justice verses welfare*. To this debate, which has continued in one form or another over the decades, we can now add the vexed issue of pre-emptive responses to the perceived risks posed by individuals. With this addition, Cohen's work maintains its relevance to our discussion of rehabilitation. Indeed, our concern in this chapter is to revisit Cohen's ideas so that they can inform our unfolding discussion of all four forms of rehabilitation – personal, judicial/legal, moral and social. In this sense, the chapter provides a broad sweep of conceptual insights to support our normative position to reimagine rehabilitation within a broader context of social action and social change.

Cohen's work also provides a cautionary tale about the relationship between rehabilitation and penal expansion. His analysis presaged the application of new technologies; at the time of its writing, the application of electronic monitoring to the management of offenders was in its infancy. This chapter, then, will include an analysis of to what extent the dystopian elements of Cohen's vision have now been realised as more recent technological developments within a digital world have extended the nature of surveillance and control. This inevitably involves an examination of the potential impact of these developments in terms of both desistance processes and wider notions of community and criminal justice.

Cohen's work assists in our consideration of current possibilities and dilemmas regarding social control and social support. Our notion of the *social*, which will be discussed and elaborated further in Chapter 6, relates to its conceptualisation as a key site *of* and provider of resources *for* successful rehabilitation. In this sense, Cohen's argument for the capacity to *do good and do justice* goes to the heart of our notions of the *moral* as well as the *social* dimensions to rehabilitation. The opening quote illuminates this but it also points to a very different world of analysis, action and response to what was perceived as the problem of crime and delinquency in the 1960s and 1970s.

## Gone fishing

The grinding logic of twenty-first-century neoliberal thinking about crime and subsequent State-sponsored responses to dealing with those who offend now usually serves to close down debate about different and alternative ways of supporting individuals – whether 'offenders', victims or both (see Burke and Collett 2016). Indeed, any discussion about the moral basis of working with those who have offended, in the political sphere at least, usually defaults to the discourse of *individual* responsibility, *personal* morality and *wickedness* (see Gove and Grayling 2016; Travis 2017; Truss 2017). Cohen, however, was faced with a period, on both sides of the Atlantic, where a *master pattern* of *destructuring* was taking place:

1.  *Away from the state* in the form of decentralization, decriminalization, diversion and non-intervention and a call to divest the state of certain control functions by creating less bureaucratic innovative agencies.
2.  *Away from the expert* by demystifying their monopolistic claims of competence in classifying and treating various forms of deviance.
3.  *Away from the institution* by creating open non-segregative measures termed variously *community treatment, community corrections* or *community care.*
4.  *Away from the mind* characterized by the call for just deserts approaches to sentencing and treatment and an impatience with individualized treatment or rehabilitation based on psychological inner-states, as well as a move towards behaviourism – focusing on the act, rather than the actor.

*(Abridged from Cohen 1985: 31)*

What Cohen found, of course, was that the destructuring movement was more imaginary than real and that by blurring the boundaries between the State and new agencies and between those who have traditionally come under supervisory control and new groups within the community, social control was extended in terms of both intensity and coverage. In addition, old forms of professional intervention were augmented rather than replaced by behaviourist approaches and an ever-growing army of therapists. Drawing on Foucault's notion of the *carceral archipelago*, Cohen developed his explanatory analogy of *society as the ocean* and the deviancy control system as something akin to a giant fishing net harvesting the sea. So, there are matters of *quantity* – 'size capacity, scope, reach, density, intensity. Just how wide are these nets being cast? Over a period of time, do they get extended to new sites, or is there a contraction – waters which are no longer fished? Do changes in one part of the industry affect the capacity of another part? And just how strong is the mesh and how large are its holes, how intensive is the recycling process?' (1985: 42). Then there is the problem of *identity*, to which Cohen asked:

Just how clearly can the net and the rest of the apparatus be seen? Is it always visible as a net? Or is it something masked, disguised or camouflaged? Who is operating it? How sure are we about what exactly is being done in all the component parts of the machine?

*(1985: 43)*

Finally, Cohen raises the problem of *ripple* – 'what effect does all this activity – casting the nets, pulling them in, processing the fish – have on the rest of the sea? Do other non-fish objects inadvertently get caught up in the net? Are other patterns disturbed: coral formations, tides, mineral deposits?' (1985: 43).

In relation to the impact of destructuring; Cohen suggested that it should deliver:

> decreasing reliance on the treatment ideology, limiting the scope of the criminal law, ending or radically decreasing incarceration, restricting the full force of the criminal justice system, minimizing formal system intervention whenever possible, screening out offenders into less intrusive alternatives. To return to the net analogy: the size and reach of the net should be decreased and so should the strength of its mesh.
>
> *(1985: 43)*

The evidence amassed in the chapter *Inside the System* tells, however, a different story – one of an increase in the total number getting into the system, many of whom would not have been processed previously (wider nets), more intensive interventions (thinner mesh) and new agencies particularly in the private sector supplementing rather than replacing the original organisations (different nets). So, Cohen's (1985: 84) analysis describes a system undergoing 'a gradual expansion of its mechanisms from more closed to more open sites and a consequent increase in the invisibility of social control and the degree of its penetration into the social body'. In its broad sweep, *Visions of Social Control* captured vividly the discourses around destructuring on both sides of the Atlantic during the 1970s and 1980s. Texts on Anti-Psychiatry (for example Szasz 1972, 1974; Boyers and Orrill 1972), deschooling society (Illich 1971) and the *Justice* movement were staples of social work/probation training course reading lists during that period in the United Kingdom, although critiques of the anti-psychiatry movement and the *justice model* were beginning to appear (for example, see Sedgwick 1982; Hudson 1987).

Like Garland's, Cohen's work can be criticised in ways that are of relevance to our own concerns about rehabilitation. He readily admits, for example, that his work is focused on what he refers to as 'bread and butter, crime and delinquency' (1985: 3) and so the crimes of the rich, powerful and organised are not discussed or analysed. There is little acknowledgement of the gradations of crime and the fact that for all the low-level crime and delinquency in the system, there are also dangerous and difficult individuals committing acts from whom the public need and should rightly expect to be protected. Indeed, issues of public protection and concepts of risk and danger are largely missing from Cohen's work, as is an analysis of the racialised or gendered aspects of net widening. But, in our quest to reimagine rehabilitation, *Visions of Social Control* offers so many insights and theoretical considerations that maintain their relevance to the operation of *the system* and it chimes with our normative and philosophical position outlined in the introductory chapter:

- Though inspired by the ideas of Michel Foucault, Cohen positioned himself within a 'humanist' tradition that opposes the denial of human agency (1985: 10). Similarly, not only do we oppose intellectual positions that deny human agency but even in the often negative and destructive environment of contemporary criminal justice and social service systems, we can still evidence the capacity of individuals to turn their lives around and of practitioners (and many others) to productively and ethically support this. Consequently, for us, *reimagining rehabilitation* is about finding appropriate social, practical and societal responses and examining the more specific organisational features of a criminal justice system that contributes to a more just social order, including by maximising the possibility for individuals to make their way in the world without recourse to crime. There has to be a bigger project of working towards social and economic equality. Reimagining rehabilitation cannot simply be about personal support and transformation. In recognising *human agency* and the utilisation of the individual's own strengths and personal capacities, we nevertheless work from the basis that, as with all of us, potential is most often realised within a comprehensive and interdependent environment of material, practical and emotional support.
- Second, in addition to Cohen's analysis of general movements or shifts in thinking, it is also the case that quite specific professional, theoretical, technical and/or political positions that shape policy and practice can deliver unintended and sometimes perilous consequences for the individuals which are hard to rectify over the short term. A recent specific example has been the introduction of the sentence of *Imprisonment for Public Protection* within the English and Welsh criminal justice system which has left many individuals marooned unjustifiably within the prison system long after the requirements of formal justice have been met (see Annison 2015). Additionally, on a more general level, the link between violation of community-based supervision and post-release imprisonment has become more problematic with recent changes in legislation affecting the supervision of all those sentenced to short (under 12 months) terms of imprisonment (see HM Inspectorate of Probation 2016). Dressed up as support but without the practical and human resources to make it meaningful (and enforced through further periods of imprisonment), this appears also to be a newly designed but classic case of net widening.
- Third, we must also be alert to those broad-based policy and practice initiatives, both local and national, that do not announce their intended outcomes in ideological terms but nevertheless carry within them similar imperatives to secure wider social, attitudinal or structural changes that extend social control into the social fabric and infrastructures of communities.
- Fourth, Cohen reminds us that:

[i]f we superimpose the newer 'inclusionary' controls onto the more traditional forms of exclusion (notably incarceration) . . . we arrive at the
likeliest future of social control. It is a future of decisive and deepening
bifurcation: on the soft side, there is indefinite inclusion, on the hard
side, rigid exclusion.

*(1985: 232)*

The prison always remains for *hard enders* and for those who fail to comply
with the less segregated inclusionary community controls. In our quest to
reimagine rehabilitation, we must not only heed this warning but develop an
approach to rehabilitation that itself does not deliver unintended injustice and
unnecessary social control.

Finally, we believe that Cohen's criterion of *moral pragmatism* underpinned by
considerations of *good* and *justice* as values that operate as a bulwark against instrumental designs has much to offer our analysis. He expands thus:

The *moral* element affirms doing good and doing justice as values in themselves.
By *doing good* I mean not just individual concern about private troubles but
a commitment to the socialist reform of the public issues which cause these
troubles. By *doing justice* I mean not equity or retribution but the sense of the
rightness and fairness of punishment for the collective good. By *values in themselves* I mean that both utilitarian and strategic consideration should, where
possible, be secondary to obtaining these values for their own sake and whatever
their other results. Or – in negative terms – utilitarian aims such as reducing
crime should not be achieved at the cost of sacrificing cherished values.

*(Cohen 1985: 252–253)*

It should therefore come as no surprise then, when Cohen revisits the opening
quote about adventure playgrounds, he is 'romantically . . . in favour of the second
strategy. It offers, instead of planning for order and control, the opportunity to
plan for human happiness and fulfilment' (1985: 264). Perhaps, any discussion of
playgrounds feels entirely anachronistic in the twenty-first-century realities of deep
austerity and a highly managed utilitarian and sanitised world of *fee for service* and *fee
for result* delivered by global private sector companies whose core business is rarely
offender rehabilitation. We believe, however, that Cohen's approach continues to
provide us with some important analytical tools and insights that can be applied to
the current world where the deployment of technologies and their environmental
capacity to control individuals expands continuously in more and more sophisticated
and potentially covert ways. As our understanding of traditional forms of supervision
becomes more sophisticated and their capacity to be experienced as both punishing
and controlling better understood, we also need to understand how *persuasive technologies* using technological hardware impact upon the ability of individuals to make
their journeys to a crime-free life. However, this is only part of the technological
equation related to the issue of social control – we also to need to better understand

the *digitised* environment within which criminal justice staff deliver rehabilitation using increasingly prescribed *technologies* of assessment and supervision. How does this environment contribute to the control through supervision of the lives of individuals? All these issues, of course, need to be located not only within the political/policy environment that determines how criminal justice resources are deployed but within the wider context of the social (and economic) support given to individuals, particularly those in difficulties, who are drawn into the criminal justice net. This requires an approach to social rehabilitation that is complementary to and capable of being integrated with the other three forms of rehabilitation – psychological, legal/judicial and moral. Ultimately, this may help us to understand what the notions of *good* and *justice* could mean in the current political and social context.

## Social control as *exerting power* and *doing good*?

The term *social control* has become something of a 'Mickey Mouse' concept, argued Cohen (1985: 2), used differentially across various academic disciplines and with little resonance in everyday language. Cohen's focus in *Visions of Social Control* was essentially 'punishment and classification' (1985: 4) and organised responses by the State, organisations operating on behalf of the State and by relatively autonomous professional groups to crime, delinquency and other problematic behaviour. In order to understand trends in punishment and classification, Cohen drew on the highly influential work of the late Michel Foucault, and particularly *Discipline and Punish* which was originally published in 1975 (and in English in 1977). Whereas Cohen sets out to demonstrate the failure of *destructuring* to achieve its goals, in the process casting the carceral net more widely and more assertively on those within or around the criminal justice system, Foucault's thesis is all encompassing in that the dispersal of punishment beyond the prison not only operates within the carceral net but penetrates everyday life:

> Carceral continuity and the fusion of the prison-form make it possible to legalize, or in any case to legitimize disciplinary power, which thus avoids any element of excess or abuse it may entail.
>
> *(Foucault 1977: 302)*

Both these works by Cohen and Foucault were published before the increased use of imprisonment – an increase so significant that the term *mass incarceration* has been used to describe what has happened in both the United States and Britain (though on quite different scales) over the past 20 years. By the time the *Culture of Control* was published in 2001, Garland could argue that, as economies had been restructured around neoliberal and global notions of the deregulated market, crime control strategies, including the extensive use of imprisonment, had adapted to late modernity – 'to the specific problems of social order produced by late modern social organisation' (2001: 210). More recently, Wacquant has seen the increasing use of imprisonment as part of a mission aiming ultimately to:

establish a new economic regime based on capital hypermobility and labour flexibility and to curb the social turmoil generated at the foot of the urban order by public policies of market deregulation and social welfare retrenchment that are the core building blocks of neoliberalism.

*(2009: 303)*

This is a nuanced and complex debate and we mention the breadth of analysis briefly as a reminder of the social and cultural forces and the political, ideological and philosophical discourses that shape notions of social control, punishment and rehabilitation. However, we need a sharper focus for our own analysis and discussion of social control and its relationship to the four forms of rehabilitation including the *social*. To that end, it is perhaps justifiable to briefly remind ourselves that within the British context, social work and probation work have been subject to searching critiques of their respective roles in social control both at the level of individual human interaction and within their respective bureaucratic settings. Travelling briefly back to the late 1970s, Bailey and Brake's *Radical Social Work* (1976) and Walker and Beaumont's *Probation Work: Critical Theory and Socialist Practice* (1981) highlighted the contradictions in attempting to help people whilst being paid officials of the State. Both publications were followed up by attempts to outline what radical practice in various settings might look like (Brake and Bailey 1980; Walker and Beaumont 1985). The dilemmas for those committed to helping individuals in trouble whilst being critical of the social control inherent within the role was neatly outlined by Cloward and Piven in the introduction to the second edition of *Radical Social Work*:

> Were we in our daily work going to defend the practices and policies of the hospitals, courts, prisons, foster care, welfare departments, and mental institutions for which we worked, or were we going to use our jobs to defend and protect the poor, the sick, the criminal and the deviant against these agencies? That is the real and difficult challenge. It is not easy to be a professional, to lay claim to professional authority and esteem, and side with ordinary folks, especially poor folks.
>
> *(1976: xii–xiii)*

Alongside these debates that sought to connect the ideological and political worlds with the reality of social work practice, the *care/control* debate, as it was often referred to, likewise exercised a range of probation practitioners and academics during the 1970s and 1980s. These discussions often reflected the particular nature of probation supervision exercised by *officers of the court* on individuals subject to the formalities of court sentences (see Fullwood 1976; Bryant *et al.* 1978; Bottoms and McWilliams 1979; Harris 1980; Senior 1984; McWilliams 1987). Some analyses concluded with organisational models for service delivery that separated the support functions of probation from control but they all reflected a desire for operational clarity about the level of punishment and intrusion that those subject to supervision could and should expect. We revisit this debate in Chapter 4 but rather than consider organisational issues of delivering punishment and rehabilitation, we will concentrate on the legal and judicial dimensions to reimagining rehabilitation.

Whether drawing on *high level* ideological, political and theoretical insights or the more immediate concerns of methods of supervision and organisational mechanisms of delivery, we are clear that care must be taken in translating their use to a world of criminal justice that has changed immeasurably over the past 30 years. We must also find a way to make sense of the mechanisms of and potential for social control within the rehabilitative endeavour that acknowledge three things:

- First, that however repressive and controlling a system of criminal justice may be, human agency and the desire and commitment of many individuals to turn their own lives around places a moral imperative of all those committed to the *rehabilitative endeavour* to finds effective and *humanistic* ways of working with people (Millar and Burke 2012).
- Second, technology has shaped the world of criminal justice in ways that seemed unimaginable 30 years ago. We therefore need to consider what is meant by technology, what are the implications for its deployment in a criminal justice system that operates within *digital* personal and social environments and how *technology* differs from *technicism*.
- Finally, the potential for control and punitiveness does not reside solely within the agencies of the criminal justice system. As the State continues to restructure its welfare services and increasingly looks to the private sector and the Voluntary and Community Sector (VCS) to deliver on its behalf, social control becomes more nuanced and potentially more punitive (Bell 2011: 4). The State has also committed and directed its ideological efforts to designing services that have become more selective and conditional, more controlling and punitive and more directed at the behaviour and thinking of the recipients and less about their material circumstances.

We need to constantly remind ourselves that social justice cannot be achieved through criminal justice and we must also ask ourselves Cohen's question of why punishing *rulebreakers* in the name of justice and helping potential and actual *rulebreakers* in the name of welfare should not continue to be seen as consistent and benevolent. This is, he argues 'the essence of humanistic civilization: to exert power and to do good at the same time' (1985: 114).

## Inside the system: Revisiting the nets

Cohen's story of net widening is, as Garland puts it, a story of *failed reductionism* (1996: 457) and although the net was cast further and deeper and its mesh strengthened, prison numbers in the UK remained pretty static during the post-war period until the 1990s. Cohen's dystopian view was focused on the breadth and depth of ever-increasing supervisory measures for delivering control over the lives of 'offenders' and the wider community whilst the *prison* remained a constant reminder of what was in store for those who failed in the community or seemed too dangerous to be allowed to remain there. However, the context of criminal justice in which we are attempting to reimagine rehabilitation is substantially different to that of the late twentieth century. Here, in the UK, the early 1990s saw a very significant change in the use of imprisonment, with incarceration rising sharply (the rise in the American prison system had already began in the 1980s). In his prescient analysis of what would become an entrenched long-term trend, Garland argued that contradictory forces of, on the one hand, an attempt to cut the cost of crime control 'have suddenly been undercut by punitive pronouncements on the part of government ministers that throw the whole process into reverse' (1996: 450). Alongside, the *new criminologies of everyday life* where crime is seen as an everyday hazard to be managed, Garland argues that there emerges a *responsibilisation strategy* – a new mode of governing crime – whereby the government seeks to commission and responsibilise new agencies, both public and private, but not the traditional crime agencies by themselves: 'The recurring message of this approach is that the State alone is not, and cannot effectively be, responsible for preventing and controlling crime' (1996: 453). The State not only extends its delivery mechanisms through a range of private and non-State sectors but at the same time exerts increasing disciplinary and managerial control from the centre on its own agencies and employees – police, courts, probation and prisons. Coupled with these pragmatic adaptations to crime control, the State acts to reassert its sovereignty, tapping into the affective discontents of an increasingly insecure public. These expressive, demonstrative adaptions centre on a show of punitive force, according to Garland, that masks the State's inability to control crime. The willingness to deliver harsh punishments to those convicted magically compensates a failure to deliver real security to a population at large:

> Unlike the penal-welfare strategy, which was linked into a broader politics of social change and a certain view of social justice – however flawed in conception and execution – the new penal policies have no broader agenda, no strategy for progressive social change and no concern for the overcoming of social divisions. They are, instead, policies for managing the danger and policing the divisions created by a certain kind of social organization, and for shifting the burden of social control onto individuals and organizations that are often poorly equipped to carry out this task.
>
> *(Garland 1996: 466)*

Garland's analysis, fully developed in the *Culture of Control* (2001), provides us with a high-level understanding not just of some of the drivers underpinning mass incarceration but also of the wider impact on communities in a world where the State punishes offenders and a range of agencies attempt to control crime. His arguments for the increasing control of the *day-to-day* operations within crime control agencies are also relevant to the way in which social control is exerted through increasing bureaucratic and technicist approaches to working with those who offend.

There is, however, a very particular story of penal growth in England and Wales which we have outlined elsewhere (see Burke and Collett 2015: 26–36). A relatively small but consistent rise in the post-Second World War prison population was interrupted between January 1992 and January 1993 by the impact of the 1991 Criminal Justice Act. During this period, it fell by some 4,000 to approximately 44,000 (Home Office 2003: 6). However, what happened next was the particularly unedifying spectacle of the political rubbishing of the largely progressive provisions of the 1991 Act, the political exploitation of the murder of James Bulger in 1993 and an enunciation of *prison works* by the then Home Secretary, Michael Howard, at the 1993 Tory Party Conference. Since then, however, except for relatively minor initiatives to relieve pressures on the prison population during crisis points, we have seen an inexorable rise in numbers of about 4 per cent per year until 2013, since when the prison population has plateaued. At the end of 2016, the total prison population stood at 84,307 and the vast majority (87 per cent) were sentenced prisoners (Ministry of Justice 2017a). The factors which largely explain this state of affairs are a combination of increased numbers of individuals sentenced to immediate custody, increased lengths of sentence (including indeterminate sentences) and finally the increase in numbers recalled to prison following breach of licence conditions (see Ministry of Justice 2016a: Figure 1, page 13). In 2000, the Average Custodial Sentence Length (ACSL) was 14.3 months but by 2015 this had increased to18.8 months with a consequent increase in the average time spent in prison from 8.1 months to 9.9 months (Ministry of Justice 2016b). These figures of course need to be put in the overall general contexts of falling levels of crime (Office for National Statistics 2018: 6), less business being dealt with by the criminal courts, reduced use of community sentences as a proportion of all sentences (Ministry of Justice 2017b) and no hard evidence of increasing violence and sexual offending (Office for National Statistics 2018: 23–25), although prosecution of historical sex offences has had an impact on the prison population.

Within the community, the new arrangements for supervising individuals following the implementation of *Transforming Rehabilitation* has resulted in a recent sharp increase in post-release supervision and in total some 260,200 individuals (including 80,890 individuals in prison) made up the National Probation Service/ Community Rehabilitation Company caseload (NPS/CRC) in 2016. In other words, some 180,000 individuals are subject to supervision in the community at any one time (Ministry of Justice 2017a: Figure 2). What we can say from all this is that over a quarter of a million individuals are within a correctional system that has come to be increasingly dominated by (increasingly lengthy) sentences of imprisonment and the conditional release and supervision of all prisoners in the community following the implementation of the Offender Rehabilitation Act 2014. All this in a system where the bureaucratic control of workers' actions and decision-making aided and abetted by continual offender assessment and classification is already seeing non-compliance as a powerful mechanism for returning individuals to custody. In other words, there appears to be an increasingly complex and problematic relationship between custody and community. This latter feature is highlighted in a pioneering analysis of the development of both *mass probation* in a time of mass incarceration in the United States by Michelle Phelps (2013). She concludes that the *paradox of probation* is that in different ways, at different times in different places, it has acted *both* as an alternative to custody and as an important net widening influence that expands penal control in terms of expanded numbers of supervision but also the potential for violations of intensive supervision to lead back to prison. From today's vantage point, Phelps suggests, 'it is clear that both probation and incarceration rates continued to a march of expansion throughout the 1980s, 1990s and for most of the 2000s, despite fluctuations and then decline in crime rates' (2013: 73).

Despite this bleak overall picture, what is particularly interesting are the examples Phelps provides of decarceration happening within specific State and US County jurisdictions. She is at pains to stress that progress is highly idiosyncratic and by no means comprehensive but her research indicates that where public policy is shaped by an understanding of the inter-relationships between sentencing cultures, effective supervision and careful management of violations, then decarceration is possible. However, it needs political support backed up by changes in sentencing, financial incentives and investment to provide quality probation services and it requires enforcement policies that support success, shorter prison sentencing and less intensive supervision. As Phelps reflects on the case studies she presents, they 'illustrate how by changing state structures, such as sentencing laws and fiscal incentives, policymakers can reshape the central institutional practices that determine the probation-prison link' (2013: 72). In more recent research, Phelps describes probation as 'neither a simple alternative nor complement to imprisonment, but a unique form of state control. Rather than a monolithic expansion, states followed diverse trajectories, likely driven by social, political, and economic conditions, producing a multi-faceted array of control strategies' (2017: 66).

Comparisons across jurisdictions are complex, not least because of diverse legal systems which define similar sounding supervisory sanctions in very different ways and at different points of the criminal justice process. Nevertheless, it seems fair to claim that most of the criminal justice systems of the United Kingdom, North America and Europe have been presiding over the development of significant expansions of penal control within and beyond prisons over the past 20 years or so. In many European countries, where *community sanctions and measures* have been promoted as *alternatives to imprisonment*, they have grown alongside it, despite falling crime rates (see Aebi *et al.* 2015). Additionally, not only is it apparent that community sanctions do not offer a clear mechanism for delivering alternatives to custody but as we have suggested, there are limitations and dangers in treating supervision and imprisonment as separate facets of penal control (the *soft* and the *hard* end, to use Cohen's terms). Increasingly, not only is release from prison conditional on community supervision but its violation is often a route back into incarceration. The probation-prison relationship is more often symbiotic than substitutional.

In their analysis of European criminal justice jurisdictions, Aebi *et al.* (2015) highlight significant variations in the ratio of incarceration to community sanctions within an overall 20-year trend of expanding carceral control at both *soft* and *hard* ends. In England and Wales, the picture is different. Until recently, the levels of community supervision (as a sentence in its own right) have declined as the prison population has grown to reach the highest rate within Europe. Between 2006 and 2016, whilst there was a gradual decrease in numbers prosecuted for indictable offences in magistrates' courts and there has been an increase in the use of immediate custody (29 per cent in 2016 compared with 22 per cent in 2006) but a decrease in community sentences from 35 per cent in 2006 to 21 per cent in 2016 (Ministry of Justice 2017b: 4). Yet, as we have seen, compulsory post-release supervision has swollen the probation caseload. Within the English and Welsh criminal justice system, therefore, we have seen the net strengthened and expanded, not just to catch more individuals per se, but to ensure that they end up in the net's deep end, remain there for longer and find their escape back into the ocean both conditional and subject to return for infringements of behavioural rules and further offending. In wanting to *reimagine rehabilitation*, it is important to recognise that the carceral net is not a monolithic structure operating in similar fashion across all the world's oceans and although we are primarily interested in the English and Welsh system, there is much to consider and learn from European and other criminal jurisdictions.

There are also further features of Cohen's net relating to *scope* and *intensity* of supervision, both for those under supervision in the community and for prisoners. Some relatively recent additions to the armoury of correctional measures available to both the courts and the executive in relation to post-release supervision move 'beyond traditionally rehabilitative measures to include unpaid work, medical, psychological or substance misuse treatment, mandatory drug or alcohol testing, exclusion orders and residence conditions, curfews, house arrest and electronic monitoring as well as other innovations' (McNeill 2013: 172). It is also worth reminding ourselves, particularly given the ever-closer links between the experience of community supervision and incarceration, that for individuals at the *hard end* of imprisonment, intensity has increased. In Crewe's words, reflecting his extensive ethnographic research in one British prison:

> Imprisonment has become 'deeper' and 'heavier' since the early 1990's. Movements are more restricted, security has been tightened, and risk has become the trump card of the system. Meanwhile, shifts in the way that power is organised and authority is exercised have created new weights and burdens, particularly around issues of powerlessness, autonomy, insecurity, and the meeting of personal needs. The carceral experience is less directly oppressive, but more gripping. It demands more and risks less.
>
> *(Crewe 2009: 449)*

We write at a time, then, when disinvestment in community sanctions and disarray in the mechanisms for their delivery in England and Wales mirrors a prison system facing a level of crisis unseen for 20 years or more and a recent Secretary of State, Liz Truss, believing against all the evidence that prisons can become sites for rehabilitation. In contrast to all this, there is evidence that rehabilitation can be reimagined in ways that support individual journeys out of crime and to new personal identities. Notwithstanding the utility of evaluating specific approaches to supervision, however, the examination of routine practices becomes more pressing and it has been argued that closer examination is required of, first, the lived experience of supervision by those *subject to* and *affected by* it; second, the cultures and practices of supervision by those who impose and deliver it; and finally the multiple contexts of supervision (material, social, political, cultural, organisational, professional and legal) that shape it (see McNeill 2013:179–183; McNeill and Beyens 2013: 6–9). It is also the case that reimagining rehabilitation cannot be effectively undertaken without considering the role of sentencing both in general terms and in relation to the racialisation and gender discrimination within front end judicial decision-making processes and this will be considered in Chapter 4.

## Social control and technological determinism

So far, in utilising the conceptual insights provided by Cohen, we have attempted to bring an analysis of net widening to the current state of affairs across both prison and community corrections. We are, however, conscious that the application of technological approaches to supervision was in its infancy when *Visions of Social Control* was published – indeed, Cohen reproduces a news article about a 1983 pilot tagging programme in Albuquerque, New Mexico, which states that 'supporters say it would ease prison over-crowding, but opponents have declared that it will bring 1984 to Albuquerque a year early' (1985: 223). Some 11 years later, the electronic monitoring of individuals subject to Radio Frequency (RF) Electronic Monitoring (EM) was introduced on a pilot basis in three localities within England and Wales and nowadays EM is an embedded feature of the various and diverse criminal justice systems of Europe and North America. The use of Global Positioning System (GPS) technology for real-time or continuous tracking is also growing. Indeed, it seems that the application of technology is about to enter a new phase as pilots in mobile phone applications for supervisors (Fagan 2017) and supervisees (McGreevy 2017), *biotech* kiosks (Stout 2012) for supervisee reporting, Remote Alcohol Monitoring (Ministry of Justice 2016c) and technology to disable a car when a previously convicted drink-driver has been drinking (Chester and Roberts 2107) are all being piloted in a variety of jurisdictions. Historically, however, as the reference to the Albuquerque pilot highlights, EM (or tagging as it is often referred to) has been the example, par excellence, of the application of *hard-end* technology to the supervision of those caught within the criminal justice net. Predictably, it has attracted both utopian and dystopian notions of the future under the application of ever-accelerating technological innovation within the human services. We will provide a brief case study of EM because it allows for a consideration of social control and net widening and importantly *doing good* and *doing justice* within the contemporary context.

The starting point for a discussion of the application of technologies to human services is a consideration of the power of technology itself to shape society. In the 1960s, a range of writers and academics, often referred to as *post-industrial prophets*, provided critical commentaries on the ever-increasing use of technology to dominate everyday life. Ellul, for example, suggested that far from being neutral tools for societal development, the technology of the *technological society* is embedded within what he refers to as *technique* through which 'the totality of methods rationally arrived at and having absolute efficiency dominate every field of human activity' (1964: xv). For Ellul, *technique* goes beyond technology and machines to an all-encompassing rationality whereby rather than being subservient to humanity, human beings have to adapt to and be subsumed by it. Herbert Marcuse, in *One Dimensional Man* (1964), offers an alternative but similarly all-encompassing critique of the technology of advanced industrial societies; technology that has the capacity to eliminate conflict by assimilating all those who in earlier forms of social order provided either forces or voices of dissent. For Marcuse, the march of technology is part of the growing union of production and destruction; the surrender of thought to those in power and the existence of unprecedented wealth alongside entrenched poverty are the greatest indictments of modern industrial states. Technological societies create false needs which are met through the *rational* nature of production – based on the technical utilisation and exploitation of human beings – the rational nature of the overall enterprise of production, however, has a double meaning – whilst technology produces vastly increased productivity of the economic, political and cultural enterprise resulting in higher standards of living:

> At the same time and on the same ground, this rational enterprise produced a pattern of mind and behaviour which justified and absolved even the most destructive and oppressive features of the enterprise. Scientific-technical rationality and manipulation are welded together into new forms of social control.
>
> *(Marcuse 1964: 120)*

This all too brief and partial description of the work of two major theorists does the issue of technological determinism scant justice. It is included simply to alert us to the possibilities of social, political and ideological control by and through technology. The work of Ellul and Marcuse in their respective 1964 publications reflects a largely pre-digital age in which the global implications of *new technology* was still some way off but – even if technological determinism has since been much disputed – their work still retains a range of profound sociological, political and philosophical arguments and insights that require us to be deeply concerned about the deployment of technology within post-industrial societies and specifically their application to human services, including within the criminal justice system.

## Technologies

In line, however, with our concern to understand the possibilities for and importance of *human agency* within criminal justice and rehabilitative process, we need to understand the impact of technology a little nearer to home and specifically within the *techno-bureaucratic* environment of the everyday world of criminal justice. The application of technology to the supervision of those who offend or are otherwise caught up in criminal justice processes is currently receiving renewed interest within the academic and research communities. Later in the chapter we will consider EM as an example, par excellence, of what Nellis refers to as a 'distinct and particular socio-technical practice' (2009: 42). However, we contend that it is important to locate such forms of control and surveillance within a wide context of separate but interlinked notions of *technologies* and *techniques*. This is necessary for two reasons – first because the overall environment within which supervision takes place has been radically transformed through the *digitisation* of the workplace in the context of Information and Communication Technology (ICT) and second, although supervision has always involved the duality of care and control, it is arguably the case that for supervisees, the technological environment of criminal justice and the target culture it supports delivers a qualitatively different experience of supervision, control and containment than in the past. The impact on the individual and their experience of supervision remains critically important but the qualitative feel of the interaction between the worker and the individual reflects not just prevailing professional knowledge and approaches and the values and ideologies of wider society but the mediating and sometimes determining aspects of the technological environment. Crewe, for example, in his ethnographic study of prisoners, comments that decency and legitimacy are delivered within prisons 'but in a manner that is faceless and impersonal. Qualities that are essential for the prison's redemptive aims – humanity, trust, faith, interest – and to which prisoners are highly sensitive are lost in the process' (2009: 452). In similar vein, Fitzgibbon and Stengel give a salutary account of the lived experience of women under community supervision in two jurisdictions:

> One of the most common themes to emerge from both the Supervisible and Chicks day projects was 'constraint' and 'control'. This emerged in images and discussions centred on limited freedom, on living under surveillance and regimes of control, on the constant perception of being watched or supervised and on the barriers that this sense of surveillance imposed on living a full and 'normal' life. Indeed, for some of the women in both the English and Hungarian research projects, the fear of being incarcerated or involved with the police was ever present.
>
> *(Fitzgibbon and Stengel 2017: 8)*

A related piece of recent research entitled 'Supervisible', across three European jurisdictions, using *photo-elicitation* as a technique to get under the skin of supervision as a lived experience. Fitzgibbon *et al.* (2017) suggest that the context of supervision within bureaucratic and increasingly routinised environments delivers supervision that is experienced in terms of real personal constraint, suspended/lost time and feelings of wasted, used up lives. Notwithstanding the common themes of judgement, labelling and stigmatisation, the images captured by the supervisees also reflected hope and growth and as the authors comment, 'suggests the experience of supervision is a much more diffuse and persuasive one; for its supervisees at least, it seems to extend in time and in impact across time, deep into the life of the supervisee' (Fitzgibbon *et al.* 2017: 317) – supervision, in essence then, can be both productive and painful and nuanced even within the context of social control.

McNeill (2018) follows up this notion of felt ambivalence by supervisees by arguing that mass supervision can be understood as *maloptical* rather than *panoptical*. He argues that through:

> the 'Malopticon', the penal subject is seen badly, is seen as bad and is projected and represented as bad. As such, it produces experiences of misrecognition and misrepresentation that constitute significant yet poorly understood pains of supervisory punishment; pains that rely neither on the architecture of confinement nor the continuous surveillance to produce their effects.
>
> *(2018: 3)*

In other words, punishment and control conceptualised by Foucault and Cohen can be further understood in terms of the complementary processes of degradation alongside discipline where the individual is misrecognised as someone who needs to be surveilled and the pains of supervision can be associated:

> with the *persistence* of supervision and its *constructions* of its subjects, rather than with its *penetration* into their 'souls' or psyches. These are the pains associated as much with civic degradation as with penal discipline. So long as a person is under supervision, he or she is constructed as untrustworthy; as unworthy of dominion.
>
> *(McNeill 2018: 19, emphasis in original)*

The relevance of these quotes relates to a wider definition of technology than the use of electronic tags – one that reflects both the means and the context of supervision and particularly the location of the rehabilitative endeavour within a bureaucratic world which allows for the measurement of everything and the routinisation of interactions between worker and worker and between supervisor and supervisee. The technologies of supervision and the technical environment seep through into *the day to day* whether we wish them to or not. Hence, McNeill notes that probation's continuing adaptations are:

> all 'technologies' of a sort and *employ* technologies of various sorts. For example, the punitive adaptation requires technologies of visibility (the ubiquitous orange vest). The rehabilitative adaptation needs technologies of behaviour change (the cognitive-behavioural programme). The managerial adaptation needs technologies not just for rationing resources (through risk assessment) but also for audit and performance measurement (the 'standards' and 'key performance indicators' *and* the infrastructure of information and communications technology that records and collates all the requisite data). Even the

reparative adaptation needs a technology (or at least a practice) of accountability and of mediation (the restorative justice conference).

*(McNeill 2017: 104)*

## Technomania and the workplace

In *Technology, Crime and Justice: the question concerning technomania*, McGuire's (2012)
expansive text covers criminal justice and the components of the justice system
in the UK in its widest sense but he is concerned with 'how a more integrated
approach to technology might contribute to a better, more just use of it within
the criminal justice process (and beyond)' (2012: 2). In developing his notion of
*technomania* – a kind of regulatory order around technology – McGuire's argument
is that 'it is not so much technology itself that has caused the problem, but our
readiness to defer to orders and regulatory practices around technology – it's technomania' (2012: 22). Ultimately if the system of technological regulation is unjust,
then it seems likely, McGuire argues, to result in a social order that is unjust:

> If we go beyond the sterile dichotomy that tells us that technology is 'some-
> times harmful sometimes not', it is essential to see technology as something
> human – no less part of us than a heart bypass or a contact lens. In which case
> the question concerning technology is certainly, as Heidegger suggested, a
> question concerning humanity – but one with an additional factor. In the
> end, it is really a question about human enhancement and how far we are
> willing, or able, to regulate the extensions that technology offers us and the
> extent to which such regulations accord with wider principles that we hold
> to be valuable.
>
> *(McGuire 2012: 223)*

This notion of technology as something human and therefore moral takes us some
way from the determinism of the post-industrial prophets. Within the context
of modern techno-bureaucracies, it offers some hope, in Cohen's terms, of *doing
good and doing justice*. The human aspect of technology is developed in the work
of Verbeek (2016) who argues that the idea of *persuasive technology* needs to be
integrated within a wider concept of technological mediation. Arguing that the
impact of technologies on human beings entails more than persuasion to adopt
the behaviours intended by their designers, Verbeek notes that technologies have
unintended consequences as well:

> First technologies help to shape how reality can be present for human beings,
> by mediating human *perception* and *interpretation*; second, technologies help
> to shape how humans are present, by mediating human *action* and *practices*.
> The first dimension can be called *hermeneutic*, since it concerns meaning and
> interpretation; the second is *pragmatic*, since it concerns human activities.
>
> *(Verbeek 2016: 3, emphasis in original)*

The concept of mediation allows for the evaluation of new technologies 'not only in terms of the quality of their functioning (including risks and unintended consequences), but also in terms of the ways in which they help to shape new practices and experiences – including technological persuasion, but not limited to it' (Verbeek 2012: 6). Second, Verbeek argues that because of the pervasive role of technologies in our daily lives, it is hard to find an activity or experience which is *not* technologically mediated – 'Rather than holding on to an interpretation of human freedom in terms of absolute autonomy and sovereignty from technology, therefore, it seems wise to reinterpret freedom as a person's *ability to relate to what determines and influences him or her*' (2016: 13, emphasis in original).

This suggests two moral imperatives in introducing technologies into the business of rehabilitation. First, as Verbeek argues, '[e]xplicit reflection on the possible mediating roles of a technology-in-design should, therefore, be part of the moral responsibility of designers' (2016: 6). Second, from the perspective of policy implementation and practice delivery, the same moral responsibility applies to those who discharge such responsibilities. This does not simply apply to individual technologies but to the techno-bureaucratic operating environment. McGuire makes this point when he argues that '[t]he wholesale penetration of ICTs into the operations of the criminal justice system has taken place with almost no debate and even less reflection upon its worth' (2012: 105).

*Probation Practice in the Information Age* (Phillips 2017) is a notable exception to this lack of consideration. Phillips elaborates on the rehabilitative endeavour from his nine-month ethnographic study of office-based practice prior to the implementation of *Transforming Rehabilitation*. Arguing that it is important not to neglect the increasing dependence on information and the concomitant use of technology, he argues that:

> whilst the rise of technology in probation has been described and documented in a range of places, the focus has primarily been on risk assessment technologies. Moreover, there has been little attempt to theorise the ways in which this has impacted on the constitution and definition of what it means to be a probation practitioner.
>
> *(Phillips 2017: 211)*

What is particularly relevant to the moral dimension of technology is his reflection that technology is often seen as a constant, almost operating in a vacuum, alongside the practitioners and their value driven approaches:

> [L]ittle has been done to think about how the technologies themselves have the power to constitute practice where a degree of interaction and interpretation is required (i.e. assessments that are more than online static risk assessment tools). In many respects, much of the work that has occurred in the context of the impact of risk has treated practice as a dependent variable and practitioners' values as an independent variable while the technology which they use is seen as a constant.
>
> *(Phillips 2017: 212)*

In other words, most analyses of probation practice and culture have, according to Phillips, tended to focus on the way in which the relationship between policies and practitioners shape practice without consideration of the technologies that mediate this important relationship; yet this is critical because even prosaic and often repeated technologically based tasks carry with them the values of the organisation. As a particular example, which we consider has far-reaching implications for practice, Phillip's ethnographic insights suggest that in the information world, knowledge becomes reified in the form of information – the *official history* of the individual that can then be cut and pasted from one document to another, used in public assessments of the individual and to play down or even ignore other forms of knowledge about the individual under assessment and supervision. This is a theme we will consider further in Chapter 4 in relation to the capacity of technologies to order court business at the expense of approaches that might support individual desistance journeys.

A different and equally compelling perspective is provided from a policy analysis by Mike Nellis, one of the foremost researchers and commentators on technological applications within the correctional services. His analysis of the Scottish government's approach to *Digital Justice* (as outlined both in its 2014 publication and in its promotion via a subsequent Holyrood conference) places the strategy in the wider context of global information and communication technologies. He argues that failure to aspire to the *corporate futurism* of the big global digital companies and to keep up to date with 'the norms, standards and vision set by these globe-spanning companies, is a manifest anxiety for both smaller companies, and now governments too, in the contemporary narrative of digitization' (2017a: 192). Furthermore, whilst the Scottish strategy sees only promise in the digital, it is:

> worryingly silent about the impact of digitization 'on the human', both the values which were once associated with humanism (such as privacy, dignity, trust and caring) and the people whose careers, workplaces and services could be adversely transformed by technology in the name of an ill-defined, or politically skewed, greater good.
>
> *(Nellis 2017a: 192–193)*

Nellis's contention is that in the search for greater efficiencies, both politicians and policymakers remain silent on the impact on digital technology on the human and professional contribution to criminal justice outcomes and this is fuelled by two contradictory assumptions. The first expects little to change, 'blindly taking for granted that old forms and patterns of professional employment will continue, assisted rather than displaced by technology' (2017a: 202). The second is premised on the opposite view 'that the endpoint of digitization will be – and must be, if efficiencies are to be maximised – disruptive and transformational of established professional practices (and the security and remuneration of the people who do them)' (2017a: 202).

Nellis laments the failure to consider the moral values or empirical evidence which can guide digitisation and argues cogently that too often *things only humans can do* are almost an afterthought, a set of actions left over from *mechanic operation*:

The ethical question is not simply what humans can do but what humans could and should do, and be encouraged and trained to do. Contrary to conventional management wisdom, technology is never merely a neutral tool which can be used for good or ill according to existing ethical criteria: the decision to use it at all, if people's lives and livelihoods are to be significantly affected by it, is itself an ethical question.

*(Nellis 2017a: 205)*

## Technicism

Operating, then, within an ever-increasing digitised environment of ICT necessarily creates moral decisions for the choice of technologies and their implementation within the framework of contemporary corrections. Furthermore, technologies create a mindset for managers and practitioners that reflects the potential of technologies to classify and control individuals subject to supervision. First, the tendency to switch from the *actor* to the *act* through approaches based on behaviourism (see Cohen 1985: 31–32) fits much better with such an environment of classification and codification. Robinson captures this perfectly when she reflects that 'Cohen's vision of the future of rehabilitation, then, seemed to imply a purely technical endeavour; a style of practice coming to dominate simply by its technical superiority, and a far cry from the moralizing style of earlier models of rehabilitation/ reform' (2008: 437). However, like Robinson, we believe that the policy and practice of rehabilitation that developed from the millennium was much more nuanced than that envisaged by Cohen's feared behaviourism. The *Effective Practice* initiative, developed in the late 1990s, which became known as 'What Works?' under New Labour's Home Office, was based on the ascendant use of cognitive-behavioural techniques that, crucially, required the active involvement of the individual as a *moral* actor with the capacity to re-evaluate choices and think differently about future choices. Robinson argues:

> Thus, effective rehabilitation is more than a technical enterprise: it also has an important moral dimension that should not be overlooked. While late-modern rehabilitation does not re-invent the sinner of pre-modern reformative efforts, it does reprise themes of personal responsibility, choice and recognition of the moral implications of those choices.
>
> *(Robinson 2008: 438)*

This view accords with the design principles incorporated within the original blueprint for 'What Works?' – the *Strategies of Effective Offender Supervision* published by HMIP (Underdown 1998). In addition to the focus on cognitive-behaviourism, it offered an all-embracing approach to rehabilitation that included the need to deal with the social circumstances of those who offend. However, in a relatively short period of time, the ascendency of *risk management*, the availability of resources and the advance of technological possibilities created a new correctional environment which abstracted the individual from their social context. In an attempt to capture the mood within the Probation Service at the time when the technologies of rehabilitation were being applied during significant organisational reform, we commented that there was now a 'correctional framework driven by the unerring requirements of public service modernisation [that] encourages a technicist and rigid response to situations rather that real engagement with individual offenders, their families and their community networks' (Burke and Collett 2008: 10).

This could clearly be seen in the way in which the balanced and integrated approach to the cognitive and social needs of supervisees outlined within *Strategies of Effective Offender Supervision* soon dissembled into a much more narrowly defined system of standardised accredited programmes designed to deliver appropriate dosages of cognitive-behavioural intervention. This reductivism was also reflected even in the design of programmes – one member of a programme accreditation panel reflected that he was 'troubled to find programme designers making submissions on the basis that the programme *is the change process. It is not; it is merely one aspect of the service required to support the change process*' (McNeill 2009: 30, emphasis in original).

Thus, we would argue that technologies and the ideological, political, bureaucratic and practice environments within which they are deployed, particularly at a time of more utilitarian forms of practice around risk reduction and public protection, lead to a partly unconscious but nevertheless insidious approach to seeing *people as things* (Burke and Collett 2010) in which the supervisee becomes less and less an active participant and more and more an object to be assessed through technologies applied by professionals whilst compulsorily engaged in structured programmes and offender management processes as required elements of legal orders imposed irrespective of consent (McNeill 2006).

In this process, the boundaries of practice and discretion, knowledge and information, punishment and proportionality become blurred and the active engagement of the individual – potentially an important mediating force on the technologies, power and discretion of the professional – is removed or at least diminished in the brave new world of offender management. As Phillips observes, the term *offender manager* has now become the preferred title for staff who work with offenders: 'This is not a matter of semantics, but an indication of the way in which the work of probation practitioners has become increasingly technicised and informationalised' (2017: 213).

Rehabilitation has been reimagined by stealth and not in the direction we will argue for.

## Spiderman moves out of Salford: The case of electronic monitoring

Cohen's reference to a 1983 newspaper article mentioned earlier in this chapter set out the potential utopian and dystopian views that novel use of radical technological means could represent both in and beyond the criminal justice system.

Now a significant feature of criminal justice across Europe and North America and beyond, the early days of EM seemed to reflect almost a sci-fi notion of the future. One of the original initiatives was developed by a Judge Jack Love who in 1983 was giving serious consideration to New Mexico's prison crisis. In a *Times* news article by Nick Cohen, the judge is quoted as being inspired by the *funny page* of his local newspaper:

> [T]he villain fitted Spiderman with an electronic bracelet and was using it to track him across the City . . . . I thought we could use this to clear our extremely crowded jails.
>
> *(Collett 1998: 4)*

By 1997, tagging was available in virtually every one of the American states (Whitfield 1997) and in England and Wales the pilot (in Greater Manchester, Berkshire and Norfolk) commenced in 1995 to tag individuals subject to community orders under the provisions of the 1991 Criminal Justice Act. It was evident to those involved early on, despite a range of opposition from criminal justice organisations and antipathy from some staff, judges and magistrates, that EM would not fade away. Perhaps the opposition was understandable in these early days where dystopian views of EM were in evidence but Nellis captures the wider context accurately when he argues that a

> conservative, nascently neoliberal, government piloted RF [radio frequency] EM as a stand-alone sanction and handed delivery of service to contracted commercial organisations, rather than to the probation service, whose social work ethos it never ceased to castigate, and whose continued existence it refused to assure.
>
> *(2017b: 236)*

One thing was clear though at the time and reflected by Dick Whitfield (who led on electronic monitoring for the Association of Chief Officers of Probation): 'Tagging cannot be re-invented and it brings with it a complex mixture of ethical, legal, technical and policy issues which have to be squarely faced' (Whitfield 1997: 121).

What is particularly interesting in looking back on this early period in the development of EM is that the issues that arose then still resonate. First, there were concerns about the potential to exacerbate the risk to others of confining an individual to his or her home particularly when quality assessments at the point of sentencing were not available. Second, issues of proportionality and where exactly tagging sat as a *restriction on liberty* within the sentencing framework of the 1991 Act were contested by both sentencers and probation practitioners and linked to this was the concern that tagging was simply expanding the level of control without any diminution in the prison population. Whitfield (2001) was already tentatively arguing that those countries with the highest rates of imprisonment also had the highest use of tagging. It was also clear from the 1995 pilots that local attitudes not only to EM but to wider issues of judicial autonomy were quickly producing significant variations across the Manchester pilot sites in terms of levels of use and types of sentence. On the plus side, there did appear to be evidence that EM might prove effective in enhancing community supervision for high-risk offenders in order to increase public protection, as a short-term adjunct to active probation intervention where the curfew order might assist compliance or buy time to undertake work on the offending-related needs of the individual. It also offered a stand-alone punishment for those with few social needs and where other forms of punishment were not appropriate (see Collett 1998: 8).

Mike Nellis has been at pains to argue that a more sophisticated conceptualisation of EM 'as the most self-evidently prison-like of all alternatives to prison – doing time at home' is required. He has argued that 'the surveillant aspects of EM curfews can be shown to be *submerged within it*, despite its predominant presentation of such curfews as "confinement"' (2009: 42, emphasis in original). EM, as mere surveillance, however, doesn't try to change attitudes or behaviour and it does not individualise 'in the sense of generating knowledge of a person's distinct idiosyncratic characteristics, as a probation officer might once have done' (Nellis 2009: 59). More recently, in a blisteringly critical and detailed account of the development of electronic monitoring within England and Wales since the mid-1990s, Nellis focuses his ire on the approach to policy under the Conservative-led Coalition government (2010–2015) and the subsequent Tory government. The reconfiguration of Probation under *Transforming Rehabilitation*, he argues, is fascinating from a policy point of view, including in relation to both the ineptitude and the ideological and commercial interests that aimed to drive massive expansion in EM and move to GPS technology (away from RF) – 'None of this owed much to academic research on good penal practice or to a nuanced understanding of penal philosophy and jurisprudence: their underpinning rationalities, in the first instance, were financial and technological, rather than penal' (2014: 185).

Contextualised within the disaster of the *Transforming Rehabilitation* reforms and the prevailing neoliberal orthodoxy of markets, competition and privatisation, Nellis is nevertheless critical of Napo, Probation Service leadership and the penal reform groups for their failure to actively engage in shaping the development and deployment of EM. In a subsequent paper, Nellis argues that:

> humanistic social welfare traditions in Britain, in which both probation and penal reform bodies have deep roots, have always been wary of 'technical fixes' being (mis)used to engineer behavioural change or social justice, especially if they are seen as likely to jeopardise or take resources from person-centred approaches. With EM technologies, this risk was undoubtedly there from the start, not intrinsic to the devices as such but associated with the dark desires – subordinating social work to surveillance and punishment, or dispensing with it altogether – to which some political and commercial interests would (still) see them put. It simply does not follow, however, that

monitoring technology is never useful, in some forms, in some degree, and that it can never be used to serve humanistic ends.

*(Nellis 2016: 119–120)*

Nellis argues that we have failed to understand EM as *coercive connectiveness* 'thinking of it merely as a penal technique that might or might not "add value" has obscured both its embeddedness in Information and Communication Technology (ICT) more generally and the broader commercial and technocultural sources of its continuing global momentum' (2016: 123):

> It can of course be represented in discursively different ways, reflecting underlying political and professional attitudes towards it, and in different times and places it has been given both utopian and dystopian inflections, often by people who have failed to conceptualise its precise nature, misunderstood its conditions of emergence in successive waves of innovation in communication technology, and failed to distinguish between its possible and plausible trajectories as a penal measure in a pervasively digitised world.
>
> *(Nellis 2017b: 218)*

Attempts to better understand the scope and diversity of EM across a number of criminal justice jurisdictions has recently seen the publication of two major studies. In 2015 a *Scottish and International Review of the Uses of Electronic Monitoring* was published (Graham and McIvor 2105) and in 2016 an *International review of the creativity and effectiveness in the use of electronic monitoring: A case study of five European jurisdictions*, co-funded by the Criminal Justice Programme of the European Union, appeared both as a summary report (Hucklesby *et al.* 2016) and with contributory reports for each of the five jurisdictions (Hucklesby and Holdsworth 2016; McIvor and Graham 2016; Beyens and Roosen 2016; Dunkel *et al.* 2016; Boone *et al.* 2016). What these studies demonstrate, taken as a whole, is that EM has become a significant feature of European criminal justice jurisdictions over the past 20 years and the deployment of RF EM happens at all stages in the criminal justice process from pre-conviction, as a sentence of the court, deployed via administrative decision-making post-sentence and as a mechanism for the early release of prisoners. Additionally, in England and Wales, it is also used (usually utilising GPS technology) as a *voluntary* addition to the supervision regime of persistent offenders (see for example, Hudson and Jones 2016). EM is used in a wide range of ways, with a wide range of people, from a stand-alone penalty for less serious offenders to part of a package of supervision for individuals who pose a risk of harm to specific victims or more generally to their community. What is also clear is that those early concerns and ideas about its use identified in the early stages of piloting EM in England and Wales are still pertinent. First, in terms of the relationship with levels of imprisonment:

> The impact of EM on the use of imprisonment is a complex question and no firm conclusions can be drawn from England and Wales . . . the prison

population rose steadily between 2002 and 2014 mainly as a result of an increasing sentenced population, suggesting that the relatively high use of EM at both sentencing and early release stages has not resulted in falls in the prison population. Indeed, England has one of the highest imprisonment rates in Europe at 147 per 100,000 population and is also a high user of EM suggesting that EM supplements rather than provides an alternative to imprisonment.

*(Hucklesby and Holdsworth 2016: 4)*

This contrasts with the use of EM in Germany which has a low prison population (and therefore little or no pressure to reduce it) and very low use of EM which in any event can only be used with more serious offenders as part of a package of supervision. It is used alongside other probation measures which focus on rehabilitation, reflecting the constitutional importance of including rehabilitation within penal sanctions (see Dunkel *et al.* 2016, 2017). Overall, as Hucklesby *et al.* conclude (2016), less extensive use is associated with long-term reductions in prison populations and reducing imprisonment rates – by contrast, high prison populations are associated with high use of EM.

The effectiveness of EM in reducing reoffending is even less clear. In a review of the evidence base, Nellis comments that like all penal measures, 'the efficiency and effectiveness of EM has been evaluated, with greater or lesser degrees of independence and sophistication, in almost all counties which have adopted it' (2017b: 229). There is some general agreement that:

- EM is more effective when integrated with the use of active supervision and social support. As Graham and McIvor put it, 'There is moderately strong consensus in the international empirical literature that electronic monitoring should be used in tandem with more rehabilitation-focused supervision and reintegrative support options (formal or informal) in order to effectively maximize opportunities for compliance and desistance from crime' (2015: 9–10).
- It appears that with greater involvement of probation agencies comes more discretionary decision-making and flexibility in the deployment of EM (Hucklesby *et al.* 2016).
- There is currently only limited empirical literature available which focuses on the perspectives and lived experiences of monitored people regarding issues of compliance, legitimacy and desistance from crime (Graham and McIvor 2015: 9).
- In even the most sophisticated research there is little analysis of ethnic and gender differences in both experience and effectiveness of EM. For example, a much quoted and high-quality piece of research (Hucklesby 2008) involved some 78 individuals of which only 7 were women and the racial prolife was unspecified.
- The influence of local factors, such as the attitude and ideologies of staff and the understanding and preferences of sentencers, which were very evident in the early days of the Greater Manchester pilot, continue to exert significant

influence. Graham and McIvor (2017: 72) argue that even standardised reporting templates and assessment processes may be mediated by the influence of localism and the professional ideologies of those involved. Most tellingly, they argue that 'There is a great variability in *whether* it gets used, and *with whom* it gets used, but once it does, there is a lack of creativity and flexibility in *how* it is used' (2017: 70, emphasis in original).

## Reimagining social control: Current realities and hopeful futures?

The business of rehabilitation has undoubtedly become increasingly complex and challenging within the last 20 years or so. This reflects in part the politicisation of crime and the expectations by both politicians and the public for the corrections industry to deliver ever more efficient and ever more effective *fixes* that control and/or turn around the lives of individuals caught up in the carceral net. As we have argued in this chapter, the bureaucratic environment of corrections is now shaped not simply by the deployment of *hard end* technologies like EM but also by Information and Communication Technologies; probation practice is significantly driven by *technologies* that reflect the wider capabilities of technological societies. In order to reimagine rehabilitation, we therefore need to reimagine practice within an environment that not only places different punishments and controls on those who offend but also significantly shapes how workers relate both to individuals caught up in the carceral net and those colleagues they work with. These relationships are not shaped simply by technology but also (as both Cohen and Garland presciently argued) by the bureaucratic, managerialised control that has been increasingly exerted by central government on those delivery agencies (State, private and voluntary) that constitute the local criminal justice system (see Chapter 5).

So, when we haul in the nets some 30 years on from Cohen's fishing trip, we do indeed find a significant increase in the catch as he predicted, but the trawlers, the tools and those fishing have changed. Although Cohen fully anticipated the continuing and ideologically critical role of incarceration as the *deep end* of corrections, the massive expansion in the use of imprisonment could not have been anticipated in the context of the politics of the time. Mass incarceration has gone alongside the anticipated increase in the *shallow end* community-based corrections so that the pattern across most European and North American criminal justice jurisdictions is one of mass supervision *and* mass incarceration, with differential and discriminatory impacts on women and members of black and minority ethnic communities. The reasons for this are complex, driven by a range of political and commercial factors and representing at an ideological level, the response of neoliberalism to the socio-economic problems it creates (Wacquant 2009).

Within England and Wales over the recent past, a slightly different picture emerges. The inexorable rise in the use of custody has contrasted sharply with a significant decline in the use of community sentences. The reasons for this are complex (see Burke and Collett 2015) but our view is that it reflects the punitive desire to use imprisonment coupled with active political disenchantment by successive political administrations with a Probation Service whose underlying humanitarian values have consistently championed community-based supervision. In the face of reducing crime rates over many years, the political climate has supported not only an increased proportion of offenders being sent to prison but also for increasing lengths of time. Additionally, poorly thought through justice policies have created what Phelps refers to as the *probation paradox* whereby community supervision can fuel re-entry into the system of incarceration. Even where fewer people enter the criminal justice system, the mesh has been thinned and the net has been lengthened to increase the intensity and depth of individual experience once in the net. The speed with which the net is pulled through the sea is increased to ensure that the slightest slip-up when released from the net and the power of the ocean will sweep the individual back into its far reaches. Phelps's (2013, 2017) work, nevertheless in relation to individual US criminal justice administrations, suggests that political commitment and strategic planning at the local level can sometimes moderate or even reduce the growth of pernicious social control and self-defeating penal measures. Within the English and Welsh context, although control from central government remains powerful, local criminal justice partners may still be able to find the space to reimagine rehabilitation as ways we will outline in the remainder of the book.

Cohen, as we acknowledge at the beginning of this chapter, posed the question as to why punishing rulebreakers in the name of justice and helping in the name of welfare should not under certain circumstances be seen as benevolent? For us, punishment in the name of justice, amongst other things, must reflect a clear and humane balance between the *coerciveness* of the sentence and level of *restriction on liberty it imposes* and the *seriousness* of the offending behaviour. We will explore such notions of individualised justice in Chapter 4, linking them to the next chapter's discussion of desistance pathways. Our concern with social control discussed in this chapter has been to understand better how changing political and techno-bureaucratic environments have created both intended and unintended consequences for individualised *justice*. In general, the social control inherent in formal court and executive sanctions has increased in its scale and intensified in its effects, but by analysing the growth of EM it is possible to discern a key relationship between imprisonment and the use of monitoring technology. All the recent reviews of EM referred to earlier lead to the conclusion that where there are high rates of imprisonment there is also a relatively high use of EM. Conversely, where there are relatively low levels of imprisonment, the deployment of EM tends to be low. Nevertheless, this significantly under-researched area also alerts us to the power of professionals to shape the deployment of these technologies to the benefit of individuals.

The grand theorists and philosophers of technological determinism remind us of the dystopian capacity of a universe dominated by technology to maintain order and control by shaping the overarching architecture. But in the relatively parochial environment of a national criminal justice system, the questions focus on what is meant by technology and on if, how and why we should deploy it. As Nellis argues in relation to EM there is nothing inevitable about the expansion and future domination of EM, although there are tendencies, contexts and conjectures . . . which favour some outcomes over others. Technological innovation only creates possibilities: it is, as the critics of technological determinism have long told us, commerce and politics which create and shape actualities.

*(2017b: 225)*

Probation and other criminal justice practitioners have in the past claimed technical expertise as part of their professional status, whether that be the application of the moral insights of Christianity, Freudian psychoanalytical techniques or the mysteries of the casework relationship. More recently, the momentum of 'What Works?' offered probation the possibility of a new set of techniques based on cognitive-behavioural approaches but still embedded within the wider social context of people's lives. It seems to us that when we stop listening to and understanding the realities of individuals' lives and their experience of supervision then we become unable to effectively challenge practice. Indeed, if supervision itself is sometimes mistakenly seen as benign and the punishment or *restriction on liberty* imposed by the courts or the executive is ignored, then we miss the necessarily punitive flip side of remaining in the community or being discharged from prison early. In turn, this assumption about 'human' supervision's benevolence misses the point of how social control may be experienced on the personal level. As McNeill puts it:

> [I]magine oneself compelled to choose between a 'simple' EM curfew between 8 p.m. and 8 a.m. for four months and a year of fortnightly hour-long meetings with a human supervisor in an office on the other side of town, who is consistently late, or whose questioning you find intrusive, or whose judgment you find questionable, or whose advice you find patronising, or who seems intent on finding any excuse to breach your probation order or have you recalled to prison. Perhaps if you like the place where you live and your own company, the choice would be easy.
>
> *(McNeill 2017: 106)*

In similar vein, in comparing RF EM with GPS tracking technology, Nellis cautions us to reflect on what different monitoring technologies might mean for individuals in different circumstances: '[T]he idea that GPS tracking is inherently more "intrusive" than RF EM may be misleading: notwithstanding the greater amount of data that GPS generates, and the behavioural inferences that may be drawn from this, some offenders may experience this as *less* "intrusive", because it permits movement rather than requires confinement at home' (Nellis 2015: 38).

This highlights the need to be professionally more curious and potentially more critical of assumptions about the automatic quality and effectiveness of traditional styles and approaches of probation practice. Specifically, there is the need for more research to ascertain individuals' perspectives and experiences of the different technologies and practices, and how they are perceived in terms of their capacity to help or hinder compliance, desistance and reintegration. This should include the capacity to reduce anti-social and well as boost pro-social capital (see Hucklesby 2008) and to ensure that all forms of supervision should be delivered in ways that actively minimise unintended and unnecessary pains both for those subject to supervision and for others affected by it.

Our discussion of the ICT context within which the supervision of individuals is now shaped and carried out also requires further reflective consideration of the tendencies towards technicism and the routinisation of procedures and practices that can represent the very opposite of approaches that help individuals develop and sustain social capital and at their worst (often in combination with commercial pressures of the business environment) use techniques for purposes for which they were never intended (see Robinson 2016). There remains the possibility to *do good* in Cohen's words and Nellis is, in our view, right when he argues that

> the broader information and communication infrastructure cannot be resisted, least of all by probation services, but the forms of EM, the regimes it can be used to create and the scale of its use are amenable to shaping, if probation services are willing to engage with the process, claim EM for themselves and contest the narratives of others.
>
> *(Nellis 2017b: 239)*

Cohen's notion of *doing good*, however, also included a commitment to the reform of *public issues which cause these troubles*. Supporting rehabilitation requires not only a commitment to listening to and understanding the experience of individuals so that the support offered by workers can enhance the social capital of the individual, it must also include a professional commitment to *contest the narratives of others* in relation to the failure to provide social resources that support rehabilitation. For example, social support in the form of housing, training, employment, substance misuse and mental health treatment that is both contingent and conditional on being under supervision is itself an invidious form of control that cannot (other than in special circumstances) be justified. Even more invidious is the process of drawing some 50,000 additional ex-prisoners (as has recently happened under the provisions of the Offender Rehabilitation Act 2014) into a system of mandatory supervision with the promise to meet their resettlement needs but without either the resources or the organisational means to deliver (Tomczak 2017; HM Inspectorate of Probation 2016).

In 'What is to be done', the final chapter of *Visions of Social Control*, Cohen asks his readers, 'just what sort of space for doing good and doing justice might actually be offered by emerging social-control systems' (1985: 245). The political argument for *doing good* and *doing justice*, treating individuals in a humanitarian way, will continue to be contentious whilst crime and those who commit it are a source of profit and where instrumental outcomes are the only justification for the allocation of resources. However, the reassertion of professional humanistic values and the better understanding of the way technologies affect the lives of both workers in their techno-bureaucratic organisations and supervisees within their relationships, homes and communities might be the basis for helping rather than constraining those who have started their travel towards a crime-free life. This chapter has sought to provide the overall context for reimagining rehabilitation in its four forms. In the next four chapters, we will discuss each of these in detail starting with the *personal*. Underpinning our analysis is the contention that there is still professional space to reassert the essence of humanistic practice or as Cohen puts it: *to exert power and to do good at the same time.*

## References

Aebi, M., Delgrande, N. and Marguet, Y. (2015) Have community sanctions and measures widened the net of the European criminal justice systems?, *Punishment and Society*, 17(5): 575–597.

Annison, H. (2015) *Dangerous Politics – Risk, Political Vulnerability and Penal Policy*, Oxford: Oxford University Press.

Bailey, R. and Brake, M. (1976) *Radical Social Work*, New York: Pantheon Books.

Bell, E. (2011) *Criminal Justice and Neoliberalism*, Palgrave Macmillan: London.

Beyens, K. and Roosen, M. (2016) *Electronic Monitoring in Belgium*, Vrije Universiteit Brussel/ Criminal Justice Programme of the European Union (JUST/2013/JPEN/AG/4510).

Boone, M., van der Kooij, M. and Rap, S. (2016) *Electronic Monitoring in the Netherlands*, Universiteit Utrecht/Criminal Justice Programme of the European Union (JUST/2013/ JPEN/AG/4510).

Bottoms, A.E. and McWilliams, W. (1979) A non-treatment paradigm for probation practice, *British Journal of Social Work*, 9(2): 159–202.

Boyers, R. and Orrill, R. (1972) *Laing and Anti-Psychiatry*, Harmondsworth: Penguin.

Brake, M. and Bailey, R. (1980) *Radical Social Work and Practice*, London: Edward Arnold.

Bryant, M., Coker, J., Estlea, B., Himmel, S. and Knapp, T. (1978) Sentenced to social work, *Probation Journal*, 25(4): 110–114.

Burke, L. and Collett, S. (2008) Doing with or doing to – what now for the probation service?, *Criminal Justice Matters*, 72(1): 9–11.

Burke, L. and Collett, S. (2010) People are not things: What New Labour has done to probation, *Probation Journal*, 57(3): 232–249.

Burke, L. and Collett, S. (2015) *Delivering Rehabilitation – The Politics, Governance and Control of Probation*, London: Routledge.

Burke, L. and Collett, S. (2016) Transforming rehabilitation: Organizational bifurcation and the end of probation as we knew it? *Probation Journal*, 63(2): 120–135.

Cavadino, M. (2010) Penology, in McLaughlin, E. and Newburn, T. (eds) *The Sage Handbook of Criminological Theory*, London: Sage.

Chester, C. and Roberts, H. (2017) Improving the effectiveness of alcohol interlocks in New Zealand, *Probation Journal*, 64(3): 286–292.

Cloward, R.A. and Piven, F.F. (1976) Notes Towards a Radical Social Work, in Bailey, R. and Brake, M. *Radical Social Work*, New York: Pantheon Books.

Cohen, S. (1985) *Visions of Social Control: Crime, Punishment and Classification*, Polity Press: Cambridge.

Collett, S. (1998) Spiderman comes to Salford – Tagging offenders: cynical Resignation or Pragmatic acceptance, *Probation Journal*, 45(1): 3–9.

Crewe, B. (2009) *The Prisoner Society – Power, Adaptation, and Social Life in an English Prison*, Oxford: Oxford University Press.

Dunkel, F., Thiele, C. and Treig, J. (2016) Electronic monitoring in Germany, Universitat Greifswald/Criminal Justice Programme of the European Union (JUST/2013/JPEN/AG/4510).

Dunkel, F., Thiele, C. and Treig, J. (2017) 'You'll never stand-alone': Electronic monitoring in Germany, *European journal of Probation*, 9(1): 28–45.

Ellul, J. (1964) *The Technological Society*, New York: Vintage.

Fagan, D. (2017) Enhancing probation practice and safety with smartphone applications, *Probation Journal*, 64(3): 282–285.

Fitzgibbon, W. and Stengel, C.M. (2017) Women's voices made visible: Photovoice in visual criminology, *Punishment & Society*, 0(0): 1–27.

Fitzgibbon, W., Graebsch, C. and McNeill, F. (2017) Persuasive Punishment: The Shadow of Penal Supervision, in Brown, M. and Carrabine, E. (eds) *The Routledge International Handbook of Visual Criminology*, Abingdon: Routledge: 305–319.

Foucault, M. (1977) *Discipline and Punish – the Birth of the Prison*, London: Penguin.

Fullwood, C. (1976) Control in Probation, After-care and Parole in Custody without Control, Papers presented to the Cropwood Round-Table Conference December 1975, in King, J.F.S with Young, W. (eds), University of Cambridge: Institute of Criminology, 23–4.7

Garland, D. (1996) The limits of the sovereign state, *British Journal of Criminology*, 36(4): 445–471.

Garland, D. (2001) *The Culture of Control*, Oxford: Oxford University Press.

Gove, M. and Grayling, C. (2016) We're getting smart on crime, not going soft, *The Sunday Telegraph*, 14 February.

Graham, H. and McIvor, G. (2015) *Scottish and International Review of the Uses of Electronic Monitoring*, Stirling: The Scottish Centre for Crime & Justice Research, Report No 8/2015.

Graham, H. and McIvor, G. (2017) Advancing electronic monitoring in Scotland: Understanding the influence of localism and professional ideologies, *European Journal of Probation*, 9(1): 62–78.

HM Inspectorate of Probation (2016) *An Inspection of Through the Gate Resettlement Services for Short-Term Prisoners – A joint Inspection by HMI Probation and HMI Prisons*, Manchester: HMIP.

Harris, R. (1980) A changing service – The case for separating 'care' and 'control' in probation practice, *British Journal of Social Work*, 10: 163–184.

Home Office (2003) *Prison Statistics England and Wales 2002*, London: Home Office.

Hucklesby, A. (2008) Vehicles of desistance?, *Criminology and Criminal Justice*, 8(1): 51–71.

Hucklesby, A. and Holdsworth, E. (2016) *Electronic Monitoring in England and Wales*, University of Leeds/Criminal Justice Programme of the European Union (JUST/2013/JPEN/AG/4510).

Hucklesby, A., Beyens, K., Boone, M., Dunkel, F., McIvor, G. and Graham, H. (2016) *Creativity and Effectiveness in the Use of Electronic Monitoring: A Case Study of Five European Jurisdictions*, Criminal Justice Programme of the European Union (JUST/2013/JPEN/AG/4510).

Hudson, B. (1987) *Justice Though Punishment: A Critique of the 'Justice' Model of Corrections*, London: Macmillan.

Hudson, K. and Jones, T. (2016) Satellite tracking of offenders and integrated offender management: A local case study, *The Howard Journal*, 55(1): 188–206.

Illich, I. (1971) *Deschooling Society*, Harmondsworth: Penguin.

Marcuse, H. (1964) *One dimensional Man*, London: Abacus.

McGreevy, G. (2017) 'Changing lives': Using technology to promote desistance, *Probation Journal*, 64(3): 276–281.

McGuire, M.R. (2012) *Technology, Crime and Justice: The Question Concerning Technomania*, Routledge: Abingdon.

McIvor, G. and Graham, H. (2016) *Electronic Monitoring in Scotland*, Stirling: University of Stirling/Criminal Justice Programme of the European Union (JUST/2013/JPEN/ AG/4510).

McNeill, F. (2006) A desistance paradigm for offender management, *Criminology and Criminal Justice*, 6(1): 39–62.

McNeill, F. (2009) What works and what's just? *European journal of Probation*, 1(1): 21–40.

McNeill, F. (2013) Community Sanctions and European Penology, in Daems, T., Snacken, S. and Van Zyl Smit, D. (eds) (2013) *European penology?*, Oxford: Hart Publishing.

McNeill, F. (2017) Post-script: Guide, guard and glue – Electronic monitoring and penal supervision, *European Journal of Probation*, 9(1): 103–107.

McNeill, F. (2018) Mass supervision, misrecognition and the 'Malopticon', *Punishment & Society* 0(0): 1–23 (advance online publication).

McNeill, F. and Beyens, K. (2013) Introduction: Studying Mass Supervision, in McNeill, F. and Beyens, K. (eds) (2013) *Offender Supervision in Europe*, Basingstoke: Palgrave Macmillan.

McWilliams, W. (1987) Probation, pragmatism and policy, *Howard Journal*, 26: 97–121.

Millar, M. and Burke, L. (2012) Thinking beyond 'utility': Some comments on probation practice and training, *Howard Journal of Criminal Justice*, 51(3): 317–330.

Ministry of Justice (2013a) *Transforming Rehabilitation: A Revolution in the Way We Manage Offenders*, London: Ministry of Justice.

Ministry of Justice (2013b) *Transforming Rehabilitation: A Strategy for Reform*, London: Ministry of Justice.

Ministry of Justice (2016a) *Guide to Offender Management Statistics England and Wales*, London: Ministry of Justice, www.gov.uk/government/statistics/offender-management-statistics-quarterly-july-to-september-2016--2 (accessed 20 April 2017).

Ministry of Justice (2016b) *Story of the Prison Population: 1993–2016 England and Wales*, London: Ministry of Justice, www.gov.uk/government/statistics/story-of-the-prison-population-1993-to-2016 (accessed 12 December 2016).

Ministry of Justice (2016c) Press Release: 'Sobriety Tags' rolled out across London, 25 February, www.gov.uk/government/news/sobriety-tags-rolled-out-across-london (accessed 15 June 2016).

Ministry of Justice (2017a) *Offender Management Statistics Quarterly, England and Wales, July to September 2016 (with Prison population as at 31 December 2016)*, London: Ministry of Justice, https://assets.publishing.service.gov.uk/government/uploads/system/uploads/ attachment_data/file/585870/omsq-bulletin-q3-2016.pdf (accessed 10 November 2017).

Ministry of Justice (2017b) *Criminal Justice Statistics Quarterly, England and Wales, October 2015 to September 2016 (provisional)*, London: Ministry of Justice, https://assets.publishing.service.gov. uk/government/uploads/system/uploads/attachment_data/file/592058/criminal-justice-statistics-quarterly-update-september-2016.pdf (accessed 10 November 2017).

Nellis, M. (2009) Surveillance and confinement: Explaining and understanding the experience of electronically monitored curfews, *European Journal of Probation*, 1(1): 41–65.

Nellis, M. (2014) Upgrading electronic monitoring, downgrading probation: Reconfiguring 'offender management' in England and Wales, *European Journal of Probation*, 6(2): 169–191.

Nellis, M. (2015) *Standards and Ethics in Electronic Monitoring: Handbook for Professionals Responsible for the Establishment and Use of Electronic Monitoring*, Strasbourg: Council of Europe.

Nellis, M. (2016) Electronic monitoring and penal reform: Constructive resistance in the age of 'coercive connectiveness', *British journal of Community Justice*, 14(1): 113–132.

Nellis, M. (2017a) Setting the parameters of 'digital (criminal) justice' in Scotland, *Probation Journal*, 64(3): 191–208.

Nellis, M. (2017b) Electronic Monitoring and Probation Practice, in McNeill, F. Durnescu, I. and Butter, R. (eds) *Probation: 12 essential Questions*, London: Palgrave Macmillan, 217–243.

Office for National Statistics (2018) *Crime in England and Wales: Year Ending September 2017*, London: Office for National Statistics, www.ons.gov.uk/peoplepopulationandcommunity/crimeandjustice/bulletins/crimeinenglandandwales/yearendingseptember2017 (accessed 16 December 2017).

Phelps, M. (2013) The paradox of probation: Community supervision in the age of mass incarceration, *Law & Policy*, 35(1–2): 51–80.

Phelps, M. (2017) Mass probation: Toward a more robust theory of state variation in punishment, *Punishment & Society*, 19(1): 53–73.

Phillips, J. (2017) Probation practice in the information age, *Probation Journal*, 64(3): 209–225.

Robinson, G. (2008) Late-modern rehabilitation: The evolution of a penal strategy, *Punishment & Society*, 10(4): 429–445.

Robinson, G. (2016) Patrolling the Borders of Risk: The new bifurcation of probation services in England and Wales, in Bosworth, M., Hoyle, C. and Zedner, L. (eds) *Changing Contours of Criminal Justice: Research, Politics and Policy*, Oxford: Oxford University Press.

Sedgwick, P. (1982) *Psycho Politics*, London: Pluto Press.

Senior, P. (1984) The Probation order – Vehicle of social work or social control, *Probation Journal*, 31(2): 64–70.

Stout, B. (2012) The future of probation: Can humans and kiosks peacefully co-exist? www.russellwebster.com/the-future-of-probation-can-humans-and-kiosks-peacefully-co-exist/ (accessed 9 March 2018).

Szasz, T.S. (1972) *The Myth of Mental Illness*, London: Paladin.

Szasz, T.S. (1974) *Ideology and Insanity*, Harmondsworth: Penguin.

Tomczak, P. (2017) The voluntary sector and the mandatory statutory supervision requirement: Expanding the carceral net, *British Journal of Criminology*, 57: 152–171.

Travis, A. (2017) Liz Truss rejects calls to cut sentences to reduce prison population, www.theguardian.com/society/2017/feb/13/liz-truss-rejects-calls-to-cut-sentences-to-reduce-prison-population (accessed 18 February 2017).

Truss, L. (2017) A speech on criminal justice reform by the Secretary of State for Justice, delivered on 13 February, www.gov.uk/government/speeches/a-speech-on-criminal-justice-reform-by-the-secretary-of-state-for-justice (accessed 18 February 2017).

Underdown, A. (1998) *Strategies for Effective Offender Supervision*, Report of the HMIP What Works Project, London: Home Office.

Verbeek, P-P. (2016) *Persuasive Technology and Moral Responsibility: Toward an Ethical Framework for Persuasive Technologies*, Paper for Persuasive06, Eindhoven: Eindhoven University of Technology.

Wacquant, L. (2009) *Punishing the Poor – the Neoliberal Government of Social Insecurity*, London: Duke University Press.

Walker, H. and Beaumont, B. (1981) *Probation Work: Critical Theory and Socialist Practice*, Oxford: Blackwell.

Walker, H. and Beaumont, B. (1985) *Working with Offenders*, London: Macmillan.

Whitfield, D. (1997) *Tackling The Tag*, Winchester: Waterside.

Whitfield, D. (2001) *The Magic Bracelet – Technology and Offender Supervision*, Winchester: Waterside.

# 3

## REIMAGINING THE REHABILITATIVE JOURNEY

## Personal rehabilitation

So what's the point of trying to change if there's nothing you can dae tae move on, you know what I mean, so. I feel kinda bad telling you this, it's just a hopeless cause [slightly laughing] really for me I'm starting tae think, it's horrible. I came oot wi all these big ideas and I went tae college, 'I'm gonnae use my experiences, I'm gonnae try and change, I'm gonnae try an let people know what it could be like in my situation'. Pfff, it just didnae happen man. Like I was saying, the thing that's really frustrating me the noo is no being able tae get a job and it's so, so annoying, so frustrating honestly it's just . . . it feels like everything's just wasted, every bit of my sentence, every effort I've made after it just, pfff, been a waste o' time that's what it's starting tae feel like. Pretty scary. ('Andy')

*(Schinkel 2015: 15)*

### Introduction: From social control to supporting change

We ended the last chapter echoing Cohen's (1985) question: what space is there for criminal justice to exert power and do good at the same time? Putting this another way, we might ask whether penal power can only ever be deployed to *coerce* change in the service of social control? Can penal power – and the institutions within which it is exercised (principally prisons and probation) – be somehow attuned or adjusted to be a means of helping citizens towards better lives? And can these institutions and interventions contribute to the wider project of social justice? These are the questions that lie at the heart of this book.

Social theorists and philosophers may seek to answer such questions on a normative level. But those who work within the penal system and those who have been subject to penal power can also bring their experience to bear. As authors with several decades of experience of probation practice between and behind us, we can all think of examples of people whose experiences of supervision did positively transform their life trajectories, social positions and prospects; and we can also think of people whose disadvantaged social positions were entrenched or exacerbated by criminal justice interventions (even those inspired by humanistic and benevolent intentions). It follows that we need to seek to understand what makes the difference between these divergent outcomes.

The chapters that follow in this book will address the legal, moral and social dimensions of rehabilitation, seeking to elaborate what rehabilitation would need to look like if it is to play a role in promoting social justice. This chapter focuses specifically on the personal dimension of rehabilitation. It explores how and why people move away from offending and towards an improved social position. It also considers what sorts of rehabilitative approaches and services might best support that journey. Change at the individual level, however positive, can never be in and of itself enough to deliver social justice. But we want to argue that it can be and often must be a part of that project.

## Personal rehabilitation and reintegration

Who needs transformation? This is a question that Marguerite Schinkel (2016) asks in her brilliant examination of how long-term prisoners make sense of *Being Imprisoned*. At a common-sense level, it might be assumed that everyone spending time as a prisoner or a probationer needs to undergo some sort of personal change, at least if they want to avoid further offending in the future. But this is not quite what Schinkel (2016) discovers. First, she finds that those who do not accept their guilt recognise no need for transformation. Second, she finds that those with no hope of change also feel no need for transformation. Third – and perhaps more surprisingly – she finds that those prisoners who are well supported and well resourced outside of prison don't require imprisonment itself to be a transformative experience. Their social situation outside allows them to imagine a crime-free future that doesn't depend on internalised or personal transformation. Those who *do* recount narratives of in-prison transformation are those for whom prison is all that stands between a spoiled past and a better future. They accept that something needs to change and – within the confines of imprisonment – perhaps the only thing that they can change is themselves. Of course, as 'Andy' identifies in the opening quote above, making that narrative stick after release is another question.

In the first development of the model of four forms of rehabilitation, McNeill (2012a: 14) referred to 'psychological rehabilitation', which, he said, 'is principally concerned with promoting positive individual-level change in the offender'. In a second paper, McNeill clarified further:

> Psychological rehabilitation means essentially what Raynor and Robinson (2009) refer to as correctional rehabilitation: that which seeks to somehow change or restore the offender, to develop new skills or abilities, and to address and resolve deficits or problems. A better, less loaded term, might be 'personal rehabilitation,' since this need not imply that any specific disciplinary perspective or set of techniques is implied in this project of personal change.
>
> *(McNeill 2014: 4204)*

The shift in language (from psychological to personal) perhaps also aims to avoid the problems inherent in medicalised or treatment-based models of rehabilitation that we discussed in Chapter 1. In reality, contemporary 'offending behaviour programmes' (OBPs) tend to rely not on a medical-somatic but rather a social-developmental paradigm (Johnstone 1996). Rather than seeking to diagnose and correct the individual flaws of 'criminal types', they aim to address and remedy social-developmental problems that they see as lying behind offending. On this logic, people who offend are not seen as being fundamentally different from anyone else; rather, they are people who – for a variety of reasons (familial, institutional, environmental, structural) – have not learned the attitudes, values or skills that they need in order to live law-abiding, satisfying and useful lives. OBPs typically seek to make good on these sorts of 'deficits' by tackling the 'criminogenic needs' associated with offending (and especially repeat offending).

Of course, such a perspective can be criticised for treating symptoms as causes, and for turning public issues into personal troubles (Wright Mills 1959). Simply seeking to 'correct' the 'offender' does nothing to remedy the socio-structural causes of crime. Indeed, rather that addressing an unjust social order, correctionalism seeks to 'responsibilise' the offender into compliance with it (Carlen 2013). However, personal rehabilitation need not be 'correctional' in this sense, even when OBPs form part of it. The wider project of personal rehabilitation might be framed in such a way as to support *both* normative personal development *and* political change. Personal rehabilitation *might* sometimes involve working through these kinds of OBPs, but they may not always be a necessary component of it and they are never sufficient for it.

In this wider sense, *personal* rehabilitation is concerned with any aspect of the normative development of the individual that is associated with movement away from offending. Most obviously, therefore, the process might be supported by any educational engagement (whether provided by others or self-directed) that affects the human resources of the learner. Equally, it might come about without any formal intervention at all. As the literature on desistance makes clear, an individual's normative development might be the result of processes of aging and maturation, or of changing social bonds or of people re-shaping their sense of themselves and their priorities (e.g. Maruna 2001). Thus, in Schinkel's (2016) study, some of those prisoners who did invest in narratives of transformation described these as self-directed processes whilst others stressed the importance of prison-based interventions of various sorts.

Whether driven by an internal or an external impetus, the idea of personal transformation – of metamorphosis – is a near universal trope in human cultures through the ages (Morland 2016). It provides a source of hope for the future and, as Andy suggests above, when frustrated by external forces beyond the control of the person concerned, a cause of profound doubt and despair. Perhaps the most famous of all journeys – Homer's *The Odyssey* – best illustrates these processes. It also provides an illustration of the complexities of finding one's way home after forced exile (see also Bottoms 2013).

## The long road home

At the beginning of *The Odyssey*, it is ten years after the fall of Troy but the victorious Greek hero Odysseus still has not returned to his native Ithaca. There, a group of misbehaving Suitors, believing Odysseus to be dead, seem intent on taking his place. Not only have they overrun his palace, they are seeking to seduce and win over his faithful – though weakening – wife, Penelope. Odysseus's son, Telemachus, is naturally worried, and sets out to track his father's journey through stories told by his former comrades.

Following the Trojan War, Odysseus and his men suffered more losses fighting the Kikones before escaping to the island of the drug-addicted Lotus-eaters, where they were tempted to stay. Next, the Cyclops Polyphemus eats many of the men before Odysseus's ingenious plan allows the rest to escape. In the process, he blinds Polyphemus and reveals his name, thus starting his personal war with the sea god Poseidon (the Cyclops's father). The wind god Aeolus provides Odysseus with a bag of winds to aid his return home, but the crew open the bag and send the ship to the land of the giant, man-eating Laistrygonians, where they again barely escape.

On their next stop, the goddess Circe tricks Odysseus's men and turns them into pigs. This time, with the help of the god Hermes, Odysseus defies her spell and changes the pigs back into men. They stay on her island for a year in the lap of luxury, with Odysseus as Circe's lover, before moving on.

Back at sea, Odysseus helps his men resist the temptations of the seductive and dangerous Sirens, steering his ship between the sea monster Scylla and the whirlpools of Charybdis. They plumb the depths of Hades to receive a prophecy from the blind seer Tiresias. Resting on the island of Helios, Odysseus's men disobey his orders not to touch the oxen. At sea, Zeus punishes them and all but Odysseus die in a storm. Odysseus reaches Calypso's island where he is imprisoned by the beautiful goddess (and taken as her lover) for eight years, until Athena arranges his release.

Odysseus sets sail on a makeshift raft but the vengeful Poseidon conjures up a storm. With Athena's help, Odysseus reaches the Phaeacians. Their princess, Nausicaa, opens the palace to the stranger. Odysseus withholds his identity for as long as he can until finally, at the Phaeacians' request, he tells the story of his adventures. When he has finished his story, the Phaeacians hospitably give him gifts and ferry him home on a ship. Athena (the goddess who has been on his side throughout) disguises Odysseus as a beggar and instructs him to seek out his old swineherd, Eumaeus; she also brings back Telemachus from his own travels. With Athena's help, Telemachus reunites with his father, who reveals his identity only to his son and the swineherd. They devise a plan to overthrow Penelope's Suitors.

In disguise as a beggar, Odysseus investigates his palace. The wicked Suitors and a few of his old servants generally treat him rudely as Odysseus assesses their loyalty and Penelope's. Penelope, who notes the resemblance between the beggar and her presumably dead husband, proposes a contest: she will, at last, marry the Suitor who can string Odysseus's great bow and shoot an arrow through a dozen axe heads. Only Odysseus can pull off the feat. Odysseus lovingly reunites with

Penelope; his knowledge of their bed that he built is the proof that overcomes her scepticism that he is an impostor. The Suitors meet their brutal end and, presumably, Odysseus and Penelope live happily ever after.

It took Odysseus about 20 years to find his way home. In him, we find a hero who is a king and a brave and successful soldier, facing all sorts of obstacles and challenges on the long road home. He is strong and clever – and he has a goddess on his side. But he also faces temptations of various sorts, has a crew of sailors who sometimes seem more of a hindrance than a help, has some very powerful enemies, and has to confront many monsters, even descending into Hades (or Hell) along the way. When he eventually returns home, he is uncertain of the loyalty of those he has loved and longed for. He doesn't know if the place and the people to whom he once belonged still exist.

Although Homer might quibble with the casting of Odysseus as a persistent offender, there is plenty of offending against gods and people in his tale. More generally, the struggle to find a way home – to find love, family and a place of belonging – offers a universal human narrative. *The Odyssey* therefore is as good a place as any to begin an examination of whether and how people who have offended – and who need to find a way home – navigate their paths to better futures.

## Inauspicious beginnings

The starting points for desistance journeys are very often spectacularly unpromising ones. Unlike Odysseus, most people who end up in the penal system are not kings and do not appear to have the gods on their side. This is important for the obvious reason that the personal and social resources that people bring to any process of personal development will have a profound bearing on their prospects of success (however defined). This, of course, is one good reason why questions of social and criminal justice cannot be separated.

Bottoms and Shapland (2011), in an important contribution to desistance theory, outline their model of a seven-step process of (or, continuing our *Odyssey* analogy, a seven-stage journey towards) desistance. We will return to the steps in this process below but, for present purposes, the more important point relates to the influence of 'pre-programmed potential' and 'social capital' on the journey. Crucially, Bottoms and Shapland (2011) note that neither the dispositions (or 'potential') of individuals nor their social positions and resources (or 'capital') are static. Rather, they can change over time, producing interaction effects in the broader process of change. Thus, for example, it is Odysseus's guile (an individual asset) that enables him to defeat the Cyclops, but in giving away his name in so doing, he alters his own social position (earning a powerful enemy in Poseidon). So, whilst his skills enable him to escape peril and move on in his journey, the shift in his social (or cosmic!) capital creates a new and significant obstacle.

If we look to the evidence about the personal dispositions and social positions of people caught up within the penal system, the picture seems bleak. Some of the clearest UK-based evidence in this regard was provided by the then New Labour government's Social Exclusion Unit (2002) in a report on *Reducing Reoffending by Ex-prisoners*. Compared to the general population, prisoners at that time were 13 times more likely to have been in care as a child, 10 times more likely to have been a regular truant from school, 13 times more likely to unemployed, 2.5 times more likely to have a family member with a criminal conviction, 15 times more likely to be HIV positive, and male prisoners were 6 times more likely to be a young father. In respect of prisoners' skills and abilities, 80 per cent had the writing skills of an 11-year-old, 65 per cent had the numeracy skills of an 11-year-old and 50 per cent had the reading skills of an 11-year-old. In relation to their health and wellbeing, 70 per cent had used drugs before coming to prison, 70 per cent suffered from at least two mental disorders, 20 per cent of male prisoners had attempted suicide and 37 per cent of female prisoners had attempted suicide. More generally, the Corston Report (2007) made clear the profound adversities that women caught up in the criminal justice system have typically faced, even before they are confronted by a justice system itself designed by and for men.

Rather than looking at the life histories and characteristics of penal subjects, some scholars have examined instead how intensely penal sanctions are concentrated in poorer communities. Thus, for example, Houchin's (2005) study of the postcodes of those in Scottish prisons on the night of 30 June 2003 found that half of all prisoners came from home addresses in just 155 of 1,222 local government wards. Although the overall imprisonment rate for men in Scotland at that time was 237 per 100,000, for men from the 27 most deprived wards in the country the rate was 953 per 100,000. At that time, about one in nine young men from Scotland's most deprived communities were spending time in prison before reaching the age of 23. Elsewhere, for example in the USA, the relationship between being at the harsh end of inequality and caught up in the penal system is also related to racial injustice (see Western and Pettit 2010).

It is problematic to over-generalise about the skills and resources of those who find their way into the penal system; there are people in prisons with considerable economic, human and social capital. But even so, in general terms, people caught up in the penal system – despite their personal potential, talents and abilities – are amongst the most marginalised, excluded and (often) damaged in our society. For some sociologists, the extent of these inequalities, and their entrenchment through the operations of 'the penal state', make talk of ex-prisoner 're-entry' or 'reintegration' ridiculous, ironic or cruel:

> Reentry programs are not an antidote to but an extension of punitive containment as government technique for managing problem categories and territories in the dualizing city. They are not a remedy to, but part and parcel of the institutional machinery of hyper incarceration (Cohen 1985), whose reach they stretch beyond bars and over the life course of convicts by keeping them under the stern watch and punctilious injunctions of criminal justice even as they return to their barren neighborhoods. Reentry must therefore be understood as an element in the redrawing of the perimeter, priorities, and

modalities of action of the state as a stratifying and classifying agency and not as an 'industry' geared to 'reintegrating' a marginalized population that was never socially and economically integrated to start with.

(Wacquant 2010: 616)

Though Wacquant is not discussing processes of desistance directly, sociologists who study desistance recognise the scale of the challenges that people face in seeking to move away from crime and punishment. As Uggen *et al.* (2006) put it:

To the extent that felons belong to a distinct class or status group, the problems of desistance from crime and reintegration into civil society can be interpreted as problems of mobility – moving felons from a stigmatized status as outsiders to full democratic participation as stakeholders.

(Uggen et al. 2006: 283)

The purpose of this short section on 'Inauspicious beginnings' has been simply to illustrate how long and difficult the journey to 'full democratic participation' might be for many people in the penal system. But equally, as we have already argued (*against* correctionalism), we might also have to accept that, in another sense, we start in the wrong place *conceptually* when we focus solely on the dispositions and social positions of *individuals* attempting desistance. We *do* need to understand what enables some people to stop offending and how they do it; we have a lot to learn from making sense of their journeys. But we also need to ask why they had to start that journey so far away from 'full democratic participation' and how and why their social mobility was so constrained by the socio-structural, legal and cultural obstacles that have been placed in their way in the past and the present. We must insist on coupling the individual and the social aspects of the journey.

## Going no/where?

So far in this chapter, we have slipped at times between discussion of personal transformation, personal development, personal rehabilitation and desistance. Of course, these terms are not synonymous. One way to clarify the distinctions between them might be to more clearly articulate their intended destinations or outcomes.

It is obvious, for example, that the terms 'rehabilitation' (at least used in the context of criminal justice as opposed to, for example, physiotherapy or occupational therapy) and 'desistance' are both concerned in some way with ending or reducing reoffending. Commonly, when people (or systems) speak of rehabilitation, they have in mind what we would term 'rehabilitative interventions' aimed at supporting an individual to change something about themselves so that the likelihood of offending is reduced. As we have noted above, this is the rationale behind offending behaviour programmes. But this confuses a mechanism (intervention) for the process itself (rehabilitation). These programmes or activities seek to support and may be part of personal rehabilitation, but they are not, in and of themselves, rehabilitation.

It is precisely this sort of framing that the desistance literature has encouraged. In that literature, desistance is seen as a (developmental) process that belongs to those that are going through it; a process that may exist 'before, behind and beyond' any intervention designed to support it (McNeill *et al.* 2012). However, we do *not* treat desistance as being synonymous with personal rehabilitation because, in our view, the desistance research also points us towards the importance of the other three forms of rehabilitation: legal, moral and social. Indeed, the four-forms model of rehabilitation was based largely on evidence about desistance processes; and it extends beyond the personal sphere because that evidence base points us towards the importance not just of personal change, but of social support of and reaction to change, of legal recognition of rights as well as responsibilities, and of the reciprocal moral reparation that might underpin restored relationships. In simple terms, desistance is not just a process of personal development, it is a social and political project that effects and is affected by a person's legal standing.

But if desistance is bigger and broader than even a capacious and person-centred conception of rehabilitation, then the notions of personal development and transformation are bigger than that of desistance. Although *transformation* perhaps implies a change more dramatic and swift than *development*, both ideas extend beyond a concern with offending. These are concepts that apply to almost any human change process, such as becoming a graduate or a parent or a marathon runner.

Again, it is notable that desistance scholars themselves have stretched the parameters of the concept beyond a concern with changes in offending behaviour. For example, Maruna and Farrall's (2004) distinction between primary and secondary desistance relates the former merely to behaviour and the latter to a related shift in identity. They posit that shifts in identity and self-concept matter in securing longer-term, sustained changes in behaviour as opposed to mere lulls in offending. The concept of tertiary desistance goes even further, referring not just to shifts in behaviour or identity but to shifts in one's sense of belonging to a (moral) community. It draws on developing evidence (for example, Laub and Sampson 2003; Bottoms and Shapland 2011; Weaver 2015) that since identity is socially constructed and negotiated, securing long-term change depends not just on how one sees oneself but also on how one is seen by others, and on how one sees one's place in society. Nugent and Schinkel (2016) have recently refined and relabelled these three forms or aspects as 'act', 'identity' and 'relational' desistance.

In fact, the links between behaviour, identity and belonging are implicit in the main explanatory theories of desistance. These are commonly divided into ontogenic theories which stress the importance of age and maturation; sociogenic theories which stress the importance of social bond and ties; and narrative theories which stress the importance of subjective changes in identity (Maruna 2001). Recently, in an important review of desistance research, Bottoms (2014) has suggested a fourth set of explanatory factors which are situational in character. Drawing on his expertise in socio-spatial criminology, as well as in desistance research, Bottoms points out that various aspects of our social environments and of our situated 'routine activities' also provide importance influences on our behaviour, for better or worse. Whilst our environments and activities are closely connected to our social bonds or ties (in intimate relationships and to families, work and faith communities), they deserve attention in their own right.

In a sense, these definitional refinements and contortions represent the efforts of desistance scholars to begin to engage with the question of destinations and outcomes with which we began this section. And, in so doing, offending itself comes to be decentred as the emphasis shifts from where we no longer wish to be (offending) to where we want to get to.

Uggen *et al.* (2006) have already provided us with one definition of the destination: they suggest that we want and need people to arrive at reintegration and thus 'full democratic participation as stakeholders' (2006: 283). However, it is fair to say that neither scholars of rehabilitation nor scholars of desistance have done a very good job of articulating what their vision of reintegration is exactly. Even Braithwaite's (1989) seminal work on *Crime, Shame and Reintegration* has more to say on the *process* of reintegration than the destination.

The importance of this question is vividly illustrated by some recent desistance studies. For example, Bottoms (2013), drawing on findings from the Sheffield Desistance Study (conducted with Shapland and others), has argued that some people desist through a form of extreme 'situational self-binding' which amounts effectively to self-imprisonment or at least self-imposed social isolation. Although Bottoms (2013) notes that this was relatively rare amongst desisters in the Sheffield study, Adam Calverley's (2009) exploration of ethnicity and desistance found that Black and Dual Heritage men in one London borough faced the greatest structural and cultural obstacles to desistance – and that they tended to desist through isolation. Nugent and Schinkel's (2016) examination of two recent Scottish studies of very different populations (released long-term prisoners and young people exiting an intensive support service) also revealed common 'pains of desistance' linked to social isolation and the failure to secure work, connection and belonging.

These findings suggest that some people desist not into 'full democratic participation as stakeholders' but into entrenched social exclusion. The fact that in so doing they cease to be a 'problem' for their neighbours or for the State is not enough. As Graham and McNeill (2017) argue, this sort of post-desistance subsistence cannot be a 'good enough' outcome of a justice process:

> We would argue that criminal justice must aim for more ambitious goals than crime reduction through self-incapacitation. Those in whose name punishment is delivered have an obligation to restore those whose debts are settled. And those whose offending flows from those social injustices and inequalities that the state permits, perpetuates and exacerbates, are owed additional duties of support.
>
> *(Graham and McNeill 2017: 446)*

In sum then, we might represent the relationships between these overlapping concepts as follows:

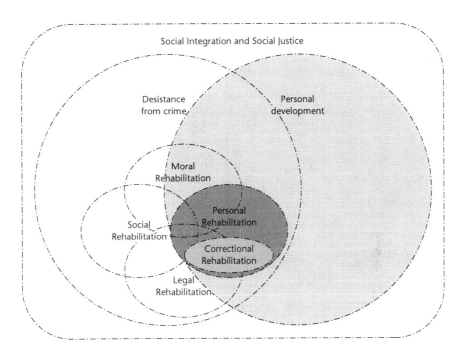

**FIGURE 3.1**  Personal rehabilitation in context

In Figure 3.1, we show how correctional rehabilitation, if it is necessary at all, is just part of personal rehabilitation, which is, in turn, part of a wider process of personal development. That wider process overlaps with the process of desistance, but desistance is about more that personal change; it requires consideration of the other three intersecting forms of rehabilitation: legal, social and moral. Both processes – development and desistance – sit within the still wider process of social integration.

One adjacent field of research does provide some resources for considering what social integration might mean and what it might require. In a recent paper, Kirkwood and McNeill (2015) compare models of reintegration that developed independently in and through studies of the experiences of people desisting from offending and people seeking asylum. As they note, these are two quite different contexts – two quite different struggles for acceptance, belonging or integration. Nonetheless, models of integration derived from research with asylum seekers may well have much to say to the criminal justice context.

For example, Kirkwood and McNeill (2015) discuss Ager and Strang's (2004) model of 'Indicators of Integration'; a model based on an extensive literature review and on empirical work with asylum seekers. The authors outlined ten 'domains' of integration, clustered in four categories:

- Means and markers: Employment; Housing; Education; Health;
- Social connections: Social bonds; Social bridges; Social links;

- Facilitators: Language and cultural knowledge; Safety and stability;
- Foundation: Rights and citizenship.

In this model, integration is founded in a person's legal status as a citizen. It is facilitated both by the sorts of skills and knowledge and the sense of safety and stability that they need in order to engage with others. Those engagements allow the development of 'social connections'. Drawing on research and theory into social capital, these connections include social bonds (usually with people similar to and connected to us through, for example, ethnic, national or religious identity); social bridges (with members of other communities); and social links (with institutions, including local and central government services). The 'means and markers' indicate the extent to which a person is 'integrated', but they also highlight the opportunities and resources that should assist people to integrate in other ways.

In common with some conceptualisations of rehabilitation, Ager and Strang's (2004) framework conceives of integration as a *process* as well as defining successful integration as *achievement* in the range of stated domains. They also recognise that if this definition was applied to members of the host society it would inevitably highlight that not all citizens are equally 'integrated', if at all. For that reason, they suggest that integration is a goal that should be worked towards for *all* citizens (Ager and Strang 2004).

Although integration or re/integration might be seen as the goal of rehabilitation, there remains an even more profound and fundamental question: integration into what and on what terms? The concept of social integration can be criticised on the grounds that – like so many liberal concepts – it tends to assume the existence of a just social order into which we should and would wish to be integrated. But if we regard the prevailing social order as unjust, integration may undesirable? As we write, there is much debate in the press about American sportspeople – many of them people of colour – 'taking the knee' during renditions of the national anthem before sporting events. They do so to protest against racial injustice and, in particular, against police brutality towards African Americans. Their protest is, in one sense, an assertion of the right to question the justice of the particular social order that anthem singing seeks to celebrate, and of their refusal to passively collude with integration into that social order.

So, it seems clear that questions of social integration – like questions of reintegration – ultimately cannot and should not be separated from questions of social justice. Nancy Fraser's (2007) wide-ranging work on social in/justice explores the relationships between redistribution (of economic resources), recognition (of social status) and representation (in political terms). She sees these three aspects of justice as being inter-related. For example, to be symbolically affirmed in terms of my equal status is not to be materially equipped to participate in social or political life. A person may have a passport and a vote, but no time, money or energy to engage politically, precisely because of lack of material resources.

Without diverting further into an extensive discussion of social justice here, it might suffice to say that this chapter is concerned with reimagining processes of personal development that might support successful integration in a just social order. Given our interest in rehabilitation, the particular type of personal development that concerns us here is associated with desistance from crime and, in particular (in this chapter), the changes within individuals that might help people who have offended move towards integration in a just order. Combining Fraser's and Uggen *et al.*'s (2006) terms, we need to understand when, how and why people come to be afforded the resources, recognition and representation that allow a person to really enjoy and fulfil 'full democratic participation as a stakeholder'.

As we have already seen, this seems like an exceptionally tall order, but the desistance literature is based largely on studying the experiences of those who somehow manage at least part of that journey (i.e. as far as desistance from offending if not necessarily integration), even against the odds. In the next section, we seek to unravel some of the twists and turns involved.

## Steps on the journey

A great deal has been written in recent decades about desistance processes and we have no intention of reviewing or summarising that literature here. We have already alluded to three key theoretical perspectives on desistance, stressing the importance of aging and maturation, social bonds and personal narratives (Maruna 2001). We have also noted that Bottoms (2014) has suggested that we should add a fourth perspective focusing on the socio-spatial dynamics of desistance. Although placing the emphasis in different places, most desistance scholars now agree that explanations of desistance require an understanding of the interplay between social and subjective factors (e.g. LeBel *et al.* 2008); and of the links and interactions between becoming more mature, developing our social ties, revising our sense of self and moving in and through different contexts and environments.[1]

Rather than trying to unpick all of these complexities here, we return to Bottoms and Shapland's (2011) seven-step model of the desistance process, as discussed above. This model, which in some respects invites comparisons to Prochaska and DiClemente's (1982) Transtheoretical Model of Change (in relation to substance use recovery) is represented in Figure 3.2. In the remainder of this section, we use this model of the process as a heuristic device, allowing us to illustrate *some* of the complex interactions involved. It is worth noting, however, that this model is derived from a study of 113 men who had been involved in persistent offending and whose mean age at the time of first interview was 20. The men, who lived in or around Sheffield, were followed up for three to four years, with an intended total of four research interviews during that period. This is not therefore a general model of desistance processes, but we suspect it has quite broad applicability.

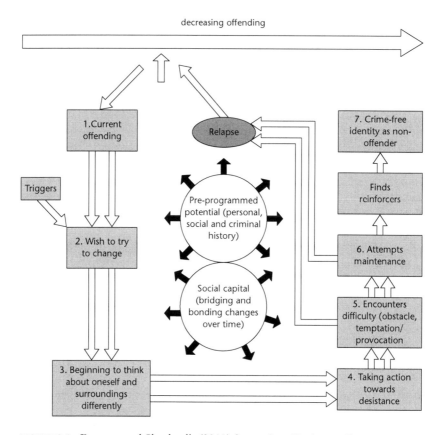

**FIGURE 3.2** Bottoms and Shapland's (2011) Seven-Step Desistance Process

## Why travel? Steps 1, 2 and 3

The first three steps in the process essentially relate to the question 'Why travel?'. For Odysseus and his crew, the answer was obvious: the war was over. Perhaps their thirst for adventure had been quelled. They wanted to go home. For people approaching desistance from crime, similar 'turning points' (Laub and Sampson 2003) or 'hooks for change' (Giordano *et al.* 2002) may come to bear.

Most of the desistance literature tends to cast these as moments of individual awakening. Common examples include a young man in his mid-twenties coming to value his relationship with an intimate partner more than spending time with his (offending) peers, or a young woman who becomes pregnant and invests herself both in the welfare of her child and the socially valorised role of mother. Positive opportunities for work or further education might also act as triggers, but so may imposed constraints (for example, conscription to military service or indeed imprisonment). Other adverse experiences like illness, injury or the loss of a loved one (or a friend and co-offender) might also trigger consideration of change. Indeed, Paternoster and Bushway (2009) have argued that a 'crystallization of discontent' with one's 'working self' as an offender, and with the 'feared self' that seems to lie ahead, may impel change.

Whether the triggering event invites hope or fear, it seems clear that the person's subjective orientation towards it is important. To return to our analogy, if Odysseus had a negative or ambivalent view of home, then the opportunity to return home after the war might have held little appeal and exercised little motivational power. Notably Odysseus felt *both* hope *and* fear about going home; he had been away for a long time and couldn't really know to what situation – or to what kind of 'welcome' – he was returning.

To some extent, *The Odyssey* also tells a story of collective journeying; Odysseus has a crew – and they often seem to be more of a burden and a problem than a resource for the journey. Nonetheless, there are questions of loyalty and camaraderie to be considered. These kinds of themes are invoked in Beth Weaver's (2015) brilliant study of 'The Del'; a small group of co-offenders who, over the course of time, mutated into a band of desisters. For them, desistance was a relational project and a relational process; as their relational commitments (to one another and to their loved ones) evolved and shifted, they produced new motivations, opportunities and resources for their desistance journeys, although not all of them travelled successfully.

Clearly, therefore, deciding to travel involves not just an external impetus but also an internal re-appraisal of one's current situation. It may be 'cued' by some shift in social context or position, but the response to that cue depends on the potential traveller's subjective apprehension of it, and on their appraisal of the prospective journey's value. It seems logical to suggest that the prospects for success may depend in part on the clarity of that apprehension of opportunity, on how unequivocally positive the assessment of the value of the journey turns out to be, and on the strength of the person's hope of succeeding in it. Indeed, there is some empirical evidence to this effect (e.g. Burnett 1992, 2000, 2004).

## Embarkation and derailment: Steps 4 and 5

It is then no small matter to set off on the desistance journey and, as we have already argued, it is entirely reasonable that many people do so unsure of their motivation and prospects, and uncertain that the venture is worthwhile. When this ambivalence meets the harsh realities of the journey and the demands that it makes, travelling backwards becomes likely. Bottoms and Shapland's (2011) model recognises this in its cyclical design; and indeed, most of the 'desisters' in their study required several 'cycles' through the process to achieve desistance.

Like Odysseus and his crew, the obstacles to finding a way home (or to a new place of belonging) are very great indeed. They faced enemies and monsters, and storms brewed by vengeful gods. The same is often true for would-be desisters. The attitudes of those around them – and the action or inaction of State (if not divine) authorities – may often conspire to block their paths.

For example, as one of us has argued recently (McNeill 2016) the State might impede desistance through its approach to economic and social policy. We have already noted that labour market de/regulation or social welfare retrenchment will have profound effects on the social contexts in which desistance is attempted. In respect of penal policy, the ways in which penal systems are ordered may exacerbate these adverse effects. Penal systems preoccupied with retribution, deterrence or incapacitation have created 'tail them, nail them and jail them' approaches to probation supervision that have contributed to mass incarceration. Cecilia Klingele (2014) has recently argued this case forcefully, not least by noting that half of all admission to jails and more than a third of all admissions to federal prisons in the USA are for probation or parole revocations. If we accept that imprisonment is, at best, a problematic context for supporting desistance and, at worst, criminogenic, then these alarming rates of breach or revocation raise important issues about the proper targeting of supervision (in ways which contribute to decarceration rather than the net widening discussed in the previous chapter) and about the effective management of compliance issues (see Robinson and McNeill 2008; McNeill and Robinson 2012; Phelps 2013). Wider aspects of penal policy – like the way in which disclosure of criminal convictions is managed – are also likely to have significant effects on labour market participation and thus on desistance. This is an issue to which we return in the next chapter in our discussion of legal (or judicial) rehabilitation.

Another kind of obstacle might be found in the sometimes pathologising language of risks and needs; an epistemic framing of practice that may serve to undermine people's resources for desistance and to construct or cement their identities as 'hopeless offenders'. As labelling theory suggests, discourses that reflect and predict failure may well provoke it (Maruna and LeBel 2003, 2010).

As McNeill sums up:

> [T]he state can make social policy choices that whip up a storm for our weary travellers, or it can calm the waves. Those that run the correctional support vessels can carry supplies and help with navigation or they can torpedo any desistance vessel that looks a little wayward. And the crews of these support vessels can encourage travellers or they can tell them (directly or indirectly) that their journeys are doomed.
>
> *(McNeill 2016: 269)*

Of course, the State is not the only potential source of obstacles. The attitudes of fellow citizens may also impede the journey. Most obviously perhaps, if employment is important to desistance, then stigmatising attitudes towards (and related discrimination against) people with convictions creates major challenges for desisters seeking to access the labour market (see McGuinness *et al.* 2013). But equally, the attitudes of those people closest to desisters may sometimes undermine rather than support change. Particularly where offending (and other problematic) behaviour has been very persistent, it may be extremely hard for close family and friends to expect anything other than disappointment. But, again as Maruna and LeBel (2010) argue, these low or negative expectations may invite relapse rather than encourage fortitude in facing the struggle.

If the notion of obstacles helpfully places the emphasis outside of the individual, then Bottoms and Shapland's (2011) mention of 'temptations' and 'provocations' draws our attention to the internal dynamics of the struggles they create. For the lonely and weary traveller, the hauntingly beautiful voices of the Sirens, or the seductions of life amongst the Lotus-eaters, might very easily end the journey prematurely. The capacity to close one's ears to the Sirens' song, and to turn away from the Lotus-eaters, might be affected by those in whose company we travel – and by the potency (or otherwise) of our hope for something better yet to come.

## Keeping going and making it home: Steps 6 and 7

Sustaining that hope depends in part on finding reinforcement which depends, in turn, on internal and external responses to the desister's efforts to maintain change. When Odysseus reaches the Phaeacians, having survived Poseidon's attempts to drown him (thanks to Athena's help), they want to hear his story; they want to know who this shipwrecked traveller is – not just in the sense of knowing his name perhaps, but in the sense of knowing his character. Their response to his reluctant telling of his story is to offer him the practical help he needs for the last part of his journey home.

Odysseus's reluctance to give himself (or his identity) away is understandable, particularly after his experience with the Cyclops and then with Poseidon. But, like all of us, if he is to secure the help of a community, he has to let himself be known by them. It is not just that the Phaeacians then are moved to meet Odysseus's material needs. The telling of his story perhaps serves another purpose; it allows Odysseus to re-craft his narrative in a way that buttresses his own positive self-identity and his motivation to take the final step of his journey.

Again, we suspect that similar dynamics apply to desisters. Maruna's (2001) seminal work on their narrative transformations reinforces these sorts of dynamics. As he notes, those in his study who were desisting from offending developed 'redemption scripts':

> The redemption script begins by establishing the goodness and convention-ality of the narrator—a victim of society who gets involved with crime and drugs to achieve some sort of power over otherwise bleak circumstances. This deviance eventually becomes its own trap, however, as the narrator becomes ensnared in the vicious cycle of crime and imprisonment. Yet, with the help of some outside force, someone who 'believed in' the ex-offender, the narrator is able to accomplish what he or she was 'always meant to do'. Newly empowered, he or she now seeks to 'give something back' to society as a display of gratitude.
>
> *(Maruna 2001: 87)*

We'll come to the importance of the 'outside force' in the next and final section of this chapter (and in the chapters that follow). For present purposes, the important point is that in the telling of such a story, the story-teller is reinforcing their own progress – and seeking both the endorsement of an audience and their further support in the journey to come. For people desisting from offending – again as for all of us – the hope, belief and endorsement of those closest to them may matter most, but endorsement from authority figures (previously associated mainly with condemnation and rejection) can also be powerful (see McNeill *et al.* 2011).

In Bottoms and Shapland's (2011) model, the end of the journey comes when sufficient reinforcement of change allows the traveller to exit with a reformed, 'crime-free' identity. As we have already said, this may be enough for desistance from offending, but even this achievement is only a staging post (even if an important one) in the journey towards social integration, far less social justice.

## Navigators, advocates and guides[2]

In discussing above some 'State-sponsored' obstacles to desistance, we drew attention to discourses and practices of punishment and supervision that might get in the way of positive change. In this final section of the chapter, we look to the desistance literature to consider in particular how supervision (and probation) might be re-modelled to support rather than impede the desistance journey.

Two seminal books, *Rethinking What Works with Offenders: Probation, Social Context and Desistance from Crime* (Farrall 2002) and *Making Good: How Ex-Convicts Reform and Rebuild their Lives* (Maruna 2001), made key contributors to debates about desistance and how best to support it. Both Farrall and Maruna drew on earlier work by Ros Burnett in her *Dynamics of Recidivism* study (Burnett 1992). Another important study of 'assisted desistance' (as opposed to spontaneous or unaided desistance) was undertaken by Sue Rex (1999), who was amongst the first to argue that:

> The knowledge we are beginning to acquire about the type of probation services which are more likely to succeed could surely be enhanced by an understanding of the personal and social changes and developments associated with desistance from crime.
>
> *(Rex 1999: 366)*

Maruna (2000) argued for a marrying of the desistance and 'What Works?' literatures, drawing together the latter literature's focus on the general principles of rehabilitative interventions and the former's understanding of the change process itself. However, the romance seemed ill-fated when Farrall's (2002) book was published. Farrall challenged both the implementation of 'What Works?' research and aspects of its methodological underpinnings. His study (based on a qualitative longitudinal study of 199 probationers and their supervising officers) suggested that motivation and social context were more clearly associated with desistance than supervision, and that the focus of supervision (on risk factors and 'criminogenic needs') neglected the crucial roles of relationships and social capital in the desistance process. Farrall's (2002) prescription was that supervision should focus less on 'offence-related factors' (or 'criminogenic needs') and more on 'desistance-related needs'.

In an effort to elaborate that proposition, McNeill (2003) suggested that 'desistance-focused probation practice' would require careful individualised assessment, focused on the inter-relationships between desistance factors (linked to age and maturation, to social bonds and to shifts in narrative identity), which built towards clear plans to support change. It would entail engaging, active and participative supervisory relationships characterised by optimism, trust and loyalty, as well as interventions targeted at those aspects of each individual's motivation, attitudes, thinking and values which might help or hinder progress towards desistance. Crucially, in McNeill's assessment – and drawing on Laub and Sampson's (2003) seminal work – it would require work not just to develop personal capabilities, but also advocacy to support access to opportunities for change, for example around labour market participation.

Beyond these prescriptions, and inspired by Farrall (2002), McNeill and Batchelor (2004: 66) went on to further elaborate the shift in practice dispositions or perspectives that desistance research seemed to us to suggest. Table 3.1 outlines their contrasting of two 'ideal-types' of practice. McNeill and Batchelor (2004) were clear that this was intended only as a heuristic device; arguably

**TABLE 3.1** Ideal-type contrasts: Offence-focused and desistance-focused practice

|  | *Offence-focused practice* | *Desistance-focused practice* |
|---|---|---|
| *Orientation* | Retrospective | Prospective |
| *Problem locus* | Individual attitudes and behaviours | Individual problems and behaviours in social context |
| *Practice focus* | Individual attitudes and behaviours | Personal strengths and social resources for overcoming obstacles to change |
| *Medium for effective practice* | Rehabilitative programmes (to which offenders are assigned on the basis of risk/ needs assessment instruments) | Individual processes and relationships |
| *Workers' roles* | Risk/needs assessor, programme provider, case manager | Risk/needs/strengths assessor, advocate, facilitator, case manager |
| *Intended outputs* | Enhanced motivation Pro-social attitudinal change Capacity/skills development | Enhanced motivation Changes in narrative/self-concept Development of inclusion opportunities |
| *Intended outcomes* | Reduced reoffending | Reduced reoffending Enhanced social inclusion |

neither of these approaches could or should exist in practice in a 'pure' form. Necessarily, an offence focus must, of course, be appropriate given that it is offending that occasions and justifies penal intervention. However, being overly offence-focused might in some senses tend to amplify precisely those aspects of a person's history, behaviour and attitudes which intervention aims to diminish. It may also tend towards misidentifying the central problems of desistance as problems of individual or personal 'malfunctioning'.

By contrast, being 'desistance-focused' implies an orientation towards the purpose and aspiration of the intervention rather than the 'problem' that precipitates it. It also requires recognising the broader social contexts and conditions required to support change. Thus, where 'being offence-focussed encourages practice to be retrospective and individualised, being desistance-focussed allows practice to become prospective and contextualised' (McNeill and Batchelor 2004: 67).

Maruna's (2001) book was less directly focused on the implications of his Liverpool Desistance Study for supervision, but his ideas (developed along with Tom LeBel) about 'strengths-based' approaches to re-entry and corrections were already developing in similar directions, informed both by desistance research and by a wider range of influences (Maruna and LeBel 2003, 2010). In essence, Maruna and LeBel (2003) exposed the limitations and problems associated with both risk-based and support- (or need-) based narratives for re-entry. The former, they argued, casts the offender ultimately as a threat to be managed; the latter as a deficient to be remedied by the application of professional expertise. By contrast, '[s]trengths-based or restorative approaches ask not what a person's deficits are, but rather what positive contribution the person can make' (Maruna and LeBel 2003: 97).

In a follow-up paper, Maruna *et al.* (2004) engaged more directly with the implications of his study for probation. Supervision, they suggested, should move away from risks and needs and towards strengths; seeking to support and encourage redemptive and generative processes, such as those involved in community service at its best. Such a discursive shift, they averred, could signal the true potential of probationers not just to them, but equally importantly to their communities. Although Maruna *et al.* (2004) supported Farrall's call for a more explicitly prospective or future-oriented form of practice, they also stressed the need for people to make sense of their pasts. They therefore suggested the need for rehabilitative processes that could support a reconstruction of personal narratives; one which recognised and repaired wrongdoing but which refused to define or delimit the person by their previous conduct.

In 2006, McNeill went further, proposing a 'A Desistance Paradigm for Offender Management' (McNeill 2006). This reflected a peculiarly British debate about how probation practice should be redesigned in the light of both changing evidence and normative arguments. He used both empirical (desistance) research and normative arguments to critique what he perceived as the misappropriation and misinterpretation of evidence in a managerialised and reductionist 'What Works?' paradigm that dominated probation policy and practice in England and Wales at that time. McNeill summed up the four paradigms as follows in Table 3.2:

**TABLE 3.2** Probation practice in four paradigms

| The Non-Treatment Paradigm | The Revised Paradigm | A What Works Paradigm | A Desistance Paradigm |
|---|---|---|---|
| Treatment becomes help | Help consistent with a commitment to the reduction of harm | Intervention required to reduce reoffending and protect the public | Help in navigating towards desistance to reduce harm and make good to offenders and victims |
| Diagnoses becomes shared assessment | Explicit dialogue and negotiation offering opportunities for consensual change | 'Professional' assessment of risk and need governed by structured assessment instruments | Explicit dialogue and negotiation assessing risks, needs, strengths and resources and offering opportunities to make good |
| Client's dependent need as the basis for action becomes collaboratively defined task as the basis for action | Collaboratively defined task relevant to criminogenic need and potentially effective in meeting them | Compulsory engagement in structured programmes and case management processes as required elements of legal orders imposed irrespective of consent | Collaboratively defined tasks which tackle risks, needs and obstacles to desistance by using and developing the offender's human and social capital |

In line with the analysis developed in the preceding sections of this chapter, McNeill's central argument ran as follows:

> Unlike the earlier paradigms, the desistance paradigm forefronts processes of change rather than modes of intervention. Practice under the desistance paradigm would certainly accommodate intervention to meet needs, reduce risks and (especially) to develop and exploit strengths, but . . . subordinated to a more broadly conceived role in working out, on an individual basis, how the desistance process might best be prompted and supported. This would require the worker to act as an advocate providing a conduit to social capital as well as a 'treatment' provider building human capital . . . Critically, such interventions would not be concerned solely with the prevention of further offending; they would be equally concerned with constructively addressing the harms caused by crime by encouraging offenders to make good through restorative processes and community service (in the broadest sense). But, as

a morally and practically necessary corollary, they would be no less preoccupied with making good to offenders by enabling them to achieve inclusion and participation in society (and with it the progressive and positive reframing of their identities required to sustain desistance).

*(McNeill 2006: 56–57)*

More recently, Maruna and LeBel (2010) again engaged directly with the promise of developing and employing a desistance paradigm for correctional practice. They began with the recognition that evaluation evidence is not the only form of evidence that matters in developing evidence-based practice (EBP). Following Lewis (1990), they argued for a shift in focus 'from programmes to lives', rejecting a medical model of change.

By better understanding the change process, Maruna and LeBel (2010) argued, we may be able to better adapt supervision to contribute to (but not to 'produce') the process. It follows that a desistance paradigm must place the person changing and *their* change process (in our metaphor, the traveller and the journey) centre stage. Notably, this is a message that finds support amongst prisoners and probationers themselves, who are often resistant to being 'treated' through programmatic interventions (Harris 2005). Although the views and voices of 'offenders' are often much too marginalised in correctional work and research, the problems of supervision violation referred to above (and of programme 'dropout') suggest that correctional practitioners and researchers would do well to hear and attend carefully to the views of those they are seeking to influence. One of the central contributions of desistance research is that it provides one way (and only one way) in which these voices can be heard.

Maruna and LeBel summed up their argument for a desistance paradigm as follows:

> [T]he desistance paradigm argues that the search for 'what works' should not begin with existing expert models of crime reduction, but rather should begin with an understanding of the organic or normative processes that seem to impact offending patterns over the life course. That is, if turning 30 is the 'most effective crime-fighting tool' (Von Drehle 2010), then we should seek to learn as much as we can about that process and see if we can model these dynamics in our own interventions.
>
> *(Maruna and LeBel 2010: 72)*

Recognising that the practical implications of such a perspective remain seriously under-developed (see also Porporino 2010), Maruna and LeBel (2010) went on to suggest one form of desistance-based intervention. Drawing on labelling theory, and on their earlier work (cited above), they made the case for an approach to supervision which employs pro-social labelling; as well as avoiding negative labelling, this requires practices and systems that expect, invite and facilitate positive contributions and activities from people subject to supervision, and that then certify and celebrate redemption or rehabilitation – de-labelling and de-stigmatising the reformed offender.

In similar vein, McNeill (2012b) argued that the field of corrections needs its own 'Copernican Correction' – one in which supervision and support services revolve around the individual change process, rather than requiring supervisees' lives to revolve around programmes and interventions. Moreover, he suggested a shift away from seeing the 'offender' as the target of the intervention (the 'thing' to be fixed) to seeing the broken relationships between individuals, communities and the State as the breach in the social fabric (or breach of the social contract) that requires repair. Importantly, this casts correctional agencies less as agents of 'coercive correction' and more as mediators of social conflicts. The objective becomes not the correction of the deviant so much as the restoration of the citizen to a position where s/he can both honour the obligations and enjoy the rights of citizenship.

Recalling the two ways in which supervision might sabotage desistance (via systems and via practices), the arguments about supporting desistance are perhaps more concerned with *reframing* systems of supervision than with *redesigning* supervisory practices. The clearest attempts at tackling the latter challenge are perhaps to be found in reports prepared for the Scottish government and the National Offender Management Service of England and Wales respectively (McNeill 2009; McNeill and Weaver 2010). Both reports responded to policymaker and practitioner requests for more explicit articulation of the practical implications of desistance research for supervision practice; both share a similar reticence in responding to these requests.

*Towards Effective Practice in Offender Supervision* (McNeill 2009) was an attempt to summarise evidence about both desistance and 'What Works?' in order to inform practice development. Instead of proposing a pre-designed and therefore homogenised intervention, McNeill tried to articulate the range of issues and questions with which a reflective practitioner would have to engage in seeking to support desistance in individual cases. The resultant 'offender supervision spine' explains in broad terms how to approach the preparatory, relationship-building stage of supervision, as well as assessment, planning, intervention and evaluation. His suggestion was that a supervisor working their way along this spine, in partnership with the supervisee, should continually develop and test 'theories of change', seeking to work out together 'why and how we think that doing what we propose to do will bring about the results they we seek', and then to implement that plan, and to evaluate its progress.

Beyond such emergent models of the supervision process, a number of broader practical implications of desistance research have been identified in the literature. In a recent overview, for example, McNeill et al. (2012) identify eight broad principles, the genesis of which is perhaps already apparent in the discussion above.

1. First, it is clear that desistance, for people who have been involved in persistent offending, is a complex process. Criminal justice supervision must be realistic about these difficulties and find ways to manage setbacks and difficulties constructively. It needs to be recognised that it may take considerable time for supervision and support to exercise a positive effect.

2. Relatedly, since desistance is an inherently individualised and subjective process, approaches to supervision should accommodate and address issues of identity and diversity.

3. Desistance research also suggests that the development and maintenance of hope may be key tasks for supervisors (see Farrall *et al.* 2014).

4. Hope may feed the discovery of self-efficacy or agency which may also be important in desistance processes. Interventions are most likely to be effective where they encourage and respect self-determination; this means working *with* would-be desisters, not *on* them.

5. Desistance can only be properly understood within the context of human and social relationships; not just relationships between supervisors and offenders (though these matter a great deal) but also between offenders and those who matter to them (Weaver 2015). Interventions based only on developing the capacities and skills of people who have offended (human capital) will not be enough.

6. It follows that supervision must address developing social capital, and with it the opportunities to apply these skills, or to practise newly forming identities (such as 'worker' or 'father').

7. Although a focus on risks and needs may be necessary, desisters also have strengths and resources that they can use to overcome obstacles to desistance – both personal strengths and resources, and strengths and resources in their social networks. Supporting and developing these capacities can be a useful dimension of supervision.

8. Finally, the language of practice should reflect this recognition of potential; striving to more clearly recognise positive potential and development and should seek to avoid identifying people with the behaviours we want them to leave behind.

This eight-principle summary was produced as part of a UK Economic and Social Research Council-funded project which aimed to develop a much more comprehensive and innovative response to the challenge to 'operationalise' desistance (explained more fully in McNeill *et al.* 2012). The partners in this project sought to foster a dialogue about supporting desistance involving academics, policymakers, managers, practitioners, ex/offenders, and their families and supporters. The project was entitled 'Discovering Desistance'.[3] Partnered in the USA by Faye Taxman's Center for Advancing Correctional Excellence (www. gmuace.org), it aimed to explore the experience and knowledge of these different stakeholders in relation to desistance from crime and how correctional supervision in the community can best support it.

Though intended to be focused on redesigning supervision, the ideas and proposals generated in and through this dialogue extended far beyond supervision practice and into much broader aspects of reintegration. For example, the participants called for the criminal justice system to make greater use of reformed offenders, not least through service-user (i.e. supervisee) involvement in the design, delivery and improvement of policies and provision across the criminal justice system. Participants argued that greater involvement of ex/offenders in mentoring schemes should be a key part of this involvement.

More generally, they argued both for a reorientation towards a more holistic and humanistic form of supervision and for correctional services to become better connected with the local communities, playing a greater role in mobilising wider community support networks to support desistance and reintegration. They called for services to work to challenge inequality and promote equality; equalising life chances and contributing to social justice (pursuing both substantive equality and equality in the criminal justice process), suggesting that this required a new approach to public and community education about the process of leaving crime behind and the lives of current and former service users in order to break down the 'them' and 'us' mentality. This, the participants suggested, would ensure better public understanding that people are capable of change, and that we all have a part to play in supporting change. Criminal justice agencies ought to model and promote the belief that positive change is possible and show that it is common, focusing on this rather than 'risks'.

Two more structural changes were routinely proposed in the workshops, both of which echo the arguments above. First, the participants called for a reduction in the reliance on imprisonment as a sanction (especially for women, black men, those with mental health issues and those on short sentences), calling for the money saved to be reinvested in community justice. Second, they argued the need to redraft the [UK] Rehabilitation of Offenders Act 1974 (which governs disclosure of criminal convictions) so as to both encourage and recognise rehabilitation, rather than to stand in the way of it.

Perhaps most fundamentally, they called for a criminal justice system that gives people hope and shows them they have a future. Given that this last prescription seems so at odds with some of the broader economic and social barriers to desistance discussed above, it is to these barriers that we return in conclusion.

## Conclusions: The limits of personal rehabilitation

In *The Odyssey*, if Athena has a job, it is not to 'fix' Odysseus. It is not even to act as his navigator. He is, after all, the captain of his own ship. Rather, her job is to *help him get home*. That sometimes requires her to help him develop new skills and tactics, but more often it means helping him find his way out of trouble and towards the material and symbolic resources that will carry him to Ithaca.

Throughout this chapter we have struggled with the tension that lies at the heart of separating 'personal rehabilitation' from the other three forms. Doing so helps us to provide conceptual clarity and allows us to focus attention on different parts of the picture, but necessarily this is sometimes at the expense of seeing the complex interactions *between* the four forms of rehabilitation and how they relate to wider processes of desistance and of personal development. And while it makes some sense to think about what personal and social resources a traveller needs in order to successfully complete such an arduous journey, the journey cannot be understood without a close examination of the terrain through which s/he must travel, and without consideration of how the climate and the weather may affect her or his prospects. The subsequent chapters will elaborate some of these important questions around rehabilitation's social, legal and organisational contexts – and turn our attention to other key players in processes of desistance and rehabilitation.

So, finally, we return to Cohen's (1985) question: what space is there for criminal justice to exert power and do good at the same time? In this chapter, we have suggested some ways in which supervision might be re-modelled so as to do some good, and we have considered some of the ways in which it might do further harm to people whose life chances are already diminished by social inequality. Hopefully, we finish with a clearer sense of how positive personal change might be better supported – but we must also confront the twin challenges of looking beyond desistance and toward social integration and social justice as our goals, and of looking beyond personal development and towards social development as our means. Penal power may be able to do some good if it can constructively build (or repair) relations of social solidarity; where it seeks only to coerce personal change, it is more likely to do harm.

## Notes

1 For those who want to explore the complexity of these interactions and of desistance theory, we would suggest reading Farrall *et al.* 2014 and/or Shapland *et al.* (2016).
2 This section of the chapter is drawn from McNeill (2016). We are grateful to the editors and publishers of the collection in which that chapter appeared for permission to re-use some of the material here.
3 The project was funded by the UK Economic and Social Research Council, award no. RES-189-25-0258.

## References

Ager, A. and Strang, A. (2004) *Indicators of Integration: Final Report*, http://webarchive. nationalarchives.gov.uk/20110218135832/http://rds.homeoffice.gov.uk/rds/pdfs04/ dpr28.pdf (accessed 24 October 2014).

Bottoms, A. (2013) Learning from Odysseus: Self Applied Situational Crime Prevention as an Aid to Compliance, in Ugwudike, P. and Raynor, P. (eds) *What Works in Offender Compliance: International Perspectives and Evidence-Based Practice*, Basingstoke: Palgrave.

Bottoms, A. (2014) Desistance from Crime, in Ashmore, Z. and Shuker, R. (eds) *Forensic Practice in the Community*, London: Routledge.

Bottoms, A. and Shapland, J. (2011) Steps towards Desistance among Young Adult Recidivists, in Farrall, S., Hough, M., Maruna, S. and Sparks, R. (eds) *Escape Routes: Contemporary Perspectives on Life After Punishment*, London: Routledge.

Braithwaite, J. (1989) *Crime, Shame and Reintegration*, Cambridge: Cambridge University Press.

Burnett, R. (1992) *The Dynamics of Recidivism*, Oxford: University of Oxford Centre for Criminological Research.

Burnett, R. (2000) Understanding criminal careers through a series of in-depth interviews, *Offender Programs Report*, 4(1): 1–16.

Burnett, R. (2004) One-to-one Ways of promoting Desistance: In Search of an Evidence Base, in Burnett, R. and Roberts, C. (eds) *What Works in Probation and Youth Justice*, Cullompton: Willan Publishing.

Calverley, A. (2009) *Cultures of Desistance: Rehabilitation, Reintegration and Ethnic Minorities*, London: Routledge.

Carlen, P. (2013) Against Rehabilitation: For Reparative Justice, in Carrington, K., Ball, E., O'Brien, E. and Tauri, J. (eds) *Crime, Justice and Social Democracy – International Perspectives*, Basingstoke: Palgrave Macmillan, 89–104.

Cohen, S. (1985) *Visions of Social Control: Crime, Punishment and Classification*, Polity Press: Cambridge.

Corston, J. (2007) *A Report by Baroness Jean Corston of a Review of Women with Particular Vulnerabilities in the Criminal Justice System*, London: Home Office.

Farrall, S. (2002) *Rethinking What Works with Offenders: Probation, Social Context and Desistance from Crime*, Cullompton: Willan Publishing.

Farrall, S., Hunter, B., Sharpe, G. and Calverley, A. (2014) *Criminal Careers in Transition: The Social Context of Desistance from Crime*, Oxford: Oxford University Press.

Fraser, N. (2007) Reframing Justice in a Globalizing World, in Lovell, T. (ed.) *Misrecognition, Social Inequality and Social Justice, Nancy Fraser and Pierre Bourdieu*, London and New York: Routledge, 17–35.

Giordano, P.C., Cernkovich, S.A. and Rudolph, J.L. (2002) Gender, crime, and desistance: Toward a theory of cognitive transformation, *American Journal of Sociology*, 107(4): 990–1064.

Graham, H. and McNeill, F. (2017) Desistance: Envisioning Futures, in Carlen, P. and Ayres France, L. (eds) *Alternative Criminologies*, Routledge: London.

Harris, M.K. (2005) In search of common ground: The importance of theoretical orientations in criminology and criminal justice, *Criminology & Public Policy*, 4(2): 311–328.

Houchin, R. (2005) *Social Exclusion and Imprisonment in Scotland: A Report*, Glasgow: Glasgow Caledonian University.

Johnstone, G. (1996) *Medical Concepts and Penal Policy*, London: Cavendish Publishing.

Kirkwood, S. and McNeill, F. (2015) Integration and reintegration: Comparing pathways to citizenship through asylum and criminal justice, *Criminology & Criminal Justice*, first published on 16 March 2015 as doi: 10.1177/1748895815575618.

Klingele, C. (2014) Rethinking the use of community supervision, *The Journal of Criminal Law and Criminology*, 103(4): 1016–1070.

Laub, J. and Sampson, R. (2003) *Shared Beginnings, Divergent Lives*, Boston: Harvard University Press.

LeBel, T.P., Burnett, R., Maruna, S. and Bushway, S. (2008) The 'chicken and egg' of subjective and social factors in desistance from crime, *European Journal of Criminology*, 5(2): 130–158.

Lewis, D.A. (1990) From programs to lives: A comment, *American Journal of Community Psychology*, 18: 923–926.

Maruna, S. (2000) Desistance from crime and offender rehabilitation: A tale of two research literatures, *Offender Programs Report*, 4(1): 1–13.

Maruna, S. (2001) *Making Good*, Washington DC: American Psychological Association.

Maruna, S. and Farrall, S. (2004) Desistance from crime: A theoretical reformulation, *Kölner Zeitschrift für Soziologie und Sozialpsychologie*, 43: 171–194.

Maruna, S. and LeBel, T. (2003). Welcome home? Examining the 're-entry court' concept from a strengths-based perspective, *Western Criminology Review*, 4(2): 91–107.

Maruna, S. and LeBel, T. (2010) The Desistance Paradigm in Correctional Practice: From Programmes to Lives, in McNeill, F., Raynor, P. and Trotter C. (eds) *Offender Supervision: New Directions in Theory, Research and Practice*, Cullompton: Willan.

Maruna, S., Porter, L. and Carvalho, I. (2004) The Liverpool Desistance Study and probation practice: Opening the dialogue, *Probation Journal*, 51(3): 221–232.

McGuinness, P., McNeill, F. and Armstrong, S. (2013) *The Use and Impact of the Rehabilitation of Offenders Act (1974): Final Report*, Scottish Centre for Crime and Justice Report 02/2013, University of Glasgow, www.sccjr.ac.uk/publications/the-use-and-impact-of-the-rehabilitation-of-offenders-act-1974final-report/ (accessed 23 April 2015).

McNeill, F. (2003) Desistance-Focused Probation Practice, in Chui, W-H. and Nellis, M. (eds) *Moving Probation Forward: Evidence, Arguments and Practice*, Harlow: Pearson Education.

McNeill, F. (2006) A desistance paradigm for offender management, *Criminology and Criminal Justice*, 6(1): 39–62.

McNeill, F. (2009) *Towards Effective Practice in Offender Supervision*, Glasgow: Scottish Centre for Crime and Justice Research, www.sccjr.ac.uk/documents/McNeil_Towards.pdf (accessed 23 April 2015).

McNeill, F. (2012a) Four forms of 'offender' rehabilitation: Towards an interdisciplinary perspective, *Legal and Criminological Psychology*, 17(1): 18–36.

McNeill, F. (2012b) Counterblast: A Copernican correction for community sentences, *Howard Journal of Criminal Justice*, 51(1): 94–99.

McNeill, F. (2014) Punishment as Rehabilitation, in Bruinsma, G. and Weisburd, D. (eds) *Encyclopedia of Criminology and Criminal Justice*, 4195–4206: DOI 10.1007/978-1-4614-5690-2, New York: Springer Science and Business Media. [A final draft version of this paper is available open access online at: http://blogs.iriss.org.uk/discoveringdesistance/files/2012/06/McNeill-When-PisR.pdf]

McNeill, F. (2016) The Fuel in the Tank or the Hole in the Boat? Can Sanctions Support Desistance, in Shapland, J., Farrall, S. and Bottoms, A. (eds) *Global perspectives on desistance. Rethinking what we know and looking to the future*, London: Routledge.

McNeill, F. and Batchelor, S. (2004) Persistent offending by young people: Developing practice, *Issues in Community and Criminal Justice*, Monograph No. 3. London: National Association of Probation Officers.

McNeill, F. and Robinson, G. (2012) Liquid Legitimacy and Community Sanctions, in Crawford, A. and Hucklesby, A. (eds) *Legitimacy and Compliance in Criminal Justice*, Abingdon: Routledge.

McNeill, F. and Weaver, B. (2010) *Changing Lives? Desistance Research and Offender Management*, Glasgow: Scottish Centre for Crime and Justice Research, www.sccjr.ac.uk/documents/Report%202010_03%20-%20Changing%20Lives.pdf (accessed 18 June 2018).

McNeill, F., Farrall, S., Lightowler, C. and Maruna, S. (2012) Re-examining 'evidence-based practice' in community corrections: Beyond 'a confined view' of what works, *Justice Research and Policy*, 14(1): 35–60.

McNeill, F., Anderson, K., Colvin, S., Overy, K., Sparks, R. and Tett, L. (2011) Kunstprojecten en What Works: een stimulans voor desistance? (Trans. Inspiring desistance? Arts projects and 'what works?'), *Justitiele verkenningen*, 37(5): 80–101.

Morland, P. (2016) *Metamorphosis: How and Why We Change*, London: Profile Books.

Nugent, B. and Schinkel, M. (2016) The pains of desistance, *Criminology and Criminal Justice*, 16(5): 568–584.

Paternoster, R. and Bushway, S. (2009) Desistance and the feared self: Toward an identity theory of criminal desistance, *Journal of Criminal Law and Criminology*, 99(4): 1103–1156.

Phelps, M. (2013) The paradox of probation: Community supervision in the age of mass incarceration, *Law & Policy*, 35(1–2): 51–80.

Porporino, F. (2010) Bringing Sense and Sensitivity to Corrections: From Programmes to 'Fix' Offenders to Services to Support Desistance, in Brayford, J., Cowe, F. and Deering, J. (eds) *What else works? Creative work with offenders*, Cullompton: Willan.

Prochaska, J. and DiClemente, C. (1982) Trans-theoretical therapy: Toward a more integrative model of change, *Psychotherapy, Theory, Research and Practice*, 19(3): 276–288.

Raynor, P. and Robinson, G. (2009), *Rehabilitation, Crime and Justice*, Houndmills: Palgrave Macmillan.

Rex, S. (1999) Desistance from offending: Experiences of probation, *Howard Journal of Criminal Justice*, 36(4): 366–383.

Robinson, G. and McNeill, F. (2008) Exploring the dynamics of compliance with community penalties, *Theoretical Criminology*, 12(4): 431–449.

Schinkel, M. (2015) Hook for change or shaky peg? Imprisonment, narratives and desistance, *European Journal of Probation*, 7(1): 5–20.

Schinkel, M. (2016) *Being Imprisoned. Punishment, Adaptation and Desistance*, Basingstoke: Palgrave.

Shapland, J., Farrall, S. and Bottoms, A. (2016) (eds) *Global Perspectives on Desistance. Rethinking What We Know and Looking to the Future*, London: Routledge.

Social Exclusion Unit (2002) *Reducing Reoffending by Ex-prisoners*, London: Office of the Deputy Prime Minister.

Uggen, C., Manza, J. and Thompson, M. (2006) Citizenship, democracy and the civic reintegration of criminal offenders, *Annals of the American Academy of Political and Social Science*, 605(May): 281–310.

Von Drehle, D. (2010) (22 February) Why crime went away: The murder rate in America is at an all-time low. Will the recession reverse that? *Time Magazine*, 22–25.

Wacquant, L. (2010) Prisoner re-entry as myth and ceremony, *Dialectical Anthropology*, 34: 605–620.

Weaver, B. (2015) *Offending and Desistance. The importance of Social Relations*, London: Routledge.

Western, B. and Pettit, B. (2010) Incarceration and social inequality, *Daedalus*, 139(3): 8–19.

Wright Mills, C. (1959) *The Sociological Imagination*, Oxford: Oxford University Press.

# 4

# REIMAGINING THE LEGAL AND SENTENCING FRAMEWORK

## Judicial rehabilitation

> In the courtroom of honor, the judge pounded his gavel
> To show that all's equal and that the courts are on the level
> And that the strings in the books ain't pulled and persuaded
> And that even the nobles get properly handled
> Once that the cops have chased after and caught 'em
> And that the ladder of law has no top and no bottom,
> Stared at the person who killed for no reason
> Who just happened to be feelin' that way without warnin'.
> And he spoke through his cloak, most deep and distinguished,
> And handed out strongly, for penalty and repentance,
> William Zanzinger with a six-month sentence . . .
> *(Bob Dylan: 'The lonesome death of Hattie Carroll' 1964)*

## With god on our side

Chapter 2 was concerned with exploring contemporary notions of control and support in order to provide a broad context for the rehabilitation in a world where, with notable exceptions, there has been an international growth in the use of both imprisonment and community supervision. But more than that, as we come to better understand the lived experience of supervision, we begin to see how that experience for individuals is mediated not only through race, gender, sexuality or personal biography and individual circumstances but within and via increasingly techno-bureaucratic environments. Workplace processes are not only supported but shaped by the application of technicist and technological approaches to the rehabilitative endeavour which also helps to shape the subjective experience of both service user and worker.

We also outlined the forces behind the inexorable rise in the prison population in England and Wales, pointing to the number of individuals sentenced to immediate custody, increasing sentence lengths and accelerating recall rates against a backcloth of declining criminal court business, reduced use of community sentences as a proportion of all sentences and little evidence of increasing violent or sexual offending. We also suggested that the decisive and deepening bifurcation that Cohen (1985: 232) described as *indefinite inclusion* in the form of community supervision or rigid exclusion within prisons is currently further exacerbated by the *probation paradox* (Phelps 2013) in which individuals are being recycled in increasing numbers between the community-based and carceral forms of punishment. All this, we argued, supports the view that mass supervision can be understood as *maloptical* rather than panoptical in the sense that punishment and control, as conceptualised by Foucault and Cohen, can be further understood in terms of the civic degradation of the individual (McNeill 2018). Then, in the last chapter, we concerned ourselves with the *personal* as one of the key forms of rehabilitation and perhaps the one that most readily chimes with the immediate preoccupations and concerns of criminal justice practitioners and managers. We began that chapter by suggesting that in addressing the various dimensions of rehabilitation throughout the chapters of this book, we are seeking to elaborate what rehabilitation would need to look like if it is to play a role in promoting social justice. Change at the individual level, however positive, can never be in and of itself enough to deliver social justice. It must already be clear therefore that, from our perspective, the challenge to reimagine rehabilitation should be much more than the integration of these four forms: *personal, social, legal* and *moral*. Ultimately, it must be about the promotion of a set of values, beliefs and behaviours that can be consistently applied to rehabilitation to support the process of desistance whilst achieving greater social justice and supporting political change.

As we have argued in the last chapter, the starting points for desistance journeys are often spectacularly unpromising ones and, unlike Odysseus, the ever-increasing numbers of those who are trawled into the contemporary penal net are not *kings* and do not appear to have *gods on their side*, certainly in socio-economic and political terms. Individual citizens will have gone through an often elaborate process reflecting policing decisions about the targeting of particular communities or groups or behaviours, a legal decision-making process where State prosecutors (in England and Wales – the Crown Prosecution Service) decide who to charge and with what offence(s) and finally, a set of decisions about what court the individual will appear in and whether bail will be granted or not. The way in which the case is ultimately dealt with may, in part, reflect the availability of Legal Aid, the quality of legal representation and the personalities and idiosyncrasies of individual magistrates and judges. Within such a complex set of processes and decisions it is not surprising that discrimination, unlawful and arbitrary, can disadvantage an individual, compound prior social and economic injustice and deliver disparate outcomes for individuals including their loss of liberty (for example, Corston 2007; Gelsthorpe 2017; Lammy 2017; Ministry of Justice 2012; Prison Reform Trust 2017a; SEU 2002).

## A focus on the *judicial*

Beyond offending, detection, arrest and prosecution, a key site for determining the future direction that an individual's life may take is the courtroom. The focus of this chapter then is the court environment, its processes and decision-making. Our particular concern is to understand how the conduct of its business and decision-making might provide opportunities for the individual to begin or sustain a journey of desistance towards a crime-free life. We will argue that the values, beliefs and behaviours that form the response to the guilty defendant – as a member of our community, as a citizen, as a member of the polity rather than an individual defined by the bad things they have done – are critical not only to personal rehabilitation but to building social and economic justice.

In the Introduction, we conceded that there would be aspects of the rehabilitative process that we must neglect in order to concentrate on those we consider either under-developed or requiring analysis within current debates about social and criminal justice. Our consideration of punishment and the sentencing process may at first seem slightly out of kilter with the more usual focus of legal or judicial rehabilitation on criminal records and the collateral consequences of criminalisation and penalisation (See Herzog-Evans 2011; McNeill 2012: 14). The significance and enduring impact of a criminal record cannot be underestimated and as Stacey (2017: 270) has recently outlined, people with convictions are the most likely disadvantaged group to be without work, making up between a quarter and a third of unemployed people. Indeed, the pernicious effects of criminal convictions, experienced by those who are often themselves victims of crime, has been highlighted by a recent challenge in the High Court from a group of ex-sex workers, who, in their middle age, still find the conviction for prostitution as young girls disbarring them from jobs. As one of the complainants, now 49 years old and forced into prostitution as a 15-year-old commented:

> I have a catalogue of offences which actually demonstrates my years of abuse.
>
> *(Topping 2018)*

Contrast this with the lives of the economist Vicki Pryce and her estranged politician husband Chris Huhne which seem to have flourished since they were both released from prison on the 13 May 2013, subject to tagging, to complete their respective eight-month sentences for Perverting the Course of Justice (see Pryce 2013). Ironically, it is rich, well-housed and well-connected people – those in least need – that offer us the basis of a sound model for rehabilitation. For most people convicted of less serious crimes than Pryce and Huhne, however, the path to restoration of full civic and legal rights is significantly more problematic and, in this sense, legal rehabilitation can be seen to be intimately intertwined with the *social, moral* and *personal*.

What's good for the well-off and well connected should be good enough for those who have little in the way of social, material and political capital. However, unsurprisingly, the evidence for the social and economic disadvantage experienced by those who are caught up in the criminal justice system has been and continues to be documented along with the collateral damage caused by the existence of a criminal record and particularly one of imprisonment (Bennett 2017). Miller and Stuart's research (2017) in the USA, for example, suggests that there is an emerging category of *carceral citizenship*, with three defining features. First, laws and policies shape how formerly incarcerated people engage with the stabilising institutions of a free society – health, housing, education, training and the labour market. Second, practices of supervision, correction and care that are otherwise unavailable to conventional members of the polity who have not been accused of a crime are applied to 'offenders'. Finally, third parties operating within the public and private sphere are empowered to manage, correct, sanction and care for the carceral citizen. Rather than disappearing at the edges of society, the carceral citizen is rendered 'super-visible' because of their criminal histories and because of their contact with institutions of punishment, coercion and care – they therefore occupy a novel form of (curtailed and constrained) political membership (Miller and Stuart 2017: 543). Whether we look, then, through the prism of *super-visible* carceral citizenship or carceral degradation, the impact of a criminal conviction can and does determine a level of *conditional citizenship* that defines access to the resources of the State. Even in such matters as the basic human requirement for housing, the collateral impact of a prison sentence affects the carceral citizen's ability and/or right to access State housing (see Cooper 2016; Carlen 2013: 96). Rather than a basic need (ironically related to the individual's capacity to desist from crime), their very status becomes a risk which justifies exclusion from a basic social service. As an alternative, they can, in certain localities, then be considered for *offender* accommodation. The level of individual degradation goes beyond being poor and having extreme housing need to being excluded because of their status as an offender.

The digital age now presents a further range of challenges for the ultimate reintegration of individuals where the internet has created profound shifts in the collective cultural experience of crime and punishment, 'particularly in creating new platforms for public involvement in the permanent stigmatization and labeling of others' according to Lageson and Maruna (2018: 127). Whether through digital tracking and stigmatisation or more traditional bureaucratic means of exclusion, the implications and collateral impact of gaining a criminal record can doom any process of desistance to ultimate failure – indeed, Maruna goes so far as to argue that treatment or reform efforts that do not address the collateral consequences of conviction do not deserve to go by the name of rehabilitation (2011b: 98). We fully accept that argument. It seems to us that the digital world exacerbates one-way communication to the detriment of many citizens with criminal records whilst further reducing the lack of civic communication and dialogue between those who look to complete their desistance journeys and the controllers of the material, economic and social resources that can support that journey.

Notwithstanding our brief discussion of legal rehabilitation and our agreement with Maruna about its ultimately defining importance, we wish to move upstream in the criminal justice process to consider judicial aspects of rehabilitation in sentencing individuals – both in terms of its immediate impact and in terms of its collateral consequences. Our overall purpose is to demonstrate that reimagining rehabilitation must engage with two basic and connected problems. The first concerns the levels of punishment routinely used by the courts and particularly the unnecessary use of imprisonment which creates spiralling levels of collateral damage from the outset of the justice process and which ultimately helps to frustrate individual desistance journeys. The second is the increasing diminution of communication and dialogue between the sentencer, the sentenced and the community, in whose name criminal justice is dispensed, which reduces the possibility for all concerned to realise their rights and responsibilities in encouraging individuals to work towards a crime-free life.

Our ultimate aim is to argue that reimagining rehabilitative processes within the confines of the court can aid the onward desistance journeys of the individual citizen. Our quest, therefore, is to envisage the court process and the act of sentencing as contributing significantly to the first three stages in Bottoms and Shapland's *Seven-Step Desistance Process* discussed in the previous chapter.

## Lonesome in the system

The quote that opens this chapter comes from Bob Dylan's album, *The Times They Are A-Changin'* (1964), which included not only 'With God On Our Side' but a song about the killing in 1963 of a black waitress at the hands of rich white tobacco farmer, William Zantzinger (Dylan purposefully misspelt his name in the lyrics). Hattie Carroll was killed as the result of a drunken racist assault at a society ball in Baltimore, Maryland. Based on medical evidence about Hattie Carroll's general health, the Maryland circuit court judges reduced the charge to one of manslaughter. According to an article which appeared in *The Guardian* in 2005:

> The judges probably thought they were being reasonable. They rejected defence claims that Carroll's precarious health made it impossible to say whether her death had been caused, or had simply occurred naturally. The judges considered Zantzinger an 'immature' young man who got drunk and carried away, but they nevertheless held him responsible for her death . . . According to the New York Herald Tribune, the judges kept Zantzinger's sentence to only six months because a longer one would have required that he serve it in state prison and they feared the enmity of a largely black prison population would mean death for him . . . The judges also let him wait a couple of weeks before beginning his sentence, so he could bring in his tobacco crop. Such dispensations were not uncommon, apparently, for offenders who had farms.
>
> *(Frazier 2005: 2–3)*

The reader might wish to question why this case, made famous by the Dylan song, which essentially juxtaposes the lives of a victim and a perpetrator in the context of the burgeoning US civil rights movement nearly 60 years ago, should have relevance to a chapter on judicial rehabilitation within an ostensibly British context. Despite the clear resonance with the Black Lives Matter movement in response to the deaths of black citizens in contemporary America and Britain, we could have chosen many cases within the English and Welsh judicial system that seem to demonstrate injustice from a victim's perspective, miscarriage of justice and inappropriate sentencing. However, the death of Hattie Carroll powerfully shines a light on the relationship between justice in court and its racial, social, economic and political contexts. Even this brief outline, we hope, demonstrates the complexities of judicial processes and decision-making that take us far beyond the notion that justice can be *blind*. On the day Zantzinger was handed a six-month sentence, 28 August 1963, Martin Luther King Jr delivered his 'I have a dream' speech to massed crowds in Washington DC. That moment stands in tragic contrast to Carroll's 'lonesome' death amongst another crowd of the *great and the good*, who failed to stand up for her and to challenge the racist abuse and physical violence that she had been subjected to that evening.

The perpetrator, Zantzinger, certainly wasn't alone. The whole racist edifice of American society at the time conspired to support him both within the court process and afterwards. He wasn't alone in the demonstrable consideration of the impact of the sentence for his personal safety and the timing of his incarceration for his and his family's future economic well-being. This leaves us with the question of whether justice was shown to Zantzinger and how, in a different time, culture and context, criminal courts might reflect the needs of the poor – male and female, black and white – appearing before the courts for much less serious offending. In essence, then, many individuals who become embroiled within the justice process whether as victims or perpetrators can suffer various degrees of being 'lonesome' – not in the obvious and brutal way that ended Hattie Carroll's life on that fateful evening but rather through the structural violence that separates some people from those resources and opportunities to make the good life possible and sustainable. The 'gods' are not on everybody's side. In Zantzinger's case, he was returned to his relatively privileged position in local society and was able to continue the life he had before his imprisonment.

## Communication, dialogue, authority and ritual

Underlining wider notions of justice, as the trial of Zantzinger demonstrates, is the need for communication (if not dialogue) between the defendant and his community and the victim and her community as mediated by judges. The court clearly communicates the racial, political and community values of that period, ostensibly favouring the interest of the defendant, and it is not difficult to imagine a very different set of values and concerns being communicated in the case of the killing of a white person by a black assailant. Here, however, we wish to examine the potential for communication and dialogue to *do good* and aid the rehabilitative process rather than to *do bad* and simply reinforce or exacerbate existing divisions between those who appear in court and the wider community.

In Chapters 1 and 3, we highlighted the problem of the individual supervisee becoming a less and less active participant and more and more an object to be assessed though techniques applied by professionals. As we have argued elsewhere, *people are not things* (Burke and Collett 2010) and locating criminal justice within a wider discussion of social and economic equality, rehabilitation can only be reimagined *as a dialogue* between citizens and as being *in dialogue* with debates about social and political change. We have also highlighted the need to resolve the process of and the implications for objectifying offending citizens, in part by conceiving of *punishment as rehabilitation* (McNeill 2014). We introduced the work of the penal philosopher Anthony Duff (2001, 2003a, 2003b, 2005) and for us, the bridge between *the legal/judicial* and the wider *social* is provided by his influential thinking, specifically his normative theory of *punishment as the communication of censure.*

In *Punishment, Communication, and Community* (2001), Duff argues that criminal punishment should communicate to the offender the censure they deserve for their crimes 'and should aim through that communicative process to persuade them to repent those crimes, to try to reform themselves, and thus to reconcile themselves with those whom they have wronged' (2001: xvii). Punishment through the communication of censure not only meets the retributivists' desire for punishment but the consequentialists' desire for reform and rehabilitation because '[c]ensure can be an efficient means of modifying conduct: the person censured may avoid such conduct in future (realising that is wrong or fearing the pain of censure)' (2001: 27–28). Although the communication of censure through court sentences for those receiving lengthy prison sentences has been questioned empirically (see Schinkel 2014), we have already argued, that working with people who have offended is ultimately and essentially a moral enterprise and in Duff's articulation of punishment – either through the reparative basis of unpaid (community) work or probation supervision – it is also communicative and censorious because through 'transparent persuasion' it aims to bring individuals to recognise the wrongs they have done and recognise that they should take steps to avoid committing such wrongs in future (2001: 101).

Duff argues for sentencing as a process; a discussion in which both the judge and the probation worker can speak to the offending citizen on behalf of the community so that the sentence reaches the individual not merely as a passive object on whom the sentence is to be imposed, but as a citizen with whom we must try to communicate about the nature and implications of his or her crime. Furthermore, and of critical importance to our desire to reimagine both legal and moral rehabilitation, such discussions should also include our readiness to be criticised by the individual for wrongs we do to her or him (2003a: 186). On this account, therefore, the offender must be treated as a full member of the normative political community and rather than excluding him or her, Duff argues that the individual:

> is also to be treated as someone who is protected by those values, and to whom we owe civic respect and concern as a fellow citizen: that is why his punishment must address him as a fellow citizen, and must seek to repair his civic relationships.
>
> *(2003a: 191)*

This responsibility to speak to the individual on behalf of the polity must, Duff argues, be reciprocated. The offender's views should be expressed to the polity, explaining what is due to the individual as well as what is due from him or her (2003a: 194). Indeed, he argues further that the unjust, oppressive and morally corrupt aspects of what passes as punishment in the United Kingdom puts all of us in a morally problematic position:

> For criminal punishment is imposed in our name, by courts that are claimed to be acting on our collective behalf; and most of us rely implicitly on the criminal law and it penal institutions for protection against a crime, and look to the police and the criminal courts for protection and satisfaction if we are victimised by crime. We are therefore all complicit in these practices, and in the injustices and the oppression that they perpetuate.
>
> *(2003b: 304)*

If the argument for communication and dialogue can be made based on its efficacy for all concerned, including the wider community, there is a further reason to justify it in relation to the direct relationship between the individual and those responsible for their supervision. Developing the conceptual thinking engendered by Bottoms and McWilliams non-treatment paradigm for probation practice (1979), through its revisions (Raynor and Vanstone 1994) and towards *A desistance paradigm for offender management*, McNeill reminds us that the original non-treatment paradigm:

> invoked a distinction between the compulsory requirements imposed by the court (with the offender's constrained consent) and the substantive content of the helping process . . . Put another way, the authority for supervision derives from the court but the authority for help resides in the offender.
>
> *(McNeill 2006: 42)*

If that is the case then, by refocusing on how change should be understood rather than how practice should be constructed (McNeill 2006: 45), we need to consider how engagement with individuals in the court process itself might kickstart, support or continue a desistance process. This seems to us to be an under-developed area of practice which needs to be linked to relatively recent developments in the philosophy of punishment. Likewise, the relationship between the sentencer, supervisor and the supervisee within the context of the court should be not only central to reimagining legal and personal rehabilitation, but as we will argue in this and subsequent chapters, the court and its processes can contribute significantly to both the *moral* and the *social*. This is because, as Faulkner and Burnett (2012: 86) argue, restricting people's liberty, even through imprisonment, does not obviate the need to regard individuals as part of a community characterised by reciprocal responsibilities.

We are also concerned about *ritual* as part of the sentencing process. As will be clear to anyone one who has visited a criminal court in operation or been a participant in its proceedings, the court process is heavily shaped by the drama of the courtroom, its physical layout and rituals – (*in the courtroom of honor, the judge pounded his gavel . . .*). Collectively, these ritual aspects of the courtroom process are often used to reinforce the power relationships of and between the professional participants at the expense of the defendant and can act to further exclude the individual from the judicial process. However, this does not necessarily need to be the case and we shall consider the application of ritual in the context of *problem-solving* approaches to sentencing later in the chapter. In *Reentry as a rite of passage*, Maruna (2011a) makes a convincing and incisive argument for the place of rituals in supporting the re-entry of prisoners into their communities and we can utilise his thinking in relation to the effective use of court-based rituals. Drawing on scholarship reflecting Durkheim's primary insights about ritual, Maruna reminds us that rituals can achieve two things: first, they can create mental states and not simply express them and, second, they can engender solidarity and social cohesion by bringing people together in common cause:

> Successful reintegration is a two-way process, requiring both effort on the part of the former prisoner (e.g. desistance, repentance), but also on the part of some wider community (e.g. forgiveness, acceptance). As such, reintegration appears to be an ideal candidate for the implementation of rituals that, by their nature, are supposed to generate feelings of solidarity and community among participants.
>
> *(Maruna 2011a: 13)*

Within this context, then, Maruna suggests that a public can learn forgiveness and reconciliation by practising it and in the process not only will public sentiments develop but the associated rituals will become more genuine. It therefore follows that rituals need to be public in order to build inclusion and engender solidarity – 'After all, whereas "treatment" is typically characterized by an insular, professionals-driven focus on the needs and risks of prisoners . . . reintegration is something that happens between the returning prisoner and the wider community' (2011a: 18). Rituals, Maruna surmises, would also offer the opportunity to focus on the person's life and character – 'accomplishments that the person can better control than an abstract concept such as risk' (2011: 20). Maruna's discussion focuses on the re-entry of prisoners but it seems to us to be equally applicable to the re-entry of citizens subject to community sanctions within the courts.

Our focus on the *judicial*, then, does not attempt to offer a jurisprudential review of sentencing (see Ashworth 2015) or to revisit philosophical debates about punishment (see Canton 2017), although it will be dependent on the insights provided by both approaches. Rather, our concern is to consider judicial decision-making within a broader context of communication and dialogue. At one end of the spectrum, this can be conceptualised in Duff's *punishment as the communication of censure* and at the other, as the active dialogue between those parties that have the potential to shape and deliver rehabilitation in social and moral terms. Whether on the philosophical, social or political level, criminal justice processes can, in our estimation, benefit from greater public engagement. Active rehabilitation processes, like those of justice itself, need to be seen to be done, as Maruna (2011b: 99) argues, if reintegration is to be meaningful 'it presumably requires comparable levels of symbolism and ritual as punishment itself'.

The death of Hattie Carroll serves to remind us that the victim deserves justice and those who offend merit an appropriate punitive response. But justice requires more than mere punishment. Our argument will be that the process of justice, even at the sharp end of sentencing individuals for their crime(s), must engage the protagonists and the wider community in a discussion that moves the polity beyond both the *utilitarian* and the *retributive*. Cohen (1985: 114) posed the question as to why society cannot at the same time punish rulebreakers in the name of justice and help potential and actual rulebreakers in the name of welfare. The capacity to exert power and to do good at the same time was for Cohen the essence of a humanistic civilisation and we now need to consider what this might mean for the judicial treatment of individuals before the court.

## Crime, sentencing and the philosophy of punishment and rehabilitation

We have, so far, outlined our reasons for considering the *judicial* aspects of rehabilitation rather the collateral damage and long-term implications of gaining a criminal record for *legal* rehabilitation. We now wish to consider the broader arguments for why certain approaches to sentencing offer the potential for sparking or reinforcing individual desistance journeys. Our approach is not to become over-absorbed in the philosophical debates about the role of the State in punishment or grand notions about the nature of humankind itself; our aims are more prosaic but, as we will argue, our purpose is to outline an approach to judicial sentencing that engages with our concern to see offenders before court treated as fellow citizens who cause *harm in* but *return to* our communities. We also wish to express our belief that however remote judges and magistrates may seem when performing their judicial functions, in a democratic society they are operating on our behalf and it follows, therefore, that rights and responsibilities apply both to those who offend and to those who require justice to be dispensed on their behalf and for the community's good. After all, it is ultimately the individual decisions of judges and magistrates in England and Wales that sentence our fellow citizens to periods of incarceration and, increasingly, that order the return to custody of those deemed to have failed under the post-release licence and supervision arrangements introduced by the Offender Rehabilitation Act 2014. They have played their part in the significant increase in the use of both supervision and imprisonment.

Before doing that, however, we need to briefly revisit past discussions of *justice* in terms of *punishment* and *rehabilitation*. This is because, whatever the more abstracted insights provided by philosophical debates about the nature of punishment and justice, the everyday reality for individuals appearing before the criminal courts in England and Wales (and elsewhere) is often contested and generally confusing. Both the judicial process and the act of sentencing is a public reality that subjects the individual to both punishment and, sometimes but not always, to measures aimed at their rehabilitation. However, this sense of being caught up in the public theatre of a criminal court where the stakes can be very high for the individual defendant is further complicated, as we have already argued, by a gap between the lived experience of certain punishments and the way they are seen and intended by those who impose or administer them. In Canton's words:

> while the pronouncement of sentence may (perhaps inevitably) give a message – even if the message is often confused, ambiguous, heard differently by different audiences and not necessarily understood as intended – the manner of the implementation of the sentence also gives a message, although one likely only to be heard by the offender.
>
> *(2017: 11)*

Stan Cohen's *Visions of Social Control* (1985) captured a period when, across the Western world, a *destructuring* movement was apparently occurring which signalled wider and deeper forms of carceral and community-based control and punishment. In discussing his seminal work in Chapter 2, we were more concerned to look at the implications for wider social control and the development of mass incarceration and mass supervision but of course, part of that destructuring process was reflective of the move to a *justice* model of sentencing. Cohen (1985: 31) saw this as a move away from *the mind* and an impatience with individualised treatment or rehabilitation based on *psychological inner-states*. The justice model was, therefore, an attack on the power of the professional worker and the injustices created through professional discretion within the justice system. This aspect of destructuring, as Cohen envisaged it, involved a move to behaviourism and a focus on the *act* rather than the *actor*. Some of the pressures behind the destructuring movement of the 1980s came, of course, from the liberal left who reflected both the burgeoning *nothing works* pessimism of that period on both sides of the Atlantic (Wootton 1959; Martinson 1974; see also Mair and Burke 2012: 119; and Cullen and Gilbert 1982/2015: Ch. 4) and significant concerns about the disproportionate impact of professional discretion in the name of correctional or psychiatric treatment.

However, in another seminal work, *Reaffirming Rehabilitation*, originally published in 1982 and recently republished, Cullen and Gilbert (1982/2015) argued for the reconsideration of rehabilitation as a key purpose of sentencing and the wider criminal justice system. Whilst accepting that there were some persuasive arguments put forward by the progressives regarding the dangers of criminal justice rehabilitation measures, Cullen and Gilbert aimed 'to warn of the dangers of embracing a punishment philosophy and to propose that we should not reject rehabilitation but rather reaffirm rehabilitation that is properly tempered by considerations limiting the coercive potential of the state' (1982/2015: 11). Their concerns regarding the abandonment of the individual by focusing on the crime (in Cohen's sense of the *act* rather than the *actor*) included the following:

- An implicit assumption that the State not only has no right but no obligation to do anything about the condition or needs of the offender – 'Yet we may ask, is a philosophy that gives legitimacy to state neglect of individual needs likely to be more benevolent than one that mandates, however imperfectly, state concern?' (Cullen and Gilbert 1982/2015: 11).
- Those who mistrust the State regarding the rehabilitative endeavour are now placing total faith in the State to punish fairly.
- When the new agenda for punishment fails to reduce crime at some point in the future, 'what will the call be for then? Less punishment – or more?' (Cullen and Gilbert 1982/2015: 12).

Nearly 40 years on and in an entirely different contemporary context, these concerns remain centrally important to our exploration of sentencing and the desistance process. The argument about deserts versus rehabilitation, however, is not simply one of differing philosophical views of justice or concerns about the abuse of power by State officials but also the underlying assumptions about human nature in relation to the criminal act. The late Barbara Hudson (1987: 56) argued that 'just as the justice model returns to a seventeenth- and eighteenth-century view of the state, so its view of the individual is a return from the determinism of the rehabilitative medical model back to the free will individual rationality model of human nature of the Enlightenment'. In other words, approaches to criminal justice sanctions that stress *deserts* also lend themselves to a view of the *actor* as rational in the choices they make about the crimes they commit (see Albertson and Fox 2014). In other words, from the individual's perspective, the benefits of crime have to be put alongside the costs (punishments) and from the court's perspective, the punishment has to carry sufficient deterrent capacity to dissuade the rational actor from continuing their life of crime.

But beyond the act and the actor (and the personal characteristics of the individual), there is the vexed and contested question about social and economic influences upon or determinants of criminal behaviour. Hudson argues that, in their consideration of the question of how one can promote legal justice in a socially unjust society, justice theorists such as von Hirsch and colleagues:

> state modestly but firmly that the law cannot bring about social justice, that it cannot alter economic relationships or change moral attitudes. The most it can do and all it should do, is to safeguard the rights of offenders as given by present laws and to make sure that the criminal justice system does not, by taking upon itself tasks which it cannot possibly accomplish, become instrumental in exacting from individual criminals the price of society's neglect of social problems.
>
> *(Hudson 1987: 58)*

More expansively, Cullen and Gilbert capture it thus:

By locating the source of illegality in the wilful calculation of the costs and benefits of crime, the deserts paradigm abandons the humanistic spirit inherent in the traditional liberal appreciation of the social injustices that victimise the less advantaged and constrain them to follow a destructive path that ends in imprisonment. It is this sensitivity to the ravaging effects of inequality, racism and youth that has allowed liberals to speak of the 'crime of punishment' and to argue that the state has an obligation to undertake general social reform as well as the reform of both its captives and the conditions under which they are held. In contrast, the model of deserts and determinacy ultimately obligates the state to do no more than to make criminal pursuits unprofitable and to provide offenders of similar sorts with the solace that they are paying their debt to society in roughly equal though, if necessary, heavy amounts.

*(Cullen and Gilbert 1982/2015: 94)*

Our commitment as authors and past practitioners, as we have argued throughout the book, is to offer a more hopeful and humanistic approach to working with individuals who often have little by way of material and social resources to build a crime-free life. This applies to the way in which courts and the sentencing process could operate. Our commitment to State-obligated rehabilitation (Carlen 1989: 8–28; Rotman 1990; Raynor and Robinson 2009) puts the role of the courts and the act of sentencing itself at the sharp end of our commitment to ensure that desistance and wider rehabilitation discourses engage with arguments for social and economic justice. This is for two basic reasons. First, appropriately applied criminal sanctions can be reflective of the causes of crime and can avoid the worsening of social inequality and injustice including the avoidance, unless absolutely necessary, of the use of imprisonment and its inevitable collateral damage for the individual and community. Second, the prior experience of individuals before the court can help us to analyse and build a plan of what needs to be done on the wider socioeconomic level before, after and outside the criminal justice system (for example Social Exclusion Unit 2002; Corston 2007).

## What's wrong with our approach to sentencing?

In *Delivering Rehabilitation* (Burke and Collett 2015), we considered the introduction of a new approach to sentencing as part of a concerted effort by the then Conservative administration in the 1980s to transform the Probation Service of England and Wales to deliver *punishment in the community* (Home Office 1988a, 1988b, 1990a, 1990b, 1991). We are concerned here, however, less with the wider political considerations and more with the government's attempt to introduce a systematic approach to sentencing that was to support the introduction of the new community penalties aimed at reducing the prison population. Surprisingly, given the context of a Thatcher-led government, Home Secretary Douglas Hurd wanted to see a coherent approach to offender rehabilitation that reduced the dominance of imprisonment, reflecting a Home Office where 'Oxbridge-educated mandarins such as David Faulkner held sway' (Silverman 2012: 7).

Hurd's Home Office, in our view, made a sophisticated attempt to deliver utilitarian outcomes whilst adhering to the basic principles of a deserts-based approach to sentencing. Amongst the flurry of publications, the White Paper, *Crime, Justice and Protecting the Public* (Home Office 1990c) and the outcome of the review of the parole system undertaken by Lord Carlisle (Home Office 1988c) provided both the philosophical background and the legislative intent for the seminal Criminal Justice Act (CJ Act) of 1991. Prior to the introduction of the 1991 Act, sentencing law had lacked a clear rationale, ostensibly relying on a leading decision of the Court of Appeal advocating retribution, deterrence, prevention and rehabilitation as the four aims of sentencing 'without providing any explanation as to how these aims are to be reconciled or which is to prevail where there is a conflict between them' (Wasik and Taylor 1994: 1). Indeed, as Faulkner has remarked, judges often spoke vaguely about 'retribution, deterrence and rehabilitation' (Faulkner 2014: 128). Under the Act, proportionality in sentencing was based on placing an offender under the appropriate level of *restriction on liberty* for the seriousness of the offence. Tripwires or thresholds were built into the sentencing framework to try to restrict the use of imprisonment – as the White Paper had famously argued:

> For most offenders, imprisonment has to be justified in terms of public protection, denunciation and retribution. Otherwise it can be an expensive way of making bad people worse. The prospects of reforming offenders are usually much better if they stay in the community, provided the public are properly protected.
>
> *(Home Office 1990c: para 2.7)*

In essence, then, this *deserts-based* approach to sentencing aimed to introduce a much clearer rationale for the use of punishments and particularly imprisonment. By separating the *quantity* of restriction on liberty from the *quality* of the intervention – *the most suitable for the offender* in the words of the Act – it gave probation the opportunity to operationally separate its traditional advising, assisting and befriending role from the control over individual offenders inherent within statutory supervision. The notion of *restriction on liberty* was in itself a useful concept for measuring the degree of punishment inflicted because it applied to fines as well as community penalties and imprisonment.

The 1991 Act also provided for more than a narrow focus on proportionality and punishment. Indeed, it built into its provisions not only the concept of sentences being *the most suitable* for the offender but within the guiding principles outlined in the White Paper (Home Office 1990c) it stated that '[e]ach order should be tailored both to the seriousness of the offence and the characteristics of the offender. A comparatively short order may make severe demands on some offenders that more severe orders would on others' (para 4.9). There was still, in Nellis's words, 'considerable scope for rehabilitative work' (2004: 118). The Act did, however, breach the principle of just deserts and proportionate punishment in relation to the commission of serious violent and sexual offences and 'began the movement towards preventive sentencing, without regard for proportionality, which culminated in the indeterminate sentences for public protection introduced by 2003 Criminal Justice Act' (Faulkner and Burnett 2012: 49).

The early signs for moving away from the use of imprisonment were positive even before the sentencing framework became operational in October 1992. A slow but fairly constant rise in the post-Second World War prison population was halted and between January 1992 and January 1993, it had fallen by some 4,000 to approximately 44,000 (Home Office 2003: 6). Our view, elaborated in Burke and Collett (2015: 29–36) was that from an operational and practitioner perspective, the legislative provisions were beginning to make sense and the Act provided for a more rational and constructive exchange between the Probation Service and sentencers, partly because of the significant resources that were put into joint training between magistrates and probation staff. Its early impact certainly reflected the fact that the training helped sentencers to anticipate the provisions and intent of the Act and possibly, as Faulkner reflected, changes in the political and public opinion in which community sentences had become more acceptable (Faulkner 2014: 137).

On a more general and ideological level, however, Garland (2001: 9) has argued that the reappearance of just deserts 'also re-established the legitimacy of an explicitly retributive discourse, which in turn, has made it easier for politicians and legislatures to openly express punitive sentiments and to enact more draconian laws'. Certainly, for an Act that was delivering on its intentions, there was a remarkable turnaround in the politics of punishment and sentencing almost from the very beginning of its implementation. Cavadino *et al.* (2013: 55) summed up the position thus – 'In terms of the philosophy of punishment, the conservative government then abandoned just deserts in favour of the assertion that "prison works" by incapacitation and deterrence'. It was not just the Conservatives in Britain but the Democrats in the United States that, as President Clinton urged, should be getting on the *right side of crime*! This overall approach, subsequently imported to Britain, was summed up pithily by Michael Tonry:

> Britain's Labour Party, after a trip to Washington by Tony Blair to meet with Clinton's political advisors, did the same thing in 1993. Since then England has adopted sentencing laws of unprecedented severity, and the prison population has reached historic highs and has increased more rapidly since 1994 than in any other Western country.
>
> *(Tonry 2006: 44)*

As the political mood towards crime and punishment changed during the 1990s and beyond, the opportunities for the 1991 Act to deliver a more rational approach to sentencing whilst reducing the prison population was lost. Specifically – the notion of punishment as *restriction on liberty* associated with all sentencing options, *suitability* for the offender as a key factor in the exact type of sentence, the understanding that the same sentence can make different demands on the individuals and finally the attenuation of the impact of previous convictions on the sentence for the current offence – all these aspects of sentencing policy (some of which still remain on the statute books) have been subordinated to a more mechanised and routinised way of sentencing individuals. The 1991 Act was then followed by a number of further statutes which were consolidated within the Power of the Criminal Courts (Sentencing) Act 2000. Further various provisions were added which were incorporated in the 2003 Criminal Justice Act 2003, which remains (with amendments) the principle statute governing sentencing in England and Wales. Andrew Ashworth, in his definitive book on sentencing within the English and Welsh criminal justice system, comments, 'The scheme of the 1991 act was abandoned in 2003, and in its place, we have a law that seems to embody the worst of "pick-and-mix" sentencing' (2015: 82).

In essence, Section 142 of the Criminal Justice Act 2003 now requires that any court dealing with an offender in respect of her or his offence must have regard to the following purposes of sentencing:

- Punishment of offenders;
- The reduction in crime (including its reduction by deterrence);
- Reform and rehabilitation of offenders;
- Protection of the public; and
- The making of reparation by offenders to persons affected by their offence.

The Act gives no guidance about how these aims are to be dealt with in individual cases, but alongside these sentencing provisions, the development of structured guidance for judges and magistrates in England and Wales has been developed and refined over the past 20 years. Ashworth's overview is that the constitutional arrangements for guidance on sentencing were altered first by the appointment of a Sentencing Advisory Panel under ss. 80–81 of the Crime and Disorder Act 1988, second by the creation of the sentencing Guidelines Council under ss. 169–170 of the Criminal Justice Act 2003, and third by the replacement of those two bodies by the Sentencing Council in the Coroners and Justice Act 2009 (Ashworth 2015: 58).

In other words, sentencers are free to deal with individual offenders within the framework laid down by Parliament and, as Ashworth reflects, the sentencing guidelines are so extensive that most of the cases in Magistrates' Courts and in the Crown Court involve the application of a guideline. He refers to the guidelines *as process* (2015: 24) and it is the case that the most recent issue of the Magistrates' Court Sentencing Guidelines stretches to some 459 pages (Sentencing Council 2017). When considered alongside the *Imposition of Community and Custodial Sentences: definitive guideline* (Sentencing Council 2016), what becomes clear is that *consistency* in sentencing is constructed around notions of seriousness in which harm and offender culpability are the key determinants.

There is certainly nothing unusual in this approach. However, the problem with the guidelines is that the list of aggravating and mitigating factors for each offence almost exclusively concerns the nature of the offending and the individual's role in carrying out the offence. Indeed, the only personal factors affecting culpability relate to mental illness or disability where they might affect the responsibility of the individual. The potential impact of a particular sentence can be considered where the circumstances of the offender (for example as a care-giver to a dependant relative) may create difficulties for others but essentially personal circumstances, particularly reflecting social and economic exclusion, do not feature in the various lists of mitigating circumstances that can be considered in determining seriousness. Other than in very specific circumstances, the notion that the same outcome for two different offenders can in practice deliver different levels of punishment has disappeared. Furthermore, in contrast to the 1991 Act, the general notion of *suitability* for the individual offender is overlaid by the four aims of sentencing and a relatively new requirement for a community penalty to include either a financial penalty or a requirement imposed for the purposes of punishment (Schedule 16, Part 1 of the Crime and Courts Act 2013).

## Justice and equality: Criminal or otherwise

In discussing the functions of sentencing, Tonry has argued that most agree that the primary functions 'are the imposition of appropriate punishments and prevention of crime. People differ on what makes a punishment appropriate and how best to prevent crime, but few people would disagree that these are legitimate functions' (Tonry 2006: 8). He acknowledges that resource management, efficiency and cost-effectiveness are legitimate *ancillary functions* of sentencing along with the need for rehabilitative community-based programmes and appropriately targeted incapacitation policies. These functions may even stretch to matters such as public reassurance, public confidence and the reinforcement of basic social norms. However, referring to the perniciousness of *latent* functions, Tonry argues that using sentencing to achieve personal, ideological, partisan political goals fundamentally obstructs performance of its primary and ancillary functions:

> Latent functions and to a lesser extent communicative functions pose a formidable problem for principled policy making. They are not primarily aimed at what goes on in courtrooms or on punishments imposed, crimes prevented, or efficiency enhanced, but on reputations developed, political goals achieved, and elections won.
>
> *(Tonry 2006: 44)*

The effects of these latent functions, operating beneath the ideological intent of incarceration that authors such as Wacquant (2004, 2018) argue meets the needs of neoliberalism, deliver devastating outcomes for many individuals. As we have noted, the prison population in England and Wales has doubled since the early 1990s and it is difficult not to relate this to the *latent* tendencies of successive political administrations to curry favour with the public for wider political and ideological advantage. Further afield, the United States incarcerates a larger share of its population that at any point in its history and as Wakefield and Wildeman argue in *Children of the Prison Boom* (2014), mass incarceration must be understood, given the disproportionate numbers of black men and women subject to it, not just in terms of its impact on those subject to it, but also in terms of how it has transformed racial inequality in America, leading to parallel paths of marginalisation for children of the imprisoned parents (Wakefield and Wildeman 2014: 129). Furthermore, and in relation to women offenders on a global level, the latest edition of the *World Female Imprisonment list* reveals that there has been an approximate 50 per cent increase in the number of women and girls held in penal institutions worldwide over the past 15 years, despite no corresponding increase in the seriousness of their offending (Institute for Criminal Policy Research 2015 quoted in Roberts and Watson 2017: 562–563).

The broad ideological thrust of criminal justice legislation and policy then shapes the operational environment of our criminal courts and sets the tone for sentencer behaviour. Individual sentencers operate, exercising some degree of independence, within the statutory minimum and maximum of sentencing guidelines and reflect a much cherished and important aspect of the British constitution – the independence of the judiciary. Approaches to sentencing have to be seen to deliver justice in a fair and efficient manner within democratic societies and *consistency* becomes the watchword. This reflects the very basis of institutionalised retributive or deserts approaches to sentencing – the use of sentencing guidelines to secure consistency by attempting to link the level of punishment to the severity of the offending based on the harm caused by the offender/offence and the culpability of the offender. At their most basic, sentencing guidelines may give primacy to the current offence(s) and previous convictions, but here is the rub in terms of substantive justice – in a telling use of Christie's view, Canton reflects:

> Yet Christie denounces such measures as 'a trained incapacity to look at all values in a situation, and instead to select only the legally relevant ones, that is, those defined by the high priests within the system to be the relevant ones' (Christie 1981: 21) What may not be taken into consideration is social justice: 'the legislators make it illegal . . . to take into consideration precisely those factors which most of the prison population have as their common background: poverty and deprivation, the absence of a share in the good life, all those key attributes of the non-productive "dangerous class"' Christie 2000: 158). All the nuances of harm, culpability and impact of sentence, then, are suppressed by the relentless logic of the grid.
>
> *(Canton 2017: 76)*

In England and Wales, sentencing guidelines, as we have already highlighted, encompass a wider range of factors than simply seriousness and previous convictions but there is still a *relentless logic of the grid* whereby culpability is focused on *offence-related* matters rather than the contexts and capacities of the individual to act as a free agent. Of freedom to act, Hudson put it this way:

> [T]he notion of free will that is assumed in ideas of culpability . . . is a much stronger notion than that usually experienced by the poor and the powerless. That individuals have choices is a basic legal assumption: that circumstances constrain choices is not. Legal reasoning seems unable to appreciate that the existential view of the world as an arena for acting out free choices is a perspective of the privileged, and that potential for self-actualisation is far from apparent to those whose lives are constricted by material or ideological handicaps.
>
> *(Hudson 1994: 302)*

Criminal justice responses to offending must, we would argue, reflect understanding of the socio-economic position of many individuals who offend for, as Box has argued, we need more understanding of the plight of individuals because many of us, in similar circumstances, might choose similar courses of action (Box 1987: 29). This is not to argue that acts of criminality and anti-social behaviour should not be responded to through criminal justice sanctions but within the British criminal justice systems there is very little latitude for reflecting the way in which social and economic inequality constrain individual choice and therefore affect culpability. Hudson brings the ideas of free will and *constraint* together in a way that points to the moral obligation of the State to support those who offend:

> States have a right to punish, they argue, because offenders do act out of choice; free will is a characteristic of human beings in normal societies, not just a legal fiction. On the other hand, choices are constrained by circumstances, and under certain social conditions people will turn to crime who in other social climates would remain law-abiding. Poverty, social and material inequalities, lack of psychiatric provision, drug and alcohol facilities, as well as experiences of abuse and harassment, lead people into crime. The state should thus recognize its role in crime causation, and its obligation towards crime prevention, by providing rehabilitative elements in sanctions to help the offender refrain from further crime.
>
> *(Hudson 1996: 66)*

A key question, then, is whether the act of sentencing can ever deliver justice in a socially and economically stratified society? Duff, for example, in arguing for punishment as a form of moral communication, recognises that the very legitimacy of punishment is undermined without attention to wider political, legal and social contexts within which it is dispensed (Duff 2003b: 305), whilst Carlen has argued that *rehabilitationism* is 'one of the many penal imaginaries whereby jurisdictions have, over the years, tried to make sense of the obviously nonsensical idea of doing justice in grossly unequal societies' (Carlen 2013: 99).

We recognise the very challenging and complex debate involved in requiring a system of sentencing to respond to civil, social and material injustices but when we invoke Cohen's *it's alright for you to talk* (1976: 95) in Chapter 2, we accept the challenge to consider the options for the *here and now*. In any event, if a system of sentencing can double England's and Wales's prison population in 25 years, surely a different approach can impact in the opposite direction. As Canton has perceptively reflected: 'Unless sentencing conventions are constantly challenged and refreshed by reflective ethical thinking, they risk becoming ossified, and a penal tariff, no matter how much it supports consistency, can degenerate into nothing more than habit' (Canton 2017: 207).

Canton, we would argue, gets to the heart of the current problem and before we consider qualitatively more sophisticated approaches to sentencing, there are a number of basic changes to current sentencing legislation and formal guidance that would help individuals to more hopefully imagine their future desistance pathways in the community rather than in prison:

- A redefined *tripwire* for the use of imprisonment that requires more than the test of *so serious* to one where the offender would have to pose *a serious threat to the community* (see Roberts and Watson 2017: 552).
- The assessment of culpability to include a greater emphasis on the personal, social and material circumstances of the individual and the responsibilities of the State to address them thorough appropriate community sentences.
- Limitations on the use of previous convictions on determining the seriousness of the current offence and instead, their recognition in relation to the suitability of an offender for a particular disposal and/or the repeat use of community rehabilitation measures.
- The acceptance that all sentences of the court involve punishment (*restriction on liberty*) which does not need to be supplemented by statutory requirements to include a punitive element in community sentences.
- A more sophisticated understanding of the relationship between what punishment means for individual offenders in terms of restriction on their liberty and capacity to respond to court orders.
- A repeal of the post-release licence and supervision arrangements of the Offender Rehabilitation Act 2014 for short-term prisoners (under 12 months) in order to reduce the recycling of individuals between the prison and the community; in its place, the reintroduction of *voluntary aftercare* arrangements where probation services have a statutory responsibility to assist for ex-prisoners.

These specific examples of changes to current sentencing do not, of themselves, deliver individual rehabilitation but as Canton (2017: 209) argues, 'community sentences should always be considered before imprisonment, which should only be used with a sense of regret and as a last resort. In reductive terms, prison blocks desistance'. Furthermore, whilst less reliance on imprisonment reduces its overall collateral and deleterious impact, it also reduces the message of exclusion both to the individual who offends and to the community affected by the offending. As Duff (2001) would argue, exclusion is a message we should be very slow to communicate.

These examples also rely on a process of sentencing that can reflect both the needs of individuals and the impact of sentences on their lives in more finely tuned ways than the current insistence on apparent consistency demands. Discretion, conceptually imagined, individually tailored and democratically accounted for, can shape sentencing for the benefit of defendants, victims and the wider community. Rather than a being a point of contention and friction, it can be the focus of ongoing communication and dialogue that strengthens civic society. Discretion is a thread running throughout the criminal justice process, sometimes operating in humane and intelligent ways and at other times as a mechanism to oppress in the most vicious of ways. As Hudson argued, restricting (discretion):

> at one stage only enhances it at another, rather as tightening a belt does nothing to reduce body fat, merely displaces it to bulge out at the midriff. What should be problematized is not discretion *per se*, but the use of discretion in discriminatory ways.
>
> *(Hudson 1987: 129)*

The challenge is to reimagine discretion as a necessary feature of a just and humane approach to sentencing and one that engenders a manner of courtroom interactions with offenders that contributes to the start or continuation of desistance journeys.

## Style as well as substance

In drawing on Anthony Duff's argument for punishment as the communication of censure, *punishment can be conceived as rehabilitation*. Whereas sentences involving reparation or supervision in the community can convey both rights and responsibilities (reciprocities between citizens), imprisonment conveys exclusion and separation both for the individual, their familial and social networks and, significantly, for the wider community. Therefore, an argument for the parsimonious use of imprisonment can be based not only on the deployment of scarce resources and the efficacy of community-based responses to individual offending, but also on a wider consideration of the importance of dialogue and communication within civic society (something we discuss in more detail in Chapter 6). Indeed, the judicious use of discretion within the process of sentencing depends on a deeper understanding from the polity about the lives of individuals at the same time as it should demand a better understanding from those who offend of the harm they have caused their communities. In this sense, then, justice really must be seen to be done but a justice that is geared to building or restoring relationships between the individual who offends, the victim and the wider community in a way that supports the ongoing dialogue and communication that underpins reintegration rather than exclusion.

We introduced the importance of ritual earlier in the chapter and drew on the work of Maruna's (2011a) *Reentry as a rite of passage*. Maruna argues that there is a relationship between wider society and those to whom rituals apply in the sense that they create mental states rather than simply expressing them: 'Rituals engender solidarity and social cohesion by bringing people together in common cause; this community bonding is then thought to serve the purpose of generating beliefs about standards of morality' (Maruna 2011a: 9).

Maruna continues that the public can learn forgiveness and reconciliation by practising it, 'by exercising this cultural muscle' (2011: 16). In other words, the process of practising and repeating rituals makes those rituals more real and more genuine and therefore they need to be open and publicly demonstrated and individually tailored:

> [R]ituals could be designed to recognize a person's efforts to 'make good' after committing an offense. These might include immediate efforts to apologize or make amends to one's victims, a period of 'good behaviour' on the outside, and efforts to recover from addiction, find productive work, give something back to one's community, or contribute to one's family responsibilities.
>
> *(Maruna 2011a: 19)*

One can readily see the relevance for the sentencing process here if it (and the review of progress in appropriate cases) involves meaningful rituals that both kick-start and reinforce efforts to desist. Not only could these rituals create a public space for communication and dialogue but in desistance terms, they could be adapted to focus on the positive attributes and potential of the individual.

Indeed, over the past 20 years or so there has been a growth (or at least greater experimentation) in different ways of engaging people both at the point of sentence and onwards by sentencers and by the court process itself. Particularly evident in parts of the US judicial system, there has been growth of problem-solving courts, based on a theoretical framework often referred to as *therapeutic jurisprudence*. Associated with specific crime-related problems such as domestic abuse, substance misuse and mental health, the problem-solving approach to the dispensation of criminal sanctions has both academic and judicial adherents. David Wexler, for example, a professor of law and Director of an International Network on Therapeutic Jurisprudence at the University of Puerto Rico, wrote a short but incisive piece – *Robes and Rehabilitation: How Judges Can Help Offenders 'Make Good'* in 2001. In it, he quotes a resolution agreed in August 2000 by the Conference of the Chief Justices and the Conference of State Court Administrators regarding problem-solving courts that use therapeutic jurisprudential principles:

> There are principles and methods founded in therapeutic jurisprudence including integration of treatment services with judicial case processing, ongoing judicial intervention, close monitoring of and immediate response

to behaviour, multi-disciplinary involvement, and collaboration with community-based and government organizations.

*(Wexler 2001: 18)*

Wexler essentially argues that courts can focus on the defendant and contribute to their rehabilitation and reform. This is not just about the development of specialised courts but rather the way in which judges as sentencers inter-react with individual defendants. Clearly influenced by the 'What Works?' literature and the deployment of cognitive-behavioural interventions, Wexler sees the court's role as promoting cognitive self-change as part and parcel of the sentencing process itself (Wexler 2001: 20). He goes further, however, as the title suggests, linking to Maruna's early work on desistance and *making good* – hence the court might say in relation to a sentence of probation:

> I am going to consider you but I want you to come up with the type of preliminary plan that we will use as a basis of discussion. I want you to figure out why I should grant you probation and why I should feel comfortable that you're going to succeed. In order for me to feel comfortable, I need to know what you regard to the high-risk situations and how you're going to avoid them or cope with them without messing up. And, speaking of messing up, I want you to tell me what happened that led you to mess up the last time, and why you think the situation is different this time around.
>
> *(Wexler 2001: 20)*

Adherents to this type of approach include practising judges and in the same publication – *Court Review* – more recently, two judges argue for the mainstreaming of the problem-solving drugs courts approach to all courts (Hueston and Burke 2016: 47). Their argument is that developing trust is absolutely key. In the case of people with drug problems they suggest:

> the court must create a place of safety that encourages offenders to seek help when they are struggling with their treatment or when barriers thwart their recovery. Judges must ensure that the probation officers will not threaten arrest of probationers who admit to drug use – otherwise, the probationers as will refuse to share their mistakes. This does not convey a license to use drugs; rather it establishes an environment where honesty is recorded and help-seeking behavior is promoted. Research suggests that, on average, high addicted offenders submitted to multiple treatment episodes before reaching sustained recovery.
>
> *(Hueston and Burke 2016: 47)*

Other proponents of problem-solving courts in the United States, likewise, underline the importance of trust along with procedural fairness – respect, neutrality and a place for the offender's voice (MacKenzie 2016). The finger-wagging judge, according to Hueston and Burke, who demands that the defendant, in this case John, 'immediately stop using drugs—will not trump John's compulsion to use'. Rather:

> John will tell the judge whatever he believes will gain his release and propel him to his next 'fix' on the streets . . . Only when John fails to comply with the court's orders will he find himself before the judge for a probation revocation or adjustment hearing—a negatively driven process, often in custody and where the tension is often palpable. The judge supervising John's case, as with most traditional court judges who are exposed to a steady diet of probation violators, is frustrated by the persistent failure of those under her supervision and by the repeat violations of her sentencing orders. Business as usual is particularly unsatisfying.
>
> *(Hueston and Burke 2016: 44)*

From an English and Welsh perspective, the most comprehensive review of problem-solving and court specialisation is to be found in Jane Donoghue's *Transforming Criminal Justice?* Tracing problem-solving justice from its origins in the United States in the 1990s, she places its use and influence within a broader sphere of community justice (Donoghue 2014: 4). It was a Labour administration in 2009 that announced the intention to mainstream aspects of problem-solving justice into the lower court system including direct judicial engagement with offenders and problem-solving intervention supported by review hearings which had been facilitated under section 178 of the Criminal Justice Act 2003.

In considering the growth of problem-solving approaches both here and in the United States, Donoghue suggests that much of the critical analyses around problem-solving justice reflects its rise as a response to the failure of traditional social institutions including the family, neighbourhood, community, schools and welfare agencies to effectively support individuals and to address local social problems – 'the process which Eric Miller has described as the "courtification" of social service provision' (Donoghue 2014: 17). Donoghue, however, argues that the picture is a more nuanced one in that problem-solving courts in both the USA and the UK might be seen as a 'windows of opportunity' to transform the lives of individuals who enter the criminal justice system (2014: 18).

> While problem-solving courts have undoubtedly in part originated as a response to the deficiencies of existing mechanisms of social control as well as failures in state welfare provision, their introduction and evolution has also opened up space for the development of a wider discourse about the purpose of punishment, how we conceptualise it, what value it has and what purpose it serves. Thus, problem-solving courts raise important questions about how we conceptualise punishment.
>
> *(Donoghue 2014: 19)*

One of the most developed examples of a community justice court and one whose operations was familiar to two of the current authors was the North Liverpool Community Justice Centre (NLCJC). In many respects, the operation and the demise of the Centre reflect many of the political and extra-judicial considerations about such provision but ultimately cost and apparent ineffectiveness (in terms of reducing reconviction) ended the experiment. Opened in September 2005, the decision was taken to close the Centre in October 2013. As Donoghue (2014: 96–101) outlines in a detailed analysis, one of the key problems appeared to be the way in which reduction in reoffending became the key measure against the relative cost of the Centre with little weight given to wider issues around community involvement and confidence in the local criminal justice system. She remains, however, positive about their potential:

> In both the US and the UK, problem-solving justice represents a subversive counter-trend that stands in opposition to existing narrative of punitivism. Above all, however, problem-solving justice is transformative in the sense that it aims to recalibrate the substantive nature of punishment to make it more socially meaningful; to provide those historically marginalized defendants with greater voice in the justice process; and to reclaim justice as a fundamental element of *local neighbourhoods* rather than central government.
>
> *(Donoghue 2014: 141)*

The problem of demonstrating effectiveness dogged the NLCJC, particularly in terms of reoffending rates, but it is also clear from the evaluation carried out by Mair and Millings (2011) that both people appearing before the judge and members of the local community spoke positively about the Centre. Criminal justice staff and those employed by agencies delivering a variety of supportive services within the Centre were highly committed and supportive of the Centre's ethos and purpose. The role of the Judge was particularly critical and the notion of *fairness* was highlighted by the vast majority of defendants. Consistency and communication were the other defining characteristics of offenders' responses: consistency in terms of regularly sitting in the court, explaining sentencing decisions and taking action when promised if offenders failed to respond; communication in terms of both clarity and engagement in the process of tackling the individual's offending behaviour:

> At the end of the day only you change things and get your shit sorted, but people need chances and support and this place helps that and throws it to you to get sorted . . . they put you on the programmes and slowly help you, and when you fall they can but don't put you in prison, and that changes everything and you get on and sort yourself which they've made happen.
>
> *(supervisee quoted in Mair and Millings 2011: 82)*

This specific example underlines Mair and Millings's more general view that:

[t]he emphasis on problem solving and the detailed case by case analysis of individuals that lies at the heart of the principles of community justice, does appear to have had a genuine impact on how many offenders viewed their life beyond the Centre. What was apparent in the way offenders talked was the way in which they appeared to be wrestling back responsibility and taking ownership of the need to address their offending behaviour. There was a strong sense that the Judge and Centre staff would mobilise to help the individual and that within that process many individuals recognised they had a role to play themselves.

*Mair and Millings (2011: 83)*

## Heading for trouble

In the review of the NLCJC by Mair and Millings, there are a number of vignettes of individual progress that convey a palpable sense of repayment made by some offenders for the faith shown in them by the court system – specifically, the process of review and acknowledgement of progress seemed to be particularly powerful – 'the positive statements presented by the Centre probation staff helped secure praise from the presiding Judge and renewed their (the individuals) efforts to desist from offending and to continue to access support' (Mair and Millings 2011: 85). Personal observation of the court process also conveyed individualisation of the sentencing process – not in the sense of removing the individual from their socio-economic status within society, but rather in a committed focus on the individual and what it might take to assist in their journey towards a crime-free life. Names were remembered, including those of family members who had been present at previous hearings. Staff from non-judicial organisations were recognised. These small but significant signs suggested a level of dialogue and communication that conveyed both interest in the individual and accountability to the wider community.

The environment, however, within which problem-solving courts such as the NLCJC developed now seems a world away from the post-*Transforming Rehabilitation* reorganisation of the Probation Service. Under the new arrangements introduced in 2014, the National Probation Service provides services to the criminal courts including the preparation of Pre-Sentence Reports (PSRs) whilst 21 separate and privately owned Community Rehabilitation Companies (CRCs) supervise the majority of those individuals subject to community sentences and post-release supervision. In addition, the management of defendants through the court process is now determined by *Transforming Summary Justice* (TSJ) and *Better Case Management* (BCM) in order to deal with more cases at first hearing (HM Inspectorate of Probation 2017: 12; National Offender Management Service 2016). The combination of these central government initiatives means that the Probation Service is required to deliver 60 per cent of its reports to the courts in oral form on the day, a further 30 per cent in written form on the day and only 10 per cent where a custodial remand may be required. The 2017 *Thematic Inspection* carried out by Her Majesty's Inspectorate of Probation (HM Inspectorate of Probation

2017) identifies a range of weaknesses emerging from these arrangements, some of which go to the core of pre-sentence assessment and sentencer confidence in it. More importantly, we would argue, is the estrangement, for the sake of speed, of sentencers from the individuals appearing before them. Indeed, the NPS has had to introduce the notion of *Safer Sentencing* where information may not be readily available on the day:

> The advice is that for a proposal to be considered safe, the report writer must form a professional judgement of whether the information would have a direct bearing on sentencing or whether the information could reasonably be followed up post-sentence for the purposes of risk management of the ensuing post-sentence.
>
> *(HM Inspectorate of Probation 2017: 20)*

In a timely and much needed analysis of current PSR preparation Robinson (2017) has analysed the demise of what is now referred to as the *Standard Delivery Report* from some 77 per cent of cases in 2007 to 5 per cent (half the current official target of 10 per cent) in the latter half of 2016 (HM Inspectorate of Probation 2017: 21). Robinson argues that the shift represents a significant cultural one in probation practice which has not attracted a great deal of academic attention. Indeed, as she comments, under the various initiatives to *speed up justice* (including those mentioned above) over the last 15 years or so – '[g]iven the probation service's role as a key actor in the courtroom – especially in relation to decisions to adjourn for Pre-Sentence Reports – it is surprising to find that it is hardly mentioned in the raft of documents associated with TJ (Transforming Justice)' (Robinson 2017: 341). Robinson's work is also based on extensive courtroom observation and whilst she acknowledges the current cultural realities of delivering assessments within the timescales and the pressures and challenges for staff tasked with responding to the targets, she comments that:

> whilst speed has become a key value for the courts, it is not the only value that matters to them: they continue to want reports that are well-informed, accurate and useful in enabling them to pass sentences that are proportionate, suitable, for the individual and unlikely to put the public at risk.
>
> *(Robinson 2017: 350)*

As Robinson notes, quality is socially constructed and what counts as good varies over time. The *National Standards for Probation* published in 2015 had little to say about court reports other than they should be prepared *within the required timescales.* Additionally, and of more relevance to our current concerns are Robinson's questions about the subject of a PSR:

> [B]ut what of the person who is the subject of the report? What is quality likely to mean to the defendant? Due to a lack of research in this area, we

currently know very little about how either the faster production or changing formats of PSRs might be perceived by defendants. However, what we
can say is that these changes present a number of risks to the quality of that
experience, such that defendants are arguably more likely (than in the past) to
feel rushed and confused, and less likely to feel fully engaged in the process.

*(Robinson 2017: 348)*

Likewise, Mair's recent review of the Probation Service's impact on advising sentencers included criticism of the increasing prevalence of tick box approaches to
providing sentencers with information. He concludes that the:

> move from expressive to instrumental reports may be speeding up justice
> but it is also leading to offenders being dehumanised. Probation has always
> helped to humanise offenders and it is vital that this remains at the core of its
> work. To do this work effectively requires credibility with the magistrates
> and judges, and the preparation of reports for courts is crucial to the estab-
> lishment and maintenance of probation credibility.

*(Mair 2016: 82)*

The emphasis on speed and efficiency, even where issues of public safety are present, reflected in the current system of processing individuals through the criminal
courts provides little space for more nuanced considerations of effectiveness, participation, and engagement with the individual's personal sense of what justice is in
qualitative terms. The imperatives of these forces of *process* are further reinforced by
the deterministic features of the ICT culture (discussed in Chapter 2) within which
practice is now driven and which can turn knowledge and assessment into timeless,
acontextual information which becomes part of the official record (Phillips 2017).
We are not arguing for the return to the days when PSRs were often lengthy and
elaborate documents, prepared in secret by professional experts on unsuspecting
clients. What we are highlighting are the paradoxical and contradictory effects of
this mystical search for efficiency, which produce opportunities lost for dialogue
that can connect sentencers, offenders and probation workers, as well as victims and
the wider community. An approach to sentencing that aspires to communicate censure in a constructive manner, reflecting discretion and nuanced decision-making,
requires both visibility and dialogue. The alternative is reliance on the *relentless logic
of the grid*, reflecting absolute notions of consistency and *desert* which may well be
delivering such high levels of incarceration by design rather than individual intent
(see Millie *et al.* 2007).

## Conclusion: Sentencing and desistance journeys

> Rehabilitationists need have no objection to their interventions being cir-
> cumscribed by retributivist limits – and as long as the burden of intervention
> is no more (and usually no less) than is deserved, retributivists need have no

objection to the pursuit of rehabilitative aims. The right to rehabilitation, so far from being at odds with retribution, is required by it: once the punishment has been served, the standing of the ex-offender should be the same as that of anybody else, and retributivists ought to welcome attempts to restore people to their due status. Moreover, unintended punitive elements – deprivation or hardships that are not part of the justly imposed sentence but may follow from it (like loss of accommodation, employment, stigma) – are retributively unjust and therefore ought to be minimised or redressed by supportive, rehabilitative interventions.

*(Canton 2017: 121)*

Individualised sentencing has atrophied over the past 25 years. Reflecting the political imperatives of successive administrations, the search for illusionary consistency in sentencing outcomes – *the relentless logic of the grid* – has contributed to a prison population in England and Wales that has grown consistently over the past quarter of a century and to the point where it is generally accepted to be in crisis. The prison population is projected to grow to an all-time high of 88,000 by 2022 (Ministry of Justice 2017). There are occasions where the sentence of imprisonment, if not the experience of it, may provide a moment of epiphany for the individual. For others, their personal, social and economic strengths may be such that incarceration makes little difference to their life trajectories. For the majority, however, prison has a damaging effect not only in terms of the future ability of the individual to desist from crime but also in the collateral damage to family, partners and children of the incarcerated, which can be devastating and have long-term consequences. In England and Wales, we have amongst the highest population of women in prison in Western Europe, often sending female shoplifters to prison, for example, ostensibly because of their previous convictions and not because of offence seriousness (Roberts and Watson 2017: 551). Our criminal justice system continues to disproportionately incarcerate Black and Minority Ethnic individuals and an alarmingly high percentage of prisoners with significant mental health and substance misuse problems fill our prisons (Prison Reform Trust 2017a). Prisons also house a disproportionately high number of individuals who are homeless at the point of sentence and will remain so at the point of discharge (Prison Reform Trust 2017b; Cooper 2016). Little wonder, then, that the reconviction rate for short-term prisoners is depressingly high with 66 per cent being reconvicted within 12 months of release (Ministry of Justice 2018: 7).

Logic and humanity dictate that we should punish less, and in this chapter we have reflected upon philosophical theories of punishment and jurisprudential insights into the criminal justice processes in an attempt to give the act of sentencing itself a more prominent and promising but less punitive place in the process of rehabilitation. As the opening quote in this conclusion highlights, retribution and rehabilitation do not have to stand in opposition to one another (McNeill 2014). Further, in embracing Duff's normative theory of punishment as the *communication of censure*, we can conceptualise the courtroom as the site for communication and dialogue on a number of levels; not simply between sentencer and sentenced but also as a place where probation can act as mediator between the victim, the wider community and those who have offended against them. Drawing on Duff's work, Canton reminds us that:

> [c]ensure is no mere scolding – not just a cry of anger and denunciation – but a communication. This communication should be open to – indeed should try to elicit – a response which in its turn merits respectful attention. Probation supervision could then be regarded as a dialogue between the community, as represented by the probation office, and the offender.
>
> *(Canton 2018: forthcoming)*

Ultimately, such a model allows for the reimagination of the courtroom as part of the response to the guilty defendant as citizen, as member of our community, as member of the polity, and as someone defined not simply by the bad things they have done but by the good things they can contribute in the future.

We have noted, drawing on both official sources of criticism (like HMIP) and Robinson's research (2017), that recent changes brought by *Transforming Rehabilitation* and other government initiatives make the reimagining of the sentencing process more difficult. An environment of diminishing resources for court and probation services, where local justice is becoming more remote and where speed appears to be the only key measure of efficiency, offers little hope at present for significant changes in the way individuals are dealt with before the courts. However, sentencing is not simply a private act *done to* the individual on our behalf behind the doors of the court but essentially a public-political act, one which binds all of us together in one of the most onerous duties the State can perform on its citizens. Finally, whatever the *harm caused by offending*, punishment places a duty on civil society to listen to the *harm done to those who offend*, particularly when the social contract between the individual and the State is insufficiently supported by the social and economic means for individuals to lead a good life.

We have highlighted the loss of discretion in sentencing with the rise of sentencing guidelines and the impact it has had on already marginalised groups. Consistency has become the holy grail of sentencing, but as we have argued, when combined with a narrow definition of offender culpability, guidelines deliver anything but consistent individual justice. The notion of culpability, constrained within a retributivist conception of justice to largely *offence-* rather that *offender*-related issues, maintains or exacerbates existing inequalities. Our position throughout this book is that individuals often have *constrained choice* in the decisions they make to offend and *bounded agency* over their attempts to determine their own futures. Nevertheless, far from excusing the individual or downplaying their culpability, discretion within the context of *communicating censure* can be interpreted as a recognition of the work expected of the individual to deal with their problems. It should also, of course, communicate to civil society the resources the individual (indeed all of us) requires to lead a good life. As we come to understand better the individual's lived and subjective experience of community penalties and imprisonment, it becomes apparent that justice or fairness or proportionality of punishment is a complex notion that the sentencing process deals with inadequately. As Van Ginneken and Hayes have commented, '[t]he significant variation in offenders' subjective experiences and definitions of punishment poses a challenge to the retributivist notion of proportionality in practice' (2017: 75). We have come a long way from the days when a government White Paper can state that a comparatively short order may make severe demands on some offenders that more severe orders would on others! As Sexton reflects – we may know the (formal) penalty better than the (lived) punishment (Sexton 2015: 133).

It seems to us, then, that consistency as the bedrock of judicial outcomes in the way sentencing guidelines envisage it is grossly simplified and substantive justice would be better served by a much more nuanced and empathetic notion of personal culpability that recognises the constraint under which individuals act. Ironically, as Hudson (2005) has argued, it is often those factors relating to reducing personal culpability that have been increasingly used as indicators of the risk of reoffending. This reality is reflected in van Stokkom's (2013) engaging discussion around the complex philosophical and practical issues in pursuing personal mitigation. Building on the work of the legal philosopher John Tasioulas, van Stokkom argues persuasively that personal mitigation should reflect elements of mercy not only where individuals are personally vulnerable including through socio-economic deprivation, but also tolerance for out of character actions, active responsibility of the offender to make good and the prevention of collateral damage to the offender and others – 'Doing justice demands a balance of competing values, and taking into account mercy, tolerance and responsibility keeps justice from being inexorable and rigid' (2013: 281).

In a telling and perceptive piece for *Criminal Justice Matters* in 2005, David Faulkner reflected that for the most part, policy, legislation and practice in sentencing is developed independently of theories of punishment and at the same time sentencer discretion is restricted and there is less room for the court to show compassion or to take account of remorse or mitigating circumstances:

> [A]t some point, the questions must arise whether punishment can be legitimate without those forms of due process, or whether punishment and the rest of the apparatus of criminal justice can properly be regarded as just another form of social intervention that is at the government's disposal.
>
> *(2005: 6)*

Sentencing becomes another form of intervention that conforms to the narrow and suffocating imperatives of the neoliberal mindset around cost and efficiencies. Furthermore, in its rigidity and adherence to procedures and guidelines rather than its wider accountability to the communities that generate and suffer from crime, sentencing can become the handmaiden of repressive social and criminal justice policies.

A system of sentencing that relentlessly plays subserviently into *the logic of the grid* is felt directly by the defendant. Speed and efficiency become the indicators of a successful system in which the individual before it becomes almost an *inorganic object* to be stress tested at speed – those stress tests include a battery of screening and risk assessment tools that determine how quickly and in what format the person before the court can be dispatched. Speed and efficiency come to shape the professional engagement of criminal justice workers in the overall operation of the courts, but measures of effectiveness then fall on the organisations responsible for their containment or supervision. The challenge of a seismic shift that would be required to move forwards the existing system of sentencing in England and Wales is daunting and would seem to require a reversal in the very policies that have been pursued over the recent past. It would require courts to operate within a justice environment that reflects a political commitment to use imprisonment as a last resource. Additionally, it would demand that sentencers, in their individual decision-making, call upon much more sophisticated and nuanced definitions of culpability within more open problem-solving approaches to defendant and community engagement. Finally, it would require the delivery of probation services to the court based on quality assessments of individuals and effective supervision in the community that retains the confidence of the judiciary and magistracy.

Our approach to considering the judicial aspects of reimagining rehabilitation has not offered an attempt to work the rough edges off the justice versus welfare debate or tweak certain jurisprudential technicalities – judicial rehabilitation must reside within the wider vision of what rehabilitation could mean in all its forms. We have chosen to concentrate on the sentencing process but we remain conscious of *legal* rehabilitation also being conceptualised deontologically as the restoration of rights and duties – ultimately as the requalification to full citizenship of the individual who has offended (McNeill 2014). Supporting individuals on the forward journey to full citizenship will always be easier from the probation office than the prison cell. Judicial rehabilitation does not stand apart from *moral* and *social* rehabilitation. Indeed, the sentencing process we have envisaged requires the moral engagement of the individual in paying back before they can be fully restored as a citizen of good character. Judicial rehabilitation also envisages our responsibilities as sentencers, criminal justice workers and citizens going beyond narrow criminal justice confines to wider ones of social and economic justice in relation to the impact of sentencing and rehabilitation:

> It follows that if we want to support desistance, much of our work will need to be with communities, civil society and the state itself. We will need to work with people with convictions in that process – not to 'correct' *them*. Rather, we need to learn from them and to work with them in a collective effort focussed not so much on crime reduction as on building a fairer society.

*(Graham and McNeill 2018: 446, emphasis in original)*

Justice and the reimagining of judicial rehabilitation is ultimately about dialogue. If individuals want ultimately be restored to full citizenship, they must speak and listen (however indirectly) to the victims and the communities they harm. If communities want peace and security, they must also speak and listen to 'offenders'. Sentencers and criminal justice workers must have concerted dialogue with those who have offended not just to assist in the restorative process but also to support their desistance journeys. Ultimately though, civic society must be engaged in open and democratic dialogue about why sentencers make the decisions they do and why the polity should be committed to meeting the social and economic needs of those same individuals who do them harm.

## References

Albertson, K. and Fox, C. (2014) *Justice, with Reason: Rethinking the Economics of Crime and Justice*, Issues in Community and Criminal Justice Series 9, London: Napo.

Ashworth, A. (2015) *Sentencing and Criminal Justice*, Cambridge: Cambridge University Press.

Bennett, C. (2017) Invisible punishment is wrong – But why? The normative basis of criticism of collateral consequences of criminal conviction, *The Howard Journal of Criminal Justice*, 56(4): 480–499.

Bottoms, A.E. and McWilliams, W. (1979) A non-treatment paradigm for probation practice, *British Journal of Social Work*, 9(2): 159–202.

Box, S. (1987) *Recession, Crime and Punishment*, London: Macmillan.

Burke, L. and Collett, S. (2010) People are not things: What New Labour has done to probation, *Probation Journal*, 53(7): 232–249.

Burke, L. and Collett, S. (2015) *Delivering Rehabilitation – The Politics, Governance and Control of Probation*, London: Routledge.

Canton, R. (2017) *Why Punish? An Introduction to the Philosophy of Punishment*, London: Palgrave.

Canton, R. (2018) Probation and the philosophy of punishment, *Probation Journal*, forthcoming.

Carlen, P. (1989) Crime, Inequality and Sentencing, in Carlen, P. and Cook, D. (eds) *Paying for Crime*, Milton Keynes: Open University Press, 8–28.

Carlen, P. (2013) Against Rehabilitation: For Reparative Justice, in Carrington, K., Ball, E., O'Brien, E. and Tauri, J. (eds) *Crime, Justice and Social Democracy – International Perspectives*, Basingstoke: Palgrave Macmillan, 89–104.

Cavadino, M., Dignan, J. and Mair, J. (2013) *The Penal System – An Introduction*, London: Sage.

Cohen, S. (1976) It's Alright For You to Talk: Political and Sociological Manifestos for Social Work Action, in Bailey, R. and Brake, M. (eds) *Radical Social Work*, New York: Pantheon Books.

Cohen, S. (1985) *Visions of Social Control: Crime, Punishment and Classification*, Polity Press: Cambridge.

Cooper, V. (2016) 'It's all considered to be unacceptable behaviour': Criminal justice practitioners' experience of statutory housing duty for (ex) offenders, *Probation Journal*, 63(4): 433–451.

Corston, J. (2007) *A Report by Baroness Jean Corston of a Review of Women with Particular Vulnerabilities in the Criminal Justice System*, London: Home Office.

Cullen, F.T. and Gilbert, K.E. (1982/2015) *Reaffirming Rehabilitation* (Second edition 2015), Abingdon: Routledge.

Donoghue, J. (2014) *Transforming Criminal Justice? Problem-solving and Court Specialism*, Abingdon: Routledge.

Duff, R.A. (2001) *Punishment, Communication, and Community*, Oxford: Oxford University Press.

Duff. R.A. (2003a) Probation, punishment and restorative justice: Should Al Turism be engaged in punishment, *The Howard Journal of Criminal Justice*, 42(2): 181–197.

Duff, R.A. (2003b) Penance, punishment and the limits of community, *Punishment & Society*, 5(3): 295–312.

Duff. R.A. (2005) Punishment and rehabilitation – or punishment as rehabilitation, *Criminal Justice Matters*, No. 60, Summer: 18–19.

Faulkner, D. (2005) Parties, politics and punishment, *Criminal Justice Matters*, No. 60, Summer: 5–6.

Faulkner, D. (2014) *Servant of the Crown – A Civil Servant's Story of Criminal Justice and Public Service Reform*, Waterside: Hampshire.

Faulkner, D. and Burnett, R. (2012) *Where Next for Criminal Justice*, Bristol: Policy Press.

Frazier, I. (2005) Life after a lonesome death, *The Guardian*, www.theguardian.com/music/2005/feb/25/bobdylan (Accessed 7 November 2017).

Garland, D. (2001) *The Culture of Control*, Oxford: Oxford University Press.

Gelsthorpe, L. (2017) Equal and different, *Scottish Justice Matters: Women and Justice (Are we making progress?)*, 5(2) November 2017: 8–9.

Graham, H. and McNeill, F. (2018) Desistance – Envisioning Futures, in Carlen, P. and Leandro, A.F. (eds) *Alternative Criminologies*, London: Routledge, 433–451.

Herzog-Evans, M. (ed) (2011) Special Issue: Judicial rehabilitation in six countries: Australia, England and Wales, France, Germany, The Netherlands and Spain, *European Journal of Probation*.

HM Inspectorate of Probation (2017) *The Work of Probation Services in Courts: An Inspection by HM Inspectorate of Probation*, Manchester: HMIP (June).

Home Office (1988a) *Punishment, Custody and the Community*, London: HMSO.

Home Office (1988b) *Tackling Offending – An Action Plan*, London: Home Office.

Home Office (1988c) *The Parole System in England and Wales – Report of the Review Committee (Carlisle Committee)*, London: HMSO.

Home Office (1990a) *Supervision and Punishment in the Community – A Framework for Action*, London: Home Office.

Home Office (1990b) *Partnership in Dealing with Offenders in the Community*, London: Home Office.

Home Office (1990c) *Crime, Justice and Protecting the Public – The Government's Proposals for Legislation*, London: HMSO.

Home Office (1991) *Organising Supervision and Punishment in the Community – A Decision Document*, London: Home Office.

Home Office (2003) *Prison statistics England and Wales 2002*, London: Home Office.

Hudson, B. (1987) *Justice through Punishment – A Critique of the 'Justice' Model of Corrections*, London: Macmillan.

Hudson, B. (1994) Punishing the poor: A Critique of the Dominance of Legal Reasoning in Penal Policy and Practice, in Duff, R.A., Marshall, S., Dobash, Rebecca and Dobash, Russell (eds) *Penal Theory and Practice: Tradition and innovation in criminal justice*, Manchester: Manchester University Press.

Hudson, B. (1996) *Understanding Justice: An Introduction to Ideas, Perspectives and Controversies in Modern Penal Theory*, Buckingham: Open University Press.

Hudson, B. (2005) Beyond punishments: Rights and freedoms, *Criminal Justice Matters*, No. 60, Summer: 18–19.

Hueston, J. and Burke, K. (2016) Exporting drug-court concepts to traditional courts: A roadmap to an effective therapeutic court, *Court Review*, 52(1): 44–50.

Institute for Criminal Policy Research (2015) *World Female Imprisonment List Women and Girls in Penal Institutions, Including Pre-trial Detainees/Remand Prisoners*, London: Institute for Criminal Policy Research.

Lageson, S. and Maruna, S. (2018) Digital degradation: Stigma management in the internet age, *Punishment & Society*, 20(1): 113–133.

Lammy, D. (2017) *The Lammy Review: An Independent Review into the Treatment of, and Outcomes for, Black, Asian and Minority Ethnic Individuals in the Criminal Justice System*, London: Lammy Review.

MacKenzie, B. (2016) The judge is the key component: The importance of procedural fairness in drug-treatment courts, *Court Review*, 52(1): 8–34.

Mair, G. (2016) What is the Impact of Probation in Advising Sentencing and Promoting Community Sanctions and Measures?, in McNeill, F., Durnescu, I. and Butter, R. (eds) *Probation – 12 Essential Questions*, London: Palgrave Macmillan, 61–83.

Mair, G. and Burke, L. (2012) *Redemption, Rehabilitation and Risk Management – A History of Probation*, London: Routledge.

Mair, G. and Millings, M. (2011) *Doing Justice Locally: The North Liverpool Community Justice Centre*, London: Bowland Charitable Trust/Centre For Crime and Justice Studies.

Martinson, R. (1974) What works? Questions and answers about prison reform, *The Public Interest*, 53: 22–54.

Maruna, S. (2011a) Reentry as a rite of passage, *Punishment & Society*, 13(1): 3–28.

Maruna, S. (2011b) Judicial rehabilitation and the 'clean bill of health' in criminal justice, *European Journal of Probation*, 3: 97–117.

McNeill, F. (2006) A desistance paradigm for offender management, *Criminology & Criminal Justice*, 6(1): 39–62.

McNeill, F. (2012) Four forms of 'offender' rehabilitation: Towards an interdisciplinary perspective, *Legal and Criminological Psychology*, 17(1): 18–36.

McNeill, F. (2014) Punishment as Rehabilitation, in Bruinsma, G. and Weisburd, D. (eds) *Encyclopedia of Criminology and Criminal Justice*, New York: Springer, 4195–4206.

McNeill, F. (2018) Mass supervision, misrecognition and the 'Malopticon', *Punishment & Society*, 0(0): 1–23 (advance online publication).

Miller, R.J. And Stuart, F. (2017) Carceral citizenship: Race, rights and responsibility in the age of mass supervision, *Theoretical Criminology*, 21(4): 532–548.

Millie, A., Tombs, J. and Hough, M. (2007) Borderline sentencing: A comparison of sentences' decision-making in England and Wales, and Scotland, *Criminology and Criminal justice*, 7(3): 243–267.

Ministry of Justice (2012) *Accommodation, Homelessness and Reoffending of Prisoners: Results from Surveying Prisoner Crime Reduction (SPCR) Survey, Research Summary 3/12*, London: Ministry of Justice.

Ministry of Justice (2017) *Prison Population Projections 2017 to 2002*, England and Wales, London: Ministry of Justice.

Ministry of Justice (2018) *Proven Reoffending Statistics Quarterly Bulletin*, January 2016 to March 2016, London: Ministry of Justice.

National Offender Management Service (2016) *Probation Instruction 04/2016: Determining Pre-Sentence Reports – Sentencing within the New Framework*, London: NOMS.

Nellis, M. (2004) Into the field of corrections – The end of English probation in the early 21st century, *Cambrian Law Review*, 35: 115–133.

Phelps, M. (2013) The paradox of probation: Community supervision in the age of mass incarceration, *Law & Policy*, 35(1–2): 51–80.

Phillips, J. (2017) Probation practice in the information age, *Probation Journal*, 64(3): 209–225.

Prison Reform Trust (2017a) *Counted Out: Black, Asian and Minority Ethnic Women in the Criminal Justice System*, London: Prison Reform Trust.

Prison Reform Trust (2017b) *Bromley Briefings Prisons Factfile*, London: Prison Reform Trust.

Pryce, V. (2013) *Prisonomics: Behind Bars in Britain's Failing Prisons*, London: Biteback Publishing.

Raynor, P. and Robinson, G. (2009) Why help offenders? Arguments for rehabilitation as a penal strategy, *European Journal of Probation*, 1(1): 3–10.

Raynor, P. and Vanstone, M. (1994) Probation practice, effectiveness and the non-treatment paradigm, *British Journal of Social Work*, 24(4): 387–404.

Roberts, J.V. and Watson, G. (2017) Reducing female admissions to custody: Exploring the options at sentencing, *Criminology & Criminal Justice*, 17(5): 546–567.

Robinson, G. (2017) Stand-down and deliver: Pre-sentence reports, quality and the new culture of speed, *Probation Journal*, 64(4): 337–353.

Rotman, E. (1990) *Beyond Punishment: A New View of the Rehabilitation of Offenders*, Westport, CT: Greenwood Press.

Schinkel, M. (2014) Punishment as moral communication: The experiences of long-term prisoners, *Punishment & Society*, 16(5): 578–597.

Sentencing Council (2016) *Imposition of Community and Custodial Sentences: Definitive Guideline*, www.sentencingcouncil.org.uk/wp-content/uploads/Definitive-Guideline-Imposition-of-CCS-final-web.pdf (accessed 12 November 2017).

Sentencing Council (2017) *Magistrates Court Sentencing Guidelines*, www.sentencingcouncil.org.uk/the-magistrates-court-sentencing-guidelines/ (accessed 2 December 2017).

Sexton, L. (2015) Penal subjectivities: Developing a new theoretical framework for penal consciousness, *Punishment & Society*, 17(1): 114–136.

Silverman, J. (2012) *Crime, Policy and the Media – The Shaping of Criminal Justice 1989–2010*, London: Routledge.

Social Exclusion Unit (2002) *Reducing Re-offending by Ex-prisoners*, London: Office of the Deputy Prime Minister.

Stacey, C. (2017) Rehabilitation in the internet age: The Google-effect and the disclosure of criminal records, *Probation Journal*, 64(3): 269–275.

Tonry, M. (2006) Purposes and functions of sentencing, *Crime and Justice*, 34(1): 1–53.

Topping, A. (2018) Former sex workers say law criminalises abuse victims, *The Guardian*, 18 January: 16.

van Ginneken, E.F.J.C. and Hayes, D. (2017) 'Just' punishment? Offenders' views on the meaning and severity of punishment, *Criminology & Criminal Justice*, 17(1): 62–78.

van Stokkom, B. (2013) Tempering Justice with Compassion: Rationales of Personal Mitigation in Sentencing, in Cornwell, D., Blad, J. and Wright, M. (eds) *Civilizing Criminal Justice: An international Restorative agenda for Penal Reform*, Hampshire: Waterside Press, 255–286.

Wacquant, L. (2004) *Punishing the Poor – the Neoliberal Government of Social Insecurity*, London: Duke University Press.

Wacquant, L. (2018) Prisoner Re-entry as Myth and Ceremony, in Carlen, P. and Franca, L.A. (eds) *Alternative Criminologies*, Abingdon: Routledge, 386–339.

Wakefield, S. and Wildeman, C. (2014) *Children of the Prison Boom: Mass Incarceration and the Future of American Inequality*, Oxford: Oxford University Press.

Wasik, M. and Taylor, R.D. (1994) *Blackstone's Guide to The Criminal Justice Act 1991*, London: Blackstone.

Wexler, D.B. (2001) Robes and rehabilitation: How judges can help offenders 'make good', *Court Review*, 38(1): 18–23.

Wootton, B. (1959) *Social Science and Social Pathology*, London: George Allen and Unwin.

# 5

# REIMAGINING PRACTICE CULTURES AND VALUES

## Moral rehabilitation

It is our choices, Harry, that show what we truly are, far more than our abilities.

*(J.K. Rowling, Harry Potter and the Chamber of Secrets 1998: 333)*

## The Dumbledore effect

The quote that starts this chapter is taken from an exchange between Harry Potter and Professor Dumbledore who acts as a guide and mentor to the young Harry. It is in response to self-doubts expressed by the young wizard, as he fears that he shares similar traits with his adversary Voldemort. Professor Dumbledore's words remind Harry that what distinguishes him from his nemesis are the *choices* he has made involving the acquisition of intellectual and moral virtues – *choices* which are far from being pre-determined. Therefore, through a process of moral mediation, Dumbledore helps him re-evaluate his position and so he is able to overcome his doubts, allowing him to take a more positive course of action. Similar to Athena's role with Odysseus, which we referred to in Chapter 3, Dumbledore does not attempt to correct Harry (or necessarily point out to him what path he should take); rather, he recognises Harry's individual agency through his acknowledgment that it is the decisions he makes which will ultimately decide his destiny. The choice that Harry has to make is essentially one between forces of good and evil and is located in a fantasy setting. Decisions to desist from crime in the real world may appear more mundane but remain profound; equally, they have an inherently moral dimension and are conspicuous by their complexity. Farrall *et al.* (2014) reflect that they invoke a range of emotional responses:

[D]esistance from crime is not confined to 'external' social factors (work, family, peers, etc.) or internal cognitive/psychological factors (identity, self-evaluation, motivation) but comprises a significant emotional component too. Desistance involves an array of emotions and feelings; it is through these emotions that individuals engaged in the processes of change that desistance requires, and through which they interpret the meaning of their past, make sense of their present and re-orientate their future. In other words, how desisters *feel* about their desistance matters.

*(Farrall et al. 2014: 214, emphasis in original)*

Engaging with moral and emotional complexity is thus an inevitable component of probation work, but it does not take place in a vacuum and is subject to a range of competing, sometimes contradictory, influences (Burke and Davies 2011). The reality – as we argued at the end of the previous chapter – is that despite the individual retaining agency, their choices will often be constrained by structural and other factors and this applies to both those delivering services and those under their supervision. Of course, whilst it is true that many individuals (especially those with entrenched criminal behaviour) may decide to stop offending, this does not mean that they will necessarily be able to carry out their intentions or that these decisions alone are sufficient for desistance (Giordano *et al.* 2002: 1001). Consequently, a change in the way that the individual weighs up their choices does not always produce a change in behaviour; support and guidance maybe required before achieving the desired state. As Anderson (2016: 31) notes, 'this is not to condone [offenders'] attitudes or their choices, but to understand them in the context in which these attitudes are formed and these choices are made'. Probation staff, we would argue, are in a good position to balance an individual's motivation to change, the opportunities available to them to do so and the skills required to take advantage of them (McNeill 2009). It is vital therefore to understand how 'interaction and communication with probation staff can support beliefs and behaviour consistent with the desistance process' (Vanstone 2018: 49). In a similar vein, Rob Canton has cogently argued:

> Offenders must find ways of negotiating through the world as they encounter it, without causing harm to others and to themselves, and criminal justice social workers should support them in these endeavours (or at least not aggravate) the injustices that oppress their clients.
>
> *(Canton 2016: 19)*

McNeill and Farrall (2013: 147–165) in their discussion of virtue and necessity argue that because desistance from crime often involves the acquisition of intellectual and moral virtues then it follows that supporting desistance requires practitioners to demonstrate those same virtues. This is because probation work involves direct engagement with people who have offended and who, in many cases, operate at the margins of society and whose stigmatisation can exist way beyond legal censure. Treating people with dignity and respect is an ethical requirement that is not dependent on its contingent outcomes as an instrumental means of reducing reoffending (Canton 2013 – see also our discussion of Stan Cohen's work in Chapter 2). Rehabilitation therefore has an inherently moral dimension. It entails a dialogue that centres on the renegotiation of shared values and mutual reparation of the harms that individual offenders, communities and the State may have done to one another (McNeill 2012, 2014).

In the preceding chapter, we explored the formal legal processes through which rehabilitative dialogues might be developed. Here our concern is with the less formal aspects of such interactions; primarily, our concern here is with the dialogue between the probation worker (as representative of the State and the punishing polity) and the supervisee. We are not suggesting that this dialogue is necessarily easy given that practitioners have to balance the authority of their role alongside its supportive aspects in what is ultimately a legally mandated one. Nor should this relationship, we should remind ourselves, be given primacy as 'social relations cannot be reduced to the influences of one person on another' (Weaver and McNeill 2015: 96). However, our contention is that at its best, good probation practice motivates people, it develops their capabilities and it seeks to secure opportunities for them to live better lives. Insights from desistance research suggests that practitioners can both contribute to and facilitate the process of desistance by focusing on improving individuals' social networks and personal competencies (King 2014; McNeill 2014). Often this might not be realised until long after the cessation of formal supervision. In their longitudinal study of desistance trajectories, Farrall and Calverley (2006: 46–57) found that probationers began to report instances of practical help and shifts in their attitudes that interactions with probation officers had engendered some years earlier. In this respect, 'the advice given by officers was "stored away" and drawn upon as personal circumstances changed' (Farrall *et al.* 2014: 281). As the authors point out, this has important implications in terms of how we conceptualise whether or not probation is effective. There is no magic intervention suggested here but more often than not the motivation to change can be sometimes stimulated by what on the face of it can appear to be *mundane* interactions between the supervisor and those under their supervision (Farrall *et al.* 2014: 140).

Shadd Maruna (2004: 274) also makes an important observation that 'desistance may be best facilitated when the desisting person's change in behaviour is recognised by others and reflected back to him in a "de-labeling process"'. The role of the practitioner is crucial here because 'de-labeling might be most potent when coming from "on high", particularly official sources' (Maruna 2004: 275). These forms of positive reinforcement are mediated through the worker's own personality, values, knowledge and skills but do not occur in a vacuum. As Canton points out, 'changes in social and political norms mean that practitioners frame the "problem" of offending – and, inevitably, law-breakers – in different terms: redeemable or damned, treatable or recalcitrant, safe or risky, motivated or unmotivated' (Canton 2011: 29) and for better or worse these relationships are profoundly affected by their institutional and organisational contexts.

## Street-level bureaucracy and beyond

In beginning to articulate the view that the process of rehabilitation is ultimately a moral one, it is nevertheless important also to recognise that it is mediated through the organisational and professional context in which it occurs. Here, we draw on Lipsky's seminal work *Street-level bureaucracy: Dilemmas of the individual in Public Service* (1980/2010) and his insightful critique of contemporary governance literature based on an analysis of the daily routines of those working in the public sector. The strengths of Lipsky's analysis, as Halliday *et al.* (2009: 423) point out, lie in the way in which it illuminates the inherent tensions that inevitably arise from the conflicting goals and pressures of contemporary public service and the human dimension inherent in delivering those services. It highlights the dissonance between the rhetoric of management control and bureaucratisation (that seeks to shape professional norms of behaviour, through target setting and performance management) with the levels of discretion (and sometimes resistance) deployed by front-line staff in public welfare organisations as they adopt coping mechanisms to deal with challenges of delivering increasingly scarce welfare resources. According to Lipsky, these coping mechanisms operate on three levels:

- Workers develop strategies to limit demands on their time and resources.
- They modify the concept of their job to narrow the gap between what is expected and what is available.
- They modify the concept of their clients to render the inevitable gap between what is expected and what can be achieved.

The operation of these coping levels helps us to understand how and why staff respond in the way that they do in response to the dilemmas involved in delivering public services. It also reminds us that policy often percolates through several political and professional levels of implementation and has been the subject of argument, dispute and compromise before it reaches street level (Evans 2011: 372). In this respect, practitioners will adopt, amend or even ignore such directives. According to Lipsky (2010: 13), street-level bureaucrats contribute to policy in two related respects. First, they exercise discretion in the decisions they take about those they interact with and second, their collective responses add up to agency behaviour (certainly in the eyes of those at the receiving end). As we shall see in this chapter, this is significant not only because of the contested nature of rehabilitative work but also because of empirical evidence that explicitly or implicitly suggests the existence of 'certain qualities that appear to give penal agents durability in the face of incessant penal change' (Grant 2016: 751). Consequently, if we are to develop a deeper understanding of penality in practice then such modes of enquiry and analyses need to be directed towards *how and why* penal-professional cultures, practices and attitudes change and resist change as well as to those practices themselves (McNeill 2009: 436). Furthermore, such analyses can be useful in understanding why a significant number of practitioners regularly go the extra mile in supporting desistance, also helping explain a range of processes including job satisfaction, morale, ethical conduct, working styles, causes of stress and coping adaptations (Brough *et al.* 2016: 15).

## Professionalisation from above, bearing down on probation

Occupational cultures are both complex and changeable and can be imposed or developed from both above and below. However, understanding the cultural dimension to an organisation is critical because it is through the transmission of values and shared practice wisdom that individuals are socialised to different degrees into their roles (Schein 1992/2004). Such cultures can be a unifying influence but can also be characterised by entrenched behaviour and attitudes as well as exclusionary practices; thus, they can become an obstacle to change. Distinctions have been drawn between organisational and occupational professionalism although to an extent both influence each other through the processes of selection and socialisation (Johnson *et al.* 2009). Professionalisation from above is based on accreditation and certification, involving hierarchical structures of responsibility and decision-making, standardised work procedures and practices and an adherence to external regulation and accountability. Professionalisation in this sense 'aims to convince, cajole, or persuade practitioners to perform in ways that are deemed appropriate, effective and efficient to promote organisational objectives that are defined by government' (Brough *et al.* 2016: 72).

Recent governments (regardless of their political affiliations) have sought to re-engineer the delivery of probation services in England and Wales as part of a broader agenda to *professionalise* public sector organisations (see Burke and Collett 2015). This has involved the deployment of a range of strategies:

- First, through the guise of *managerialism*, the adoption of market sector disciplines has been encouraged as a way of improving public service standards and increasing government control over what is delivered. This has involved redefining the relationship between public sector professionals and users of their services to one of provider and consumer evaluated through quantitative measurement of performance and target setting (see Chapter 6 for a fuller discussion of this). In probation practice, this has been accompanied by a change in language towards *offender management*, a term which has paradoxically been criticised for implying a deprofessionalisation or objectification of those individuals subject to supervision (Grapes 2007). These *top-down* constructions of quality and processes of quality assurance have also been associated (in and beyond the UK) with the development of national standards and/or performance indicators for probation work. *Official* constructions of quality have been criticised as being managerially driven and concerned more with controlling staff than enhancing the quality of practice. In turn, this has increased the bureaucratic demands upon front-line probation practitioners and reduced the time and space available for face-to-face contact with those under their supervision. This negatively impacts not only on supervisors, in the sense of displacing 'the centrality of practitioners as agents of change with tools and procedures that are not sensitive enough to the multi-faceted nature of the cultures, practices and practitioners that they seek to change' (Graham 2016: 164) but also on those subject to supervision, by failing to acknowledge their human subjectivity and rendering them as policy objects to be moulded on behalf of the general public (Anderson 2016: 409). Lipsky warns of the dangers inherent in this approach, claiming that 'society does not want computerised public service and rigid application of standards at the expense of responsiveness to the individual situation' (2010: 23).

- Second, as part of the modernisation agenda of the New Labour government in England and Wales, probation has been encouraged to work in partnership with other relevant criminal justice organisations. Robinson *et al.* (2014: 137) observe that collaborative working has become 'part of the cultural fabric of probation practice in England and Wales'. This has involved a redefining of professionalism whereby the values of occupational professionalism have sometimes been viewed as an impediment to more efficient system goals. Grant (2016) argues that in the contemporary landscape, penal agents strive to gain legitimacy and traction within the competitive and status-laden justice field and so claims for occupational distinctiveness are tempered by organisational drives to increase and embed more inter-agency working under the guise of public protection. Nash (2008), for example, claims that rehabilitative roles and responsibilities between the police and probation or criminal justice social work have become increasingly blurred.

- Third, there has been the relentless drive towards *marketisation* in the form of direct competition through privatisation, outsourcing and competitive tendering shaped by a commercial logic. This logic assumes that, through the creation of internal markets, competitive bidding for contracts and incentivisation, services can be provided more efficiently and cheaply as well as driving up the quality of the service. From this perspective the break-up of probation in England and Wales as a unified public service can be viewed within a broader context whereby 'the ideologies of the market, entrepreneurship, consumerism, and individualism have "colonized" public sector cultures' (Waring 2015: 350). This trend raises fundamental questions regarding the migration of public sector workers into the private sector in terms of 'how these cultural differences are reconciled, whether public values are substituted for those of private enterprise, and if new "hybrid" cultures are emerging' (Waring 2015: 345). According to Honig (1996) these neoliberal marketisation strategies have turned public service provision into a dilemmatic space. It is within this dilemmatic space that professionals and street-level bureaucrats strive to balance colliding value systems, managing the tensions that are inherent in public life (Lipsky 1980/2010). Consequently, the room for trust and discretion has tended to become narrower, with these pressures increasing as a result of these agendas. Eadie *et al.* (2013) argue that what they term the 'art of thinking in practice' has been marginalised in a climate in which technical *solutions* are prioritised in order to process individuals more efficiently through their orders. Similarly, Graham (2016: 164) argues that:

[c]oncentration on the tools and technologies of practice and their standardisation has surpassed and, arguably, neglected attention being given to issues that remain important to practitioners – identity, values, legitimacy and future purpose (who they are and why they do what they do).

The practical outcomes of the issues identified by Graham are highlighted in the study of probation work by Mawby and Worrall (2013). They highlight the relentless pressures probation workers experienced when trying to balance the contact time spent with clients (described as emotionally taxing) and doing effective work with them and satisfying the demands of paperwork and keeping records updated. Workers often felt unsupported by management and were made to feel that inability to cope was due to their personal shortcomings. This, together with what officers experienced as constraints on their professional autonomy coupled with high levels of accountability, resulted in a form of psychological exit (i.e. thinking about leaving) and an increase in cynicism as a result of the breaking up of the 'psychological contract' between themselves and their management. Interestingly, a corollary to this drawn from Europe is the study by Vogelvang *et al.* (2014) of resilience amongst Dutch probation officers which found that an appropriate management style, clear communication and manageable workloads were important factors in empowering officers in the face of increasing stress levels and role complexity.

## Professionalism from within

The forms of *professionalism from above*, outlined in the previous section, contrast with notions of *professionalism from within* (Graham 2016). The latter is often characterised by the divergent views, experiences and roles of different subgroups and individuals within the organisation and how they relate to others in the field. These in turn are often backed up by an informal culture which also provides the means to alleviate stress, particularly during periods of change, through the support and camaraderie of fellow workers (Brough *et al.* 2016: 24). All of these practical and organisational arrangements profoundly shape the culture of the agency as it is played out in the interactions between workers and the norms that develop around routine tasks. This is important because as Graham (2016: 67) points out: 'There is no point in conceptualising and analysing rehabilitation work merely as a technical and instrumental exercise if the workers involved make sense of it as a normative experience, incorporating affective labour and ideological dimensions'.

Grant's (2016: 755) study of criminal justice social workers in Scotland suggests that practice cultures and therefore occupational behaviours are underpinned by more than just the knowledge and skills required to do the job; they are inculcated by values and principles. Successive studies (Annison *et al.* 2008; Deering

2011; Grant 2016) have found that whilst probation occupational culture has, in some ways, changed and adapted, in other respects it has proven to be remarkably resilient and that practitioners appear to share common sets of values and principles regardless of how these subjective elements are forged. These can be broadly centred around a commitment to welfare-oriented approaches based upon more *relational* and *humanistic* dispositions. This tends to indicate a preference for discretion and the need to respond creatively to each individual case (Grant and McNeill 2015 – see also Burke and Millar 2012). Robinson *et al.* 2014, in their study of probation practitioners' perspectives on the meaning of *quality* in their work, found that this was articulated in terms of: building rapport; treating the offender respectfully; listening; being open and honest; following up on promised actions; taking time to get to know the person; being consistent; involving the offender in setting goals; establishing boundaries; and building trust.

It thus becomes apparent that professionalism from above will almost inevitably create tensions with professionalism from within. Lipsky, for example, contends that conflicts are inevitable given the client focus of professional norms and the dominant framework of the institutions in which professionals operate. In the past, probation practitioners have been able to resist policy changes perceived as managerial and punitive by 'adaptively and strategically interpreting, evaluating, [and] reconstructing central priorities' (Cheliotis 2006: 324). As Grant (2016: 759) points out, practitioners 'attempt to navigate through competing objectives and organizational pressures by adopting transgressive methods' that cut across the formal organisational culture. This may also include what Mawby and Worrall (2011) refer to as 'a controlled form of risk-taking'. Each of these authors are keen to point out this is not about behaving recklessly or disregarding the organisation's objectives. Nor is it merely about a nostalgic return to a largely mythical golden age of probation when workers enjoyed largely unfettered autonomy and professional discretion. Rather, it is about putting their skills to the test for the good of the offender, victims, the public and the organisation (Mawby and Worrall 2011, 2013). In this respect, as Robinson has argued:

> by employing degrees of creative agency . . . practitioners may also have active capacities to prevent external punitive discourse from drilling too deeply into their habitus. The room allowed for professional discretion and the agency of probation workers can thus be used to mitigate against pervasive managerialism and people-processing.
>
> *(Robinson 2013: 94)*

Indeed, Worrall and Mawby contend that 'a degree of edgework is essential for both the morale of workers and the health of the service as a whole' (Worrall and Mawby 2013: 116).

These findings support McNeill and Farrall's (2013) contention that it is not so much the merits of a specific technical approach that matter in securing outcomes but rather the qualities of the worker. These qualities were identified by the authors as being characterised by a combination of (largely soft/relational) skills, professional training (for those qualified staff) and experiences accrued on the job, coupled with the values, personal experiences and qualities that participants brought to their work. Rather than adopting a uniform conformity to organisational behaviours, the literature on professional ideologies and behaviours suggests that workers often do what they have always done in the past despite changes to the organisation. As Rudes *et al.* (2014: 19) contend, 'these past ideologies and behaviours are often not based in research evidence, but rather are learned behaviours formed from gut-level, intuition, informal team socialization processes, training or a lack of training, learned behaviours, lacking resources, and so forth'.

## What then matters in the delivery of rehabilitative services?

As the previous discussion demonstrates, given their particular ideology, the approach taken by staff as they undertake their responsibilities can have important consequences for both the organisation and those under their supervision. However, as valuable as insights into the way in which practitioners operate are, it is also important that there are more objective means to measure the impact probation practice can have on the process of desistance (Raynor 2018). In recent years, there has been increasing international attention given to the skills involved in supervision and the methods that underpin the supervisory process. Furthermore, the evidence suggests that staff who are trained to develop appropriate skills tend to produce better results both in terms of reconviction and compliance (Trotter 1996; Trotter and Evans 2012). Indeed, the most developed approach to evaluating the skills used by staff was that developed by Bonta *et al.* (2011). Using audio tapes of interviews, the researchers sought to assess the effects of a training programme – the *Strategic Training Initiative in Community Supervision* (STICS) – which was broadly based on principles of risk, needs and responsivity (RNR). Those officers trained in the STICS programme were instructed to assess and focus their efforts on the criminogenic needs of those under their supervision. These included positive relationship building and a structured approach to supervision, incorporating the use of cognitive-behavioural techniques, problem-solving, decision-making, consequential thinking and victim awareness (Bourgon *et al.* 2010). Their findings suggested that those probation officers who were trained using STICS were more effective in reducing reoffending than those who had not been trained and tended to have a more clearly defined structure of intervention, better relationship skills and employed more cognitive techniques. The amount of time workers spent discussing probationers' needs as opposed to the conditions of probation in their meetings was also positively associated with recidivism reductions in that the difference between the control group and the experimental group was 15 per cent (25.3 per cent for the experimental group and 40.5 per cent for the control group). Similar findings were produced in the quasi-experimental Jersey Supervision Skills Study (Raynor *et al.* 2014) which identified a range of skills used by staff in videotaped interviews and found significantly lower reconviction rates amongst people supervised by more skilled staff.

In England and Wales, the *Skills for Effective Engagement and Development* (SEED) training package was developed by the National Offender Management Service (NOMS). This initiative aimed to provide probation staff with additional training and continuous professional development in skills they could use in supervising offenders, particularly in one-to-one meetings. Like STICS, SEED was designed broadly in accordance with RNR principles, but it was also informed by emerging evidence about desistance from crime (Sorsby *et al.* 2018: 193). Although the implementation of SEED was effectively derailed by the *Transforming Rehabilitation* reforms, there were indications that practitioners valued it. Aspects of SEED that were particularly appreciated involved teams training together and discussing cases together between further training sessions. Interestingly, SEED was also appreciated because of the very fact that the framework for supervision was based on empirical evidence (Sorsby *et al.* 2018: 211). Finally, although evidence of the impact of SEED training on supervisees' experience of supervision was limited, there were some indications that practitioners in the trained group were perceived as using a fuller range of SEED skills overall, compared with those in the comparison group (Sorsby *et al.* 2018: 212).

The importance of these models of supervision is that they were not simply concerned with risk management or even a reductionist focus on offender compliance in accordance with the expectations of the court. Rather they attempted to locate the individual under supervision within a wider professional and organisational context and thereby tailor supervision to the drivers of criminal behaviour and the degree to which the individual made progress (Toronjo and Taxman 2018). This is critical because as Pereira and Trotter (2018) point out, research shows that supervision approaches that predominantly focus on formal compliance and performance management and that fail to balance the supervisory functions of accountability with education and support, limit the space for reflection and skills development by both supervisor and supervisee. Although they differ in the details of skill assessment and measurement, all these well-designed studies support the main finding of the current study that more skilled officers produce better results. They also show that levels of skill can in fact be improved by appropriate training (Raynor *et al.* 2014).

In the light of the importance attached to both training and ongoing supervision in these studies, the current arrangements in England and Wales are concerning. As Dominey and Gelsthorpe (2018) note, Community Rehabilitation Companies are not obliged to employ qualified staff in offender management roles nor are they required to adopt evidence-based practice tools such as SEED, although they will need to ensure that their staff are adequately equipped to meet the contractual requirements set by the Ministry of Justice. Toronjo and Taxman (2018: 217) highlight the importance of staff *buy-in* and as Vanstone (2018: 27) similarly argues, '[t]raining staff in this way is one thing, but ensuring that learned skills become ingrained and maintained in everyday practice is another' (Vanstone 2018: 27). In the STICS programme, for example, those staff involved were provided with ongoing clinical support in the form of monthly meetings to review and discuss practice skills and were able to participate in refresher courses. Indeed, the reconviction rate amongst those supervised by the STIC trained officers who participated in the monthly clinical supervision sessions was further reduced from 25 per cent to 19 per cent (Bourgon *et al.* 2010; Bonta *et al.* 2013). This would seem to suggest that the dialogue that occurs between practitioners is just as important as that which takes place within the supervisory relationship.

## The politics of delivering rehabilitation and experiencing organisational change

The evidence that more skilled supervisors deliver better outcomes means that the importance of identifying and promoting evidence-based skills appears incontrovertible. However, as Raynor points out, contemporary policies have often been marked by the absence of such an approach:

> The twenty-first century so far shows a progression from being *guided* by evidence, to using evidence as a *resource to support* policy decisions already made, to *creating* evidence to support policies and eventually to dispensing with evidence altogether.
>
> *(Raynor 2018: 70, emphasis in original)*

This would appear particularly pertinent in the case of England and Wales following the implementation of the *Transforming Rehabilitation* reforms which were both untested and unsupported by research (see Chapter 1 for an overview of *Transforming Rehabilitation* reforms). It is perhaps unsurprising that the vast majority of probation stakeholders disagreed with the proposal to split the service and saw this as the most damaging aspect of the reforms, believing the process to be 'arbitrary, artificial and permanent' (Deering and Feilzer 2015: 62). The emotional costs involved in the restructuring of probation were evident in the reactions of the majority of those interviewed by Robinson *et al.* (2016); respondents expressed '*hurt*', '*anger*', '*confusion*' and '*uncertainty*'. One practitioner described it as an '*unwanted divorce*' (Robinson *et al.* 2016: 167). Staff generally believed that the timescales for implementing the split had been unrealistic and that the failure to develop and test the changes had resulted in what some viewed as an indecent rush to prepare themselves for these two almost arbitrary organisations (Robinson *et al.* 2016). Respondents questioned the ethics of the new organisations and, like those whose views were canvassed in a similar study by Deering and Feilzer (2015), believed that although probation values had already come under pressure and been compromised before *Transforming Rehabilitation*, that this had been exacerbated by the structural split, producing a negative effect on all those involved.

Burke *et al.* (2016) applied the notion of 'splitting and fracturing', 'adapting and forming' and 'exiting or accommodating' to explore the processes involved in the migration of probation staff into the new organisational arrangements. Splitting and fracturing refers to the period immediately following the allocation of staff between the National Probation Service (NPS) and the Community Rehabilitation Company (CRC) as probation staff established new roles and responsibilities within the CRC but also experienced fractured emotional bonds and relationships, most notably with former colleagues. Many of those interviewed mentioned the physical loss of former colleagues to the NPS (felt to be exacerbated by structural impediments to communication across the *interface* between the two organisations) and/or the loss of human capital (in the forms of knowledge, skills and experience) through voluntary redundancies. Associated with these perceived losses was, for some, the threat to professional identity of reconciling the notion of a public service ethos with the values of the private sector. There was also a further powerful theme of loss expressed in relation to the local identity of the previous organisations (see also Robinson *et al.* 2016). For others there was a feared loss of professional identity where working for the CRC was perceived as a sign of 'professional failure' (Robinson *et al.* 2016; see also Kirton and Guillaume 2015) in contrast to the status secured by NPS colleagues working with high-risk individuals. In terms of the NPS, there were those who saw demands to attend to high-risk cases exclusively as being more likely to utilise valued probation skills. Others, however, feared that the NPS, organisationally at least, would become too centrally controlled and too focused on management and surveillance. Phillips *et al.* subsequently found that the unrelenting pressure of working only with high-risk supervisees appeared to have a variable impact upon NPS practitioners but overall the change was seen as responsible for raising levels of stress. The authors concluded that this was 'untenable in the long term' (2016: 189).

The second element of the migration process – *adapting and forming* – concerned how workers adapted to their changed circumstances. In an earlier study, Waring and Bishop (2011) identified three emergent identities amongst staff as they adapted to the changed organisational field. The first of these *ideal* types Waring and Bishop identified as *pioneers* who had felt inhibited by public sector bureaucracy and welcomed the outsourcing of provision, seeing it as an opportunity to re-invigorate their practice. This form of *intrapreneurship* whereby workers embrace change, engage in creative work, develop new initiatives using entrepreneurship and innovation (Graham and White 2015; Graham 2016) could be seen as an attempt to regain a level of control over externally imposed changes. The second emergent identity type in Waring and Bishop's study generally viewed change in more critical terms and sought to sustain established values, practices and relationships within the new working environment. These so-called *guardians* viewed change as an opportunity to build a new organisational identity and culture that was distinct from, but true to, the traditions of the occupation's past. The third group identified by Waring and Bishop were classified as the *marooned* because they felt abandoned by their former employer and were struggling to adapt to the changes in their work. Some found it difficult to reconcile what they perceived as public sector values within a new working environment that emphasised competition and entrepreneurialism. Compared to the *pioneers* and *guardians* in Waring and Bishop's study, the *marooned* exhibited less agency or capacity to reconstruct their identities. They displayed an overwhelming sense of nostalgia about the former organisational structures and a desire to return 'home', even though this might result in a loss of pay or occupational status.

During their research, Burke *et al.* (2016) observed elements of each of these types, although the *guardian* and *marooned* types tended to be most prevalent amongst longer-serving staff. For some staff, the organisational split and creation of the CRC had provided an opportunity to develop their careers and take on new responsibilities; they displayed characteristics of the pioneering spirit identified by Waring and Bishop. Despite significant anxieties about the wider application of commercial enterprise to probation practice, some staff in the CRC had also been energised – particularly by the prospect of improved IT systems, relaxation of national standards and a renewed emphasis on rehabilitation and meaningful engagement with service users. As mentioned previously, a number of those interviewed had chosen to work in the CRC because they felt that the NPS would be too preoccupied with the management and surveillance of high-risk cases and would remain tightly controlled by the centre. In this respect they felt *liberated* from what they saw as the overly *command and control* approach adopted by the (former) National Offender Management Service which they believed had restricted the autonomy of the former Probation Trust and had made it less responsive to local issues.

Staff often conceptualised their guardianship role in terms of wanting to minimise the impact on service users of the organisational upheaval that had resulted from the implementation of the *Transforming Rehabilitation* reforms. Guardianship in this sense revolved around an enduring commitment to delivering quality probation services. In one respect, these *ambivalent pragmatists* (arguably the largest group) were driven by a sense of *business as usual* and their pragmatism informed a sense of not dwelling upon or being distracted by the wider context of reform. But for others their stance was very much informed by a defence of a vocational profession and ethos they valued. They blended resilience with pragmatism in an attempt to mediate and manage the impact of the reforms and ensuing organisational changes, in order to sustain their commitment to a probation ethos and set of probation values.

The number of staff presenting *marooned* characteristics was small but they were often vocal. In the most extreme cases the sense of being marooned led workers to exit or to be seriously contemplating leaving the organisation. Those marooned employees who stayed were also characterised by their ideological opposition to what they saw as a shift 'from the logic of the public good to the logic of the market' (White 2014: 1002). For some staff the sense of being disempowered and harbouring deep antagonism towards the *Transforming Rehabilitation* reforms led to a *defiant resilience*. Their resilience was marked by their commitment to probation values and their service users to keep performing their roles in spite of their deep opposition to organisational reform and the compromised job satisfaction they reported. Where individuals' defiant resilience was played out most powerfully it revolved around the pressures they reported in meeting performance targets set within the contracts for CRCs. These targets were viewed as more onerous than previous expectations and the perceived heightened organisational emphasis on delivering on them was viewed as undermining their professionalism and added to their sense of feeling marooned.

The final focus of the migration study concerned how workers reconciled their misgivings about the organisational changes that had been imposed upon them. In general, those probation staff encountered in the research displayed a high level of pragmatism and resilience in order to ensure that it was *business as usual* despite their internal ideological opposition to *Transforming Rehabilitation* and apprehensions regarding the new arrangements. This in turn appeared to serve as a coping mechanism that enabled them to sustain and protect their professional habitus within the changed organisational structures. For some staff, as previously discussed, the process of migration from the Probation Trust to the CRC was marked by a further migration in the form of leaving the organisation. Drawing on the model developed by Hirschman (1970), Mawby and Worrall (2011) identify 'exit' as one of a number of ways that employees respond to adverse workplace conditions. Exiting can involve the actual process of leaving the organisation or psychologically withdrawing and therefore no longer identifying with it.

## The impact of *Transforming Rehabilitation* on the culture of probation

In the previous sections, we introduced studies that evidence practitioner responses to the *Transforming Rehabilitation* reforms in order to highlight how the cultural change and market dynamics of these changes could or might undermine moral rehabilitation. Studying the experiences of probation staff following the implementation of *Transforming Rehabilitation* therefore provides a particularly instructive insight into the impact of migration/diaspora upon occupational cultures, although as Burke *et al.* (2016) point out, their experiences have some unique features that distinguish *probation migration* from other public to private sector migrations. First, whilst the authors did not observe the wholesale substitution of public values and altruistic dispositions for private enterprise during the course of their research, it was clear that the imperatives and language of the private sector were increasingly infusing CRC thinking. Some staff were finding this more difficult than others to reconcile with what they viewed as the traditional ethos of probation. Nearly all those workers interviewed were keen to hold on to a notion of *public service*, even if this was no longer *located* within the public sector, and their hopes for new ownership were often implicitly tied to their perceived ability to do this. Their anxieties in this respect often revolved around uncertainty in how profit maximisation could be reconciled with the delivery of *public service*, and the operational credibility of their organisation in the eyes of service users and criminal justice practice partners.

Second, the restructuring of established working relationships, both within and external to the case study area, had renegotiated the distribution of status and power between the various stakeholders in offender management, particularly in respect of the interface between the NPS and the CRC. Some staff clearly resented what they perceived to be the creation of new hierarchical professional identities. This would appear to support Graham's (2016) assertion that hierarchies of knowledge and care have developed in contemporary rehabilitation work as status and personal capital are experienced differently by practitioners depending on the type of rehabilitation they are involved in. The speed with which some staff appeared to adopt new organisational identities in relation to their former colleagues based on status differentials could be seen as somewhat surprising given the previously documented resilience of the probation ethos in the face of externally imposed changes and may have longer-term repercussions for the occupational culture of probation. This is not merely a question of the potential fragmentation of service delivery, as undesirable as this may be, which many critics of *Transforming Rehabilitation* feared. Probation workers may now be located in separate organisational territories but they share a common heritage that transcends organisational and sectoral boundaries. These are the ties that have bound probation workers to 'an honourable profession' (Mawby and Worrall 2013: 154). Ultimately, the success of the reformed organisations will be shaped by their ability to recruit those individuals to their organisations that have the right skills and aptitudes as identified by Robinson *et al.* (2014) and Grant and McNeill (2015). It will also involve enabling existing employees to build meaningful relationships with those under their supervision, encourage creative thinking, intellectual curiosity, and build collaborative relationships with other stakeholders. This will not be easy for, as Robinson *et al.* note, the moral obligation to help improve offenders' lives which has animated probation work throughout its history is now sharpened by a new instrumental imperative to deliver profits for shareholders' (Robinson *et al.* 2017: 16). However, as Dominey and Gelsthorpe (2018: 214) point out, those responsible for overseeing the future direction of rehabilitative services 'will be wise to take note of the research that suggests that organisational quality, alongside staff and programme quality, contributes to work that reduces recidivism'.

## Privatisation and the legitimacy of rehabilitative practices

If, as we have argued in the previous sections, the moral performance of practitioners is implicitly linked to both the legitimacy of the organisation and its effectiveness then this raises profound questions regarding the legitimacy of outsourcing rehabilitative services. Indeed, legitimacy is not simply a reflection of the values that establish the moral basis of probation practice, it is also reflective of the effectiveness of the organisation. In this sense, values, moral purpose, and outcomes are all related components of the legitimacy of an organisation. Implied in our perspective is the notion that legitimacy can only be established with reference to the external world, particularly in such contentious areas as punishment and rehabilitation. This is because 'legitimacy is best understood as a social process: a product of evaluations of social audiences or constituencies which may bring different norms, values and expectations to bear on their judgements' (Robinson *et al.* 2017: 138).

Organisational legitimacy in the way that we have conceptualised it, however, plays out at the day-to-day operational level through the use of authority. Both the internal world of probation and its external stakeholders (particularly sentencers and the criminal court) will have expectations about its legitimate use and in this regard the work of Jackson *et al.* (2013) regarding legitimate authority is helpful. For these authors, legitimate authority has three basic components. First, it requires *legality* in terms of acting according to the authority's own rules and being seen to follow those rules. Second, it relies upon *shared values* between authority and those subject to that authority. Third, it requires *consent* drawn from the subject's recognition of a moral obligation to obey the authority (Brough *et al.* 2016: 22). We have already argued that, for probation practitioners, the *Transforming Rehabilitation* reforms have left a significant *legitimacy deficit* because they neither consented to nor shared the values behind the changes, which they considered to be politically and ideologically driven. In addition, those important stakeholders who contribute to the external legitimacy of probation services, particularly sentencers, appear to have lost confidence in the new arrangements. This can be evidenced by the decline in court orders, with the number of individuals commencing supervision dropping by 11 per cent since 2013 (Ministry of Justice 2017). This contrasts sharply with the situation in Scotland, where the use of community sentences has increased from 12 per cent of all sentences to 19 per cent (Scottish Government 2017). These trends are not attributable to changes in the volume of sentencing cases nor in the offence mix within those cases, which have been broadly similar in both countries (Bowen 2017).

McNeill and Robinson (2013) suggest that service users' views of the legitimacy of community sentences are particularly important in fostering active engagement rather than simply formal compliance. They introduce the concept of *liquid legitimacy* to explain how the legitimacy of, and compliance with, community sentences changes over the course of the court order and examine how both may be built, maintained or eroded during the supervision process. Enforcement practices that privilege formal compliance over substantive engagement are identified by the authors as a significant threat to the legitimacy of community sanctions and to developing positive supervisory relationships. In this respect, the style and approach taken by the practitioner is at least as important as the formal content and structure of the sanction. However, the ability of practitioners to influence the scope of the supervisory relationship is also constrained by the conditions in which they work which can serve to limit the quality and the authenticity of the practitioners' moral performance thus weakening their legitimacy.

McNeill and Robinson (2013) argue that community sanctions face particular legitimacy problems arising from several of their features. In particular, their purposes are perennially contested, and are often cast somewhat differently in pursuit of both external legitimacy (e.g. with sentencers, the public and politicians) and internal legitimacy (with those subject to such sanctions). For the latter audience, the fluid or *liquid legitimacy* of community sanctions is a function of their changing forms and shapes; of the ways in which they are negotiated, constructed, contested and reconstructed by the actors involved. However:

[t]he lived reality of being on a community sentence is relationally constructed, not architecturally bounded (as in the prison). This liquid quality
can allow legitimacy to flow in (when the relationship is working well
and trust and loyalty have been established), but also to 'ebb away' (when
promises are broken, services fail to materialise or enforcement is perceived
as unjust).

*(McNeill and Farrall 2013: 158)*

Notably, recent research by The Centre for Justice Innovation suggests that current enforcement practices place unnecessary restrictions on the use of discretion
of offender managers, are too focused on the drawn-out processes of instituting a
formal court hearing and can appear arbitrary and opaque to offenders (Centre for
Justice Innovation 2017*)*.

## Privatising legitimacy and authority

As we have argued, probation staff (and systems) need to model the values and
virtues they want supervisees to adopt. If they do not, and if the wider system
lacks legitimacy in the eyes of supervisees, then it loses the right to influence and
persuade. Ironically, the inculcation of private sector involvement within criminal
justice has to a large extent been presented as a response to a perceived 'crisis of
state legitimacy' (Garland 1996). Initially, New Labour's approach to the crisis
of State legitimacy was an attempt to decentralise rehabilitative services whilst at
the same time trying to maintain control over the operation of the probation
service it had redesigned through the tyranny of targets, league tables, performance indicators etc., orchestrated through New Public Management (NPM)
(Burke and Collett 2015). New Labour, however, sowed the seeds of privatisation of the probation service in England and Wales through the introduction of
'contestability' and in many respects the *Transforming Rehabilitation* initiative of
the current Conservative administration reflects the logical end-game of contestability that sought to introduce the concept of *market tension* into the monopoly
of community-based corrections (Burke and Collett 2015: 4). This has enabled
the State to delegate coercive tasks to non-State actors without compromising the
State's role as 'the *ultimate* repository of legitimate coercion' (Fitzgibbon and Lea
2017: 3, emphasis in original). However, according to Adam White (2010), within
the security market, private sector organisations have themselves struggled to gain
legitimacy and 'the interference of commercial interests in the provision of security
for citizens offends against this general sensibility . . . creates a cultural resistance
to the security market and those who wish to enter it' (Robinson *et al.* 2017: 5).
Following the collapse of Carillion and concerns regarding the financial health of
Interserve, one of the main providers of probation services, the outsourcing model
on which the *Transforming Rehabilitation* reforms are predicated has been brought
into focus, raising fundamental questions about the relationship between the State
and private corporations (Soames 2018).

Fitzgibbon and Lea (2017) identify two stages in the development of private sector legitimacy in relation to the State. In the first instance, companies try to get as close as possible to the State by efficiently delivering the outsourced requirements and sheltering in the shadow of the State's own legitimacy. The message here is one of *business as usual*, with an emphasis on the maintenance of professional standards but with an added dash of innovation and efficiency. The second stage aims to establish the private sector as a legitimate provider of coercive services *in its own right*, 'establishing the corporation as a responsible "citizen" through the promotion of the corporation's own values and standards' (Fitzgibbon and Lea 2017: 11). For example, the two largest CRC contractors, Sodexo and Interserve, respectively promote themselves as a *world leader in Quality of Life services* and *helping to create improved and better environments where people can live and work*. Stressing their public interest credentials in this way serves to deflect criticism that the ultimate aim is profit maximisation to meet the interests of shareholders.

According to Fitzgibbon and Lea (2017: 11), over time a *lock-in* effect occurs whereby these companies become essential to the functioning of the State and become 'too big to fail' (*see also* White 2016). Lock-in not only enhances the power of the private sector but also changes the character of the outsourcing agent itself. This is because the State gradually loses the capacity in its personnel and expertise to provide the services it has outsourced. This makes it increasingly difficult for the State to resume control of the services it has outsourced 'even in the face of major demonstrations of incompetence and suspected corruption' (Fitzgibbon and Lea 2017: 9). The authors claim that 'the growth in the size and power of the security-industrial complex and the state's growing dependency on it through lock-in and state dehabilitation increases the *independent* power of the security-industrial complex as policymaker in its own right' (Fitzgibbon and Lea 2017: 11). This, in turn, further embeds the symbiotic relationship between private corporations and the State as 'claims to rightful authority by private corporations become commonplace' (Fitzgibbon and Lea 2017: 14). It also has had a negative impact on the voluntary sector as we discuss in Chapter 6.

However, Hansen Lofstrand *et al.* (2015) contend that the more the private security industry assumes public functions the more it runs the risk of becoming embroiled in the moral dilemmas and legitimation struggles characteristic of public sector service delivery. These cannot simply be resolved through an economic logic of efficiency, cost cutting and profit seeking. This is because market-based behaviours cannot supplant the 'moral tensions, trade-offs and conflicts, and the attendant social struggles over meaning' (Hansen Lofstrand *et al.* 2015: 14) that delivering public services inescapably entails. As such, market actors operating in the field of criminal justice also are re-shaped by the terrain they have entered and are subject to its cultural and moral logic. The scale of the challenges facing the private sector in the delivery of rehabilitative services is becoming increasingly apparent and perhaps greater than envisaged by those private sector companies who have found it extremely difficult to reconfigure and re-engineer probation to their operational models.

In October 2017, some four years on from the implementation of the *Transforming Rehabilitation* reforms, the Chief Executive of the National Offender Management Service declared that the new system of offender supervision 'wasn't working' as it should (Shaw 2017). Shortly after, in her assessment of probation services, Dame Glenys Stacey – the Chief Inspector of Probation – reflected that 'we are in a very unsettling position' and expressed concern that 'rather than seeing a large amount of activity . . . we are seeing less happening than any of us would be comfortable with' (Stacey 2017: NPN). Although inspection reports found examples of innovative and well-focused practices, these tended to be the exception rather than the norm. Overall, high caseloads were offering inadequate levels and forms of contact and intervention. The Chief Inspector claimed that 'CRCs are too often doing little more than signposting and form-filling' (HM Inspectorate of Prisons 2017a: 17) and in some instances supervision amounted to little more than a phone call or cursory meeting in a public place. Overall, the public sector NPS was delivering noticeably better quality services than the privately owned CRCs (HM Inspectorate of Prisons 2017a: 23). The contracting for *Transforming Rehabilitation* seems to have led to a situation where CRCs are incentivised to pursue profit (or minimise losses) through *efficiencies* rather than effectiveness; financial returns are sought through volume of business rather than delivery of rehabilitative support for reparative and reintegration outcomes. Instead, they focus primarily (and in some cases exclusively) on ensuring compliance with court orders or post-release licences. Whilst this might be appropriate for some individuals (if indeed they deserve or require probation supervision at all), it is a wholly inappropriate response to those individuals who have complex needs and often chaotic lifestyles.

Later in October 2017, the Justice Select Committee, having questioned a range of stakeholders about the reasons for the challenges with the implementation of the programme, launched an inquiry into the *Transforming Rehabilitation* reforms. It became clear that the new owners of privatised probation services were also facing financial challenges as the number of service users they were engaging was smaller than anticipated. This was partly the result of sentencing trends, with fewer convictions for theft and drugs offences and increases in convictions for sexual offences (Ministry of Justice 2017) resulting in a greater number of higher risk offenders being retained by the NPS. It was also believed that the new owners of the CRCs had overestimated their ability to make cost savings despite redundancies and a scaling back of the original ambitions of the operating models (National Audit Office 2017). In response, the Ministry of Justice increased the value of the contracts, by around £278 million. No additional requirements were attached to the payments. Combining this with the additional payments of £42 million and £22 million (to keep the CRCs afloat) gives the total additional projected payments of £342 million. The Ministry estimates the maximum fee for service payments will increase to £2.5 billion. This is below the £3.7 billion projected in 2016 but covers much lower volumes of activity than projected at that time (National Audit Office 2017). However, as Carr (2018) contends, this is not just about the financial burden to the public but is illustrative of the flawed logic of the risk-based means of allocation that underpinned the *Transforming Rehabilitation* reforms. In reality, the risks and needs of individuals are fluid. Individuals do not fit neatly into these boxes, and nor do they stay in one. Putting organisational boundaries between risk types and levels was always going to be problematic.

## How can we reimagine the moral?

Whilst there appears to be little evidence of a positive transformation in rehabilitation in England and Wales, recent policy changes have undoubtedly brought about a cultural transformation in probation work as 'the moral obligation to help improve offenders' lives which has animated probation work throughout its history is now sharpened by a new instrumental imperative to deliver profits for shareholders' (Robinson *et al.* 2017: 16). In her submission to the Justice Committee, the Chief Inspector highlighted the impact on the organisational and occupational culture of probation brought about by the *Transforming Rehabilitation* reforms: '[The reforms were] a very significant cultural challenge and change for probation. It is a caring profession . . . yet this wholesale move to fragment the service and to give it a commercial edge has been enormously difficult' (HM Inspectorate of Prisons 2017b).

As we noted in our discussion of personal rehabilitation (see Chapter 3) when considering personal rehabilitation, cessation of offending is a process involving a complex array of factors that include the strengthening of social bonds through changes in identity and motivation at significant junctures in the life course (Farrall and Calverley 2006). Professional interventions, we have argued, should always be designed to contribute to that process by enabling practitioners to build meaningful relationships with those under their supervision, encourage creative thinking, intellectual curiosity, and build collaborative relationships with other stakeholders. This requires a continuing reassessment of both the *quality* of service and of professional *performance* (Graham 2016: 179). This reassessment must, we contend, go far beyond delivery systems, performance incentives and measures of apparent effectiveness. It must include the *moral* basis of rehabilitative work. This is exactly why we highlighted, in Chapter 2, Cohen's argument that *doing good* and *doing justice* are values in themselves and do not have to be justified by utilitarian and strategic considerations. Indeed, Cohen goes as far as to argue that reducing crime should not be achieved at the cost of sacrificing these values.

Anderson (2016) has recently argued that not enough attention has been paid to the 'moral space in which [desistance] narratives are co-constructed' resulting in a situation where 'the voices of people who have offended are silenced and their experiences of victimisation or structural violence are written out' (2016: 409). This is not to underestimate or condone the harm done by individuals to themselves and others. Crimes and offences can be seen as breaches of a social contract of reciprocal obligations and in Chapter 4, drawing on the work of Antony Duff, we considered the potential of *punishment as the communication of moral censure*. However, Duff, like Anderson also recognised the lack of social and political reciprocity to those who offend and those who society harms or ignores.

Whilst we would contend that offers of reparation and acceptance of help and support should be voluntary as far as possible, we accept that if a person does not volunteer to make good, then the State has the power (and the right) to impose compulsory losses. Similarly, if a person refuses help (for example, help that might reduce the risk of serious offending as well as supporting reintegration), then the State has the appropriate authority (and some would say duty) to impose restrictions on the individual in an attempt to secure public safety. In sum, then, the role of probation is (or should be) to implement court-imposed sanctions in a way that maintains the integrity of the judicial process whilst encouraging 'making good' (Maruna 2001) as part of a moral communication between those engaged in the supervisory relationship. This requires communication not only with the individual victim(s) but to the wider community. Reciprocally, the community and its social, economic and political institutions – the polity – may often have a responsibility to respond to the harms done to those who offend. In pursuit of its ultimate goal of reintegrating individuals into their communities, probation inevitably has a role to play in working for a just social and economic order.

The dilemma for us then is how to reimagine rehabilitation such that its practitioners might remain committed to change those policy and practice directives that potentially oppress individual service users whilst offering help and support that recognises both personal *agency* and the needs of victims. Geoff Pearson in a telling contribution to *Radical Social Work* argued that social workers:

> urgently need an education in how to place themselves in the world of politics. But they still require an education in how to relate to clients whose lives have become unstuck. When social work does not do that, and only mouths slogans about 'clients in general', it is no longer doing social work.
>
> *(1976: 43)*

This chimes with Cohen's notion of the *unfinished* (developed from the work of the Norwegian sociologist Thomas Mathieson) in relation to both theory and practice. He argued in *It's alright for you to talk* that workers should not be ashamed of dealing with short-term humanitarian goals but should also keep in mind longer-term political prospects (Cohen 1976: 95). This must be done with the individual in trouble, particularly as current research is helping us to better understand not only the lived experience of probation supervision but also how individuals experience the levels of punishment (both quantitative and qualitative) contained within their supervision. In addition, we are now better able to understand the immediate and ongoing collateral impact of criminal convictions, including the implications for the long-term civic status of convicted citizens. We also know from research across Europe that the experiences of supervision are very different in different countries, especially in relation to the extent of practical help offered, but overall supervisees generally find it helpful. Respect and fairness from supervisors, good relationships between supervisors and supervisees in which they work *together* to address problems, and the provision of practical assistance all seem to help. This is consistent with other studies (Shapland *et al.* 2014: 141). To a large extent these sorts of factors influence the way people engage (or fail to engage) in changing their offending behaviour through supervision.

Whilst supervision has many diverse forms, they share an imminent, pervasive quality in which people are made subject to life-altering and freedom-limiting conditions and live under the constant threat of further (worse) sanctions being imposed should they be judged as somehow 'failing'. Their status as semi-free citizens feels precarious. Being supervised in a fair and helpful way may make these pains easier to bear, but it does not remove them (McNeill and Beyens 2016). Sarah Anderson has recently argued that:

> [m]ainstream criminal justice responses can isolate the offence from its context and write out the 'offender's' victimisation and dehumanisation by individuals, language, institutions and structures. Far from healing the relational breaches, this treatment creates further distance between us and the 'other'. 'Bearing witness' situates offending within a whole life which includes both victimisation and offending, emphasising our shared humanity, acknowledging shared culpability, and offering hope that we can live together. In contrast, 'turning away' risks turning relational breaches into irreparable relational chasms.
>
> *(Anderson 2016: 421)*

This brings us to the crux of the issue about reimagining moral rehabilitation. Rather than maintaining our fetish for techniques and technologies of supervision, the criminal justice system needs to reimagine and expand the moral space within which the supervision of individuals who offend takes place. That space needs to be big enough for people who have offended to acknowledge and make reparation for the harm they cause themselves, their friends and family, and the wider community. It needs to be big enough for workers to offer qualitative help and support in helping individual desistance journeys. It also needs space for civil society and the polity to recognise and embrace the harm done to individuals through social and economic inequality and discrimination. If we move away from *moralising crime* to *understanding the moral dimensions of crime and punishment* then everyone has something to gain in seeking together to become better citizens contributing to a better society. The paradox for practice is that the *virtuous qualities* identified by McNeill and Farrall, which we referred to at the start of this chapter, are

> as necessary at the social and political level as it is at the individual level, and that to seek to model and support it in practice compels us to engage in politics, since we depend on one another's virtues to build the sort of polity in which we can thrive together.
>
> *(McNeill and Farrall 2013: 160)*

If one accepts that personal virtue is about the development of good citizenship, then it follows that collective virtue is about the character of the polity to which we all belong, for better or worse. It also raises fundamental questions about the values and virtues of the communities in which rehabilitation endeavours are located and to which we turn our attention in the next chapter.

## References

Anderson, S.E. (2016) The value of 'bearing witness' to desistance, *Probation Journal*, 63(4): 408–424.

Annison, J., Eadie, T. and Knight, C. (2008) People first: Probation officer perspectives on probation work, *The Probation Journal*, 55(3): 259–271.

Bonta, J., Bourgon, G., Rugge, T., Gress, C. and Gutierrez, L. (2013) Taking the leap: From pilot project to wide-scale implementation of the Strategic Training Imitative in Community Supervision (STICS) justice, *Research and Policy*, 15(1): 17–35.

Bonta, J., Bourgon, G., Rugge, T., Scott, T-L., Yessine, A., Gutierrez, L. and Li, J. (2011) An experimental demonstration of training probation officers in evidence based community supervision, *Criminal Justice and Behaviour*, 38(11): 1127–1148.

Bourgon, G., Bonta, J., Rugge, T., Scott, T-L. and Yessine, A.K. (2010) Technology Transfer: The Importance of On-going Clinical Supervision in Translating What Works to Everyday Community Supervision, in McNeill, F., Raynor, P. and Trotter, C. (eds) *Offender Supervision: New Directions in Theory, Research, and Practice*, Cullompton: Willan.

Bowen, P. (2017) *Community Sentences Across Borders*, London: Centre for Justice Innovation.

Brough, P., Brown, J.M. and Biggs, A. (2016) *Improving Criminal Justice Workplaces: Translating Theory and Research into Evidence-based Practice*, Abingdon: Routledge.

Burke, L. and Collett, S. (2015) *Delivering Rehabilitation: The politics, Governance and Control of Probation*, Abingdon: Routledge.

Burke, L. and Davies, K. (2011) Introducing the occupational culture and skills in probation practice, *European Journal of Probation*, 3(3): 1–14.

Burke, L. and Millar, M. (2012) Thinking beyond 'utility': Some comments on probation practice and training, *Howard Journal of Crime and Justice*, (51)3: 317–330.

Burke, L., Millings, M. and Robinson, G. (2016) Probation migration(s): Examining occupational culture in a turbulent field, *Criminology and Criminal Justice*, 17(2): 192–208.

Canton, R. (2011) *Probation: Working with Offenders*, Abingdon: Routledge.

Canton, R. (2013) The point of probation: On effectiveness, human rights and the virtues of obliquity, *Criminology and Criminal Justice*, 13(5): 577–593.

Canton, R. (2016) Why Do People Commit Crimes? in McNeill, F., Durnescu, I. and Butters, R. (eds) *Probation: 12 Essential Questions*, London: Palgrave Macmillan, 9–34.

Carr, N. (2018) Transforming rehabilitation? Destination unknown, *Probation Journal*, 65(1): 3–6.

Centre for Justice Innovation (2017) *Written Evidence from the Centre for Justice Innovation (TRH0057)*, www.data.parliament.uk/ (accessed 19 March 2018).

Cheliotis, L.K. (2006) How iron is the iron cage of new penology? The role of human agency in the implementation of criminal justice policy, *Punishment and Society*, 8(3): 313–340.

Cohen, S. (1976) It's Alright For You to Talk: Political and Sociological Manifestos for Social Work Action, in Bailey, R. and Brake, M. (eds) *Radical Social Work*, New York: Pantheon Books.

Deering, J. (2011) *Probation Practice and the New Penology: Practitioner Reflections*, Aldershot: Ashgate.

Deering, J. and Feilzer, M. (2015) *Privatising Probation: Is Transforming Rehabilitation the End of the Probation Ideal?* Bristol: Policy Press.

Dominey, J. and Gelsthorpe, L. (2018) Competing to Control in the Community: What Chance for a Culture of Care?, in Hucklesby, A. and Lister, S. (eds) *The Private Sector and Criminal Justice*, London: Palgrave Macmillan.

Eadie, T., Wilkinson, B. and Cherry, S. (2013) 'Stop a minute': Making space for thinking in practice, *Probation Journal*, 60(1): 9–23.

Evans, T. (2011) Professionals, managers and discretion: Critiquing street-level bureaucracy, *British Journal of Social Work*, 41(2): 368–386.

Farrall, S. and Calverley, A. (2006) *Understanding Desistance from Crime*, Crime and Justice Series, London: Open University Press.

Farrall, S., Hunter, B., Sharpe, G. and Calverley, A. (2014) *Criminal Careers in Transition: The Social Context of Desistance from Crime*, Oxford: Oxford University Press.

Fitzgibbon, W. and Lea, J. (2017) Privatization and coercion: The question of legitimacy, *Theoretical Criminology*, (advance online publication).

Garland, D. (1996) The limits of the sovereign state, *British Journal of Criminology*, 36(4): 445–471.

Giordano, P.C., Cernkovich, S.A. and Rudolph, J.L. (2002) Gender, crime and desistance: Towards a theory of cognitive transformation, *American Journal of Sociology*, 107(4): 990–1064.

Graham, H. (2016) *Rehabilitation Work: Supporting Desistance and Recovery*, Abingdon: Routledge.

Graham, H. and White, R. (2015) *Innovative Justice*, London: Routledge.

Grant, S. (2016) Constructing the durable penal agent: Tracing the development of habitus within English probation officers and Scottish criminal justice workers, *British Journal of Criminology*, 56(4): 750–768.

Grant, S. and McNeill, F. (2015) What matters in practice? Understanding 'quality' in the routine supervision of offenders in Scotland, *British Journal of Social Work*, 45(7): 1985–2002.

Grapes, T. (2007) Offender Management, in Canton, R. and Hancock, D. (eds) *Dictionary of Probation and Offender Management*, Cullompton: Willan.

Halliday, S., Burns, N., Hutton, N., McNeill, F. and Tata, C. (2009) Street-level bureaucracy, interprofessional relations and coping mechanisms: A study of criminal justice workers in the sentencing process, *Law & Policy*, 31(4): 406–428.

Hansen Lofstrand, C., Loftus, B. and Loader, I. (2015) Doing 'dirty work': Stigma and esteem in the private security industry, *European Journal of Criminology*, 13(3): 297–314.

Hirschman, A.O. (1970) *Exit, Voice, and Loyalty: Responses to Decline in Firms, Organizations, and States*, Fellows of Harvard College.

HM Inspectorate of Prisons (2017a) HMI Probation annual report 2017, www.justice inspectorates.gov.uk/hmiprobation/corporate-documents/annualreport2017/ (accessed 18 March 2018).

HM Inspectorate of Prisons (2017b) Written evidence from HM Inspectorate of Probation (TRH0052) http://data.parliament.uk/writtenevidence/committeeevidence.svc/ evidencedocument/justice-committee/transforming-rehabilitation/written/73909.html (accessed 18 March 2018).

Honig, B. (1996) Difference, Dilemmas, and the Politics of Home, in Benhabib, S. (ed.) *Democracy and Difference: Contesting the Boundaries of the Political*, Princeton, NJ: Princeton University Press, 257–277.

Jackson, J., Bradford, B., Hough, M., Myhill, A., Quinton, P. and Tyler, T. (2013) Why do people comply with the law? Legitimacy and the influence of legal institutions, *British Journal of Criminology*, 52(6): 1051–1071.

Johnson, S.D., Hian Chye Koh and Killough, L.N. (2009) Organizational and occupational culture and the perception of managerial accounting terms: An exploratory study using perceptual mapping techniques, *Contemporary Management Research*, 5(4) December.

King, S. (2014) *Desistance Transitions and the Impact of Probation*, Abingdon: Routledge.

Kirton, G. and Guillaume, C. (2015) *Employment Relations and Working Conditions in Probation after Transforming Rehabilitation: With a Special Focus on Gender and Union Effects*, Centre for Research in Equality and Diversity, School of Business and Management: Queen Mary University of London.

Lipsky, M. (1980/2010) *Street-Level Bureaucracy: Dilemmas of the Individual in Public services*, New York: Russell Sage.

Maruna, S. (2001) *Making Good: How Ex-convicts Reform and Rebuild Their Lives*, Washington DC: American Psychological Association.

Maruna, S. (2004) Pygmalion in the reintegration process: Desistance from crime through the looking glass, *Psychology, Crime and Law*, 10(3): 271–281.

Mawby, R.C. and Worrall, A. (2011) Probation workers and their occupational cultures, University of Leicester/Keele University, www2.le.ac.uk/departments/criminology/documents/Final_report_Nov_2011%20-17%20Nov%202011.pdf (accessed 11 April 2018).

Mawby, R. and Worrall, A. (2013) *Doing Probation Work – Identity in a Criminal Justice Occupation*, Abingdon Oxon: Routledge.

McNeill, F. (2009). *Towards Effective Practice in Offender Supervision*, SCCJR Discussion Paper No. 01/2009, Glasgow: SCCJR.

McNeill, F. (2012) Four forms of 'offender' rehabilitation: Towards an interdisciplinary perspective, *Legal and Criminological Psychology*, 17(1): 18–36.

McNeill, F. (2014) Punishment as Rehabilitation, in Bruinsma, G. and Weisburd, D. (eds) *Encyclopaedia of Criminology and Criminal Justice*, New York: Springer, 4195–4206.

McNeill, F. and Beyens, K. (2016) *Offender Supervision in Europe*, Basingstoke: Palgrave Macmillan.

McNeill, F. and Farrall, S. (2013) A Moral in the Story! Virtues, Values and Desistance from Crime, in Cowburn, M., Duggan, M., Robinson, A. and Senior, P. (eds) *Values in Criminology and Criminal Justice*, Bristol: Policy Press.

McNeill, F. and Robinson, G. (2013) Liquid Legitimacy and Community Sanctions, in Crawford, A. and Hucklesby, A. (eds) *Legitimacy and Compliance in Criminal Justice*, Routledge: Abingdon, 116–138.

Ministry of Justice (2017) *Written Evidence to the Justice Committee* (TRH0032) http://data.parliament.uk/writtenevidence/committeeevidence.svc/evidencedocument/justice-committee/transforming-rehabilitation/written/73856.html. (accessed 18 March 18).

Nash, M. (2008) Exit the 'polibation' officer? De-coupling police and probation, *International Journal of Police Science & Management*, 10(3): 302–312.

National Audit Office (2017) *Investigation into Changes to Community Rehabilitation Company Contracts: Report by the Comptroller and Auditor General*, HC 676 Session 2017–2019, London: NAO.

Pearson, G. (1976) Making Social Workers: Bad Promises and Good Omens, in Bailey, R. and Brake, M. (1976) (eds) *Radical Social Work*, New York: Pantheon Books.

Pereira, C. and Trotter, C. (2018) Staff Supervision in Youth Justice and its Relationship to Skill Development: Findings from Australia, in Ugwudike, P., Raynor, P. and Annison, J. (eds) *Evidence-Based Skills in Criminal Justice*, University of Bristol: Policy Press.

Phillips, J., Westaby, C. and Fowler, A. (2016) Spillover and work-family in probation practice: Managing the boundary between work and home life, *European Journal of Probation*, 8(3): 113–127.

Raynor, P. (2018) From 'nothing works' to 'post-truth': The rise and fall of evidence in British probation, *European Journal of Probation*, 19(1): 59–75.

Raynor, P., Ugwudike, P. and Vanstone, M. (2014) The impact of skills in probation work: A reconviction study, *Criminology and Criminal Justice*, 14(2): 235–249.

Robinson, A. (2013) Transforming rehabilitation: Transforming the occupational identity of probation workers? *British Journal of Community Justice*, 11(2/3): 91–103.

Robinson, G., Burke, L. and Millings, M. (2016) Criminal justice identities in transition: The case of devolved probation services in England and Wales, *British Journal of Criminology*, 56 (1): 161–178.

Robinson, G., Burke, L. and Millings, M. (2017) Probation, privatisation and legitimacy, *Howard Journal of Crime and Justice*, 56(2): 137–157.

Robinson, G., Priede, C., Farrall, S., Shapland, J. and McNeill, F. (2014) Understanding 'quality' in probation practice: Frontline perspectives in England and Wales, *Criminology and Criminal Justice*, 14(2): 123–142.

Rowling, J.K. (1998) *Harry Potter and the Chamber of Secrets*, New York: Bloomsbury.

Rudes, D.S., Viglione, J. and Taxman, F.S. (2014) Professional Ideologies in United States Probation and Parole, in Durnescu, I. and McNeill, F. (eds) *Understanding penal practice*, Abingdon: Routledge, 11–30.

Schein, E.H. (1992/2004) *Organisational Culture and Leadership*, San Francisco: Jossey-Bass.

Scottish Government (2017) *Reconviction Rates in Scotland: 2014–15 Offender Cohort*.

Shapland, J., Sorsby, A., Robinson, G., Priede, C., Farrall, S. and McNeill, F. (2014) What Quality Means to Probation Staff in England and Wales, in Durnescu, I. and McNeill, F. (eds) *Understanding penal practice*, Abingdon: Routledge, 139–153.

Shaw, D. (2017) Ex-prisoners lack support, says probation head, www.bbc.co.uk/news/uk-41595826 (accessed 18 March 2018).

Soames, R. (2018) Carillion halted stupid, unthinking outsourcing. Now it's time for change, *The Guardian*, 25 February 2018.

Sorsby, A., Shapland, J. and Durnescu, I. (2018) Promoting Quality in Probation Supervision and Policy Transfer: Evaluating the SEED Programme in Romania and England, in Ugwudike, P., Raynor, P. and Annison, J. (eds) *Evidence-Based Skills in Criminal Justice*, University of Bristol: Policy Press, 193–217.

Stacey, G. (2017) *Can Probation Services Deliver What We All Want and Expect?* Keynote speech of the Criminal Justice Management Conference 19 September 18, www.justiceinspectorates.gov.uk/hmiprobation/wp-content/uploads/sites/5/2016/10/Westminster-forum-November-2017-1.pdf (accessed 18 March 2018).

Toronjo, H. and Taxman, F.S. (2018) Supervision Face-to-face Contacts: The Emergence of an Intervention, in Ugwudike, P., Raynor, P. and Annison, J. (eds) *Evidence-Based Skills in Criminal Justice*, University of Bristol: Policy Press.

Trotter, C. (1996) The impact of different supervision practices in community corrections, *Australian and New Zealand Journal of Criminology*, 28(2): 29–46.

Trotter, C. and Evans, P. (2012) An analysis of supervision skills in youth probation, *Australian and New Zealand Journal of Criminology*, 45(2): 255–273.

Vanstone, M. (2018) The Effective Practice of Staff Development in England and Wales: Learning from History and Contemporary Research, in Ugwudike, P., Raynor, P. and Annison, J. (eds) *Evidence-Based Skills in Criminal Justice*, University of Bristol: Policy Press, 17–37.

Vogelvang, B., Clarke, J., Sperna Weiland, A., Vosters, N. and Button, L. (2014) Resilience of Dutch probation officers: A critical need for a critical profession, *European Journal of Probation*, 6(2): 126–146.

Waring, J. (2015) Mapping the public sector diaspora: Towards a model of inter-sectoral cultural hybridity using evidence from the English healthcare reforms, *Public Administration*, 93(2): 345–362.

Waring, J. and Bishop, S. (2011) Healthcare identities at the crossroads of service modernisation: The transfer of NHS clinicians to the independent sector?, *Sociology of Health and Illness*, 33: 661–676.

Weaver, B. and McNeill, F. (2015) Lifelines: desistance, social relations and reciprocity in Criminal, *Justice and Behavior*, 42(1): 95–107.

White, A. (2010) *The Politics of Private Security: Regulation, Reform and Re-legitimation*, Basingstoke: Macmillan.

White, A. (2014) Post-crisis policing and public-private partnerships: The case of Lincolnshire Police and G4S, *British Journal of Criminology*, 54(6): 1002–1022.

White, A. (2016) *Shadow State: Inside the Secret Companies That Run Britain*, London: Oneworld publications.

# 6

# REIMAGINING CIVIL SOCIETY AND COMMUNITY ENGAGEMENT

## Social rehabilitation

> A society that does not care is a society that you do not care about.
>
> *(Bobby Cummines, The Road from Crime)*

### Why do we need to reimagine community and civil society?

In this chapter, we examine the potential contribution that civil society could make to enriching rehabilitation through the lens of citizenship, social capital and community. As one of us has already noted, rehabilitation involves more than just the criminal justice system and its concerns are not solely limited to reducing individual reoffending.

> Rehabilitation is a social project as well as a personal one. Whether we cast it in deontological terms as being concerned with the requalification of citizens, or in utilitarian and correctional terms as being concerned with their re-education or resocialization, it raises profound political questions about the nature of (good) citizenship, about the nature of society, about the relationship between citizenship, society and the state, and about the proper limits of legitimate state power.
>
> *(McNeill 2012: 14)*

This is because rehabilitation is an important component in the dispensation of justice that has both a social and moral dimension. As we noted in the previous chapter, it is moral in that rehabilitation involves renegotiating whether, how and on what terms the 'offender' and society might live together in the future (Raynor and Robinson 2009). It is social in the sense that rehabilitation seeks to promote the restoration or establishment of social bonds that will support the (re)integration of the individual offender into the community and in doing so, strengthens collective efficacy. As Snacken (2016: 62) points out, those delivering community sanctions have the difficult task of combining *internal* legitimacy – in order to foster compliance by the offender – with *external* legitimacy, aimed at wider audiences. In practice, this involves a reciprocal set of duties that are owed by the 'offender', the community and the State in relation to one another. In addition to the individual's obligation to make good, we would argue that the community and the State must accept a duty to support rehabilitation. That duty rests on two principles. First, to the extent that the community and the State bear some complicity in permitting or exacerbating criminogenic social inequalities, they too must make good. Second, even under a retributivist approach to punishment, the polity has a duty to make sure that the punishment ends and that there is no punishment beyond the legal sanction (McNeill 2016: 76).

Ultimately, individual behaviour change is unlikely to occur if the social context that residents inhabit is not taken into account and if it fails to engage communities in that process. This is because, regardless of the intrinsic qualities of rehabilitative agencies, they can never replace the informal supports and social controls provided by families, neighbours and wider community organisations. As we discuss later, notions of *community* are highly contested but, as a recent report has highlighted, the *community* is often absent from *community corrections* in which the term too often merely describes the location of the person under supervision, rather than the meaningful engagement of community resources in reintegration efforts (Executive Session on Community Corrections 2017: 6).

Increasingly, demands to re-position rehabilitative practices around risk management and public protection, whilst seemingly seeking to appease community concerns, have paradoxically led probation in England and Wales to retreat from – or certainly become less visible – in communities. Instead, probation has aligned itself more closely with other criminal justice agencies. In doing so, contact between those under supervision and their supervising officers has become focused mainly on enforcement purposes. A recent report from the United States (addressing issues that are by no means unique to that country) has highlighted that in contemporary practice:

> [m]ost interactions between people under supervision and community corrections staff occur across a desk in a central office building. These locations and the nature of these interactions send the wrong message – that behaviour is to be either 'punished' or 'cured' in a fortress-like environment, divorced from the atmosphere in which it took place.
> 
> *(Executive Session on Community Corrections 2017: 7)*

At the individual level, this is unlikely to enhance the relationship aspects of supervision since research has shown that those under supervision are unlikely to develop relationships with their officers if they do not feel that they are being *invested in*. In turn, this is likely to have a detrimental impact on retention and compliance (Laub *et al.* 1995). At the community level, when the local connectedness of probation is weakened, this 'restricts opportunities for representation at local strategic and policy levels and consequently reduces the potential for local involvement in the governance of the service itself' (Senior *et al.* 2016: 19). Yet, as Faulkner contends, if probation aspires to be an agent of social justice 'its authority, legitimacy and strength must in the end come not from government but from the citizens and communities it serves' (Faulkner 2003: 308).

The ability of the penal system to exercise more positive forms of power – in the form of integrative rehabilitative strategies that aim to repair the damage caused by crime and provide a sense of public reassurance – will always be somewhat constrained by its dependency on other services, systems and actors. However, those resources such as housing, education, health and welfare are often beyond the control of the penal system. Indeed, a recent attempt to establish the essence of probation work identified four major systems of social organisation which exist in various formations in all Western social democratic societies and many other jurisdictions (Senior *et al.* 2016: 10). These are the correctional system, the social welfare system, the treatment system and the community respectively. It follows that the scope of probation work should extend to engaging with wider civil society because, as Harding (2000: 148) states, '[i]t takes us beyond the courtroom and the jail house to the problems that local people face, identifies the causes and how they might be addressed'. Such an approach, though, raises a series of fundamental questions in terms of how the infliction of State punishment can avoid compounding the isolation of individuals and instead be about strengthening communities and repairing broken relationships. In order to address these questions, it is necessary to begin by examining what we mean by the terms *community* and *civil society*.

## Community, trust and social capital

Notions of what constitutes *community* are contested and convey a variety of meanings and associations, not all of them necessarily favourable to the exercise of citizenship. Exhortations towards *civil society* and *community* can sometimes invoke images of neighbourliness and a sense of belonging that suggest a form of inclusiveness that is confined to the so-called *law-abiding*. However, in reality, membership of different social groups 'are not mutually exclusive; rather they are plural and most individuals will have cross-cutting loyalties, which operate with different strengths in different circumstances' (Deakin 2001: 5). As a result, the same concerns that identify one community may cause rivalry or competition with another and even spill into direct conflict. In reality, communities can just as easily be characterised by their homogeneity, self-interest and exclusionary attitudes as by their reciprocity, self-reliance and mutual aid. Faulkner and Burnett make this point in the context of criminal justice:

> [N]otions of 'community' may be used positively to promote non-custodial sentences, and to reinforce notions that offenders are still members of the

community whose laws they have broken and that they are both entitled to its rights and benefits and subject to its obligations. Equally though the interests of the 'community' can be used negatively, to impose restrictive or intrusive conditions on people's behaviour, or to exclude those who do not 'fit' or who have 'forfeited' or do not 'deserve' their right to membership.

*(2012: 74)*

According to Raynor and Robinson, in public-political debate, 'the offender's interests are always counter poised to those of the "community" and weighted against them or assumed to be in conflict' (2009: 12). Personal rehabilitation fails to address (or challenge) this conflict, since where 'rehabilitation operates solely on the individual "offender" and not on the conflict itself, the victim, or the community it will struggle to offer moral redress or meet demands for more expressive forms of justice' (McNeill 2016: 76).

Nevertheless, it is increasingly accepted that communities have many resources, networks, groups and relationships that can serve rehabilitative goals. The concept of social capital has been employed as a means of explaining how an environment of mutual trust, once created, helps to build up a bank of resources that can be used to support a whole variety of organisations and initiatives and serve a succession of different social functions. In *Making Democracy Work* and *Bowling Alone* (Putnam 1993, 2000), the American political scientist Robert D. Putnam highlighted the critical role played by social capital in generating the norms, reciprocity, generalised trust and voluntarism that he presented as the critical ingredients of good governance and democracy. Putnam draws an important distinction between capital that *bonds* communities and capital that *bridges* communities. The former occurs when people socialise with others like themselves, fostering connections based on ethnic, social, religious and financial similarity. Bridging capital is much more outward facing, diverse and inclusive in its ability to make connections across groups. Putnam's central argument is that societies characterised by generalised reciprocity tend to be more successful than distrustful ones; within such societies, bridging capital encourages the development of inclusive public policies. They also provide the opportunities and resources to support integration and demonstrate the extent to which the individual is integrated into the wider community.

Taking a lead from Putnam's work, Barker argues that trust 'is the social glue that holds communities and nations together' as it 'makes it less risky and more rewarding for [citizens] to participate in community and civic affairs, and helps to build the social institutions of civil society upon which peaceful, stable and efficient democracy depends' (2016: 83). Barker continues, 'those societies with high degrees of confidence in State authorities have a propensity towards less crime, high norm compliance and policing that is less brutal and more fair' (2016: 84) and conversely, those societies relying on mass incarceration and other forms of criminal justice sanctions involving the expulsion of offenders from a shared future are generally 'associated with a denial of reciprocity and low social trust' (Barker 2016: 84).

For the subjects of repression, as Barker points out, 'criminal justice policies and practices that are perceived or experienced as hostile and invasive [regardless of whether they are acted out in prison or the community] tend to breed political alienation, distrust, and withdrawal' (2016: 86). The implications of this are clear, as the authors of a recent attempt to reimagine penal policy in England and Wales point out:

> We need to think about the ways in which ideas and practices of solidarity, democracy, trust and legitimacy (and their partial application, or even absence) shapes practices of crime control and punishment. But we also need to explore the reverse idea – namely that police, criminal justice and penal institutions can be civic agents, part of whose purpose is to contribute to the maintenance, repair and strengthening of social bonds and to extending and deepening processes of democratic inclusion.
>
> *(Farrall et al. 2016: 3–4)*

Beckett Wilson (2014: 64) observes that those individuals who find themselves in conflict with the justice system tend to have different types of social capital ranging from the 'licit' (socially legitimate, promoting cohesion, law abiding) to the 'illicit' (socially illegitimate, often self-serving and illegal). The process of desisting from offending, therefore, involves a shift in the balance of licit and illicit social capital, though this will differ according to the individual involved. Examining the portfolios of social capital amongst problematic drug users, she found that they generally tended to rely on illicit social capital, lacking its licit forms (Beckett Wilson 2014: 65). If this is the case, then one of the goals of rehabilitation should be about securing licit social capital, so as to reduce the reliance on its illicit forms; that requires connecting at-risk individuals with more mainstream networks.

Farrall (2004) suggests that strengthening social capital through work with employers and families is much more likely to engender positive outcomes for people trying to stop offending. In his research, social capital in these forms appeared more likely to foster permanent rather than short-term desistance, because the support of peers, families and associates in the community was more accessible than and likely to outlast any specific intervention. Building social capital required not only the provision of legitimate opportunities (for example, by finding new accommodation or at least time away from other offenders or drug users) but also, as we noted earlier, through an investment in the rehabilitative process and sense of *ownership* of it by the individual (Farrall 2004: 67).

Considering the relational aspects of supervision in these terms suggests that the role of the supervising officer can be important in terms of providing brokerage; supporting the individual in building relationships (in the form of bridging social capital) which offer access to licit resources. Beckett Wilson (2014) nicely sums up the objective of intervention as: 'to increase individual motivation; to devalue illicit social capital; to make licit social capital a more attractive investment; and to aid that process through social capital brokerage' (2014: 75). Of course, developing the social capital of a vilified, marginalised and excluded group is undoubtedly testing and raises a fundamental challenge in terms of how communities can themselves be better encouraged and supported to engage in the rehabilitative process. Having fleetingly considered some of the debates around notions of community and social capital, we now turn our attention to exploring how civil society has developed and been moulded by contemporary policies.

## Civil society: From the *agora* to the shadow state

In its contemporary form, civil society is generally conceptualised as, 'the culmination of voluntary activities and associations that people undertake in contexts that are not determined by requirements issuing from the state' (Jacobs 2016: 10). However, this simple definition conceals a complex and problematic concept that over time has produced a variety of different and sometimes conflicting interpretations. The space occupied by civil society has evolved as part of the dynamic process of adaptation and social change. Gaps have opened up, new opportunities have appeared and voluntary bodies have taken up different roles and started to perform them in different ways, in response to shifts in the external environment (Deakin 2001). This makes our task of reimagining civil society even more challenging. What is it that we are trying to reimagine? Is it a physical or metaphorical *space, place* or *location* that is characterised within the realm of voluntary initiative, the sphere of the market place, the private or domestic domain or 'the proper location for morality in a liberal state' (Boyd 2004: 603). Is it the means of creating and sustaining democracy in which the evolving rights and responsibilities of citizenship are forged? Is it the arena in which voluntary action could form relationships with the State that would supplement – perhaps even eventually supplant – the State's role, in particular as a means of delivering welfare? Or alternatively, as Deakin (2001: 204) suggests, 'does civil society represent the space in which activity at the local level facilitates linkages between families and groups (both formal and informal) that can build and sustain communities and create social capital'. In reality, it is probably the case that civil society has been conceptualised in different ways and at different times to signify all these different perspectives. However, whatever stance is taken, conceptualising civil society inevitably raises questions about 'its relationship with the state, the relative emphasis on individual or collective action, the relative weighting of political democracy and the democracy of the markets' (Atkinson 2012: 18).

The notion of civil society has deep historical roots that can be traced back to the classical political philosophy of Ancient Greece. In its earliest conception, civil society was indistinguishable from the State because the end-point of individual development was viewed as being achieved through a realisation of political life. The *polis* (the city-state) was the pinnacle of human development and hence 'the state represented the civil form of society' (Atkinson 2012: 18). *Civitas* was thus understood 'as the pursuit of civic virtue through good governance' (Powell 2007: 37). One of the fundamental rights implicit within the formulation of civil society was defined by the basic democratic freedom to associate. Zygmunt Bauman likens the contemporary idea of civil society to the ancient Greek concept of the *agora* as a site for political assembly, a town square, an interface between the public and private spheres of social life that created the idea of a political community or republic based upon active citizenship (Bauman 1998: 86). The organisation of the ancient *civitas* and *polis* combined what we today call public and private spaces and the secular and religious dimensions had an obvious moral, normative dimension in that 'civility and toleration were seen as an essential aspect of a proper understanding of civil society' (Ayhan Akman 2012: 322).

With the emergence of the modern nation-state, notions of civil society were subsequently based on *court society* with 'an elaborate state apparatus, religious uniformity, a subordinated public sphere and an economy subject to mercantilist policies, presided over by an absolute monarchy' (Perez Diaz 2014: 813). Citizenship was determined from the centre of power (Okri 2018). This provided a unified conceptual schema to understand modern Western societies whose components complemented one another and emerged in an open system combining a liberal (later, a democratic) polity and a market economy within a plural society. However, social contract theorists such as Hobbes and Locke parted company with this idea of society being a fusion of the individual, civil society and their rulers. Instead, civil society involved 'a contractually produced and politically guaranteed instrument of individuals who came together to attain some common purpose' (Ehrenberg 1999: 91). As such, civil society acted as an antidote to State power and its strength was closely related to the democratic quality of the polity. As Ayhan Akman (2012: 323) points out, 'the stronger civil society is, the better are the prospects of reigning in the authoritarian tendencies of the state and the higher the quality of democracy'. From this perspective civil society was recast as essentially political, involving individual struggles 'to become free and liberate themselves from oppression' (Powell 2007: 630). Similarly, De Tocqueville saw civil society as a defence against an over-powerful State that might threaten 'newly realized individual rights and freedoms organized through the medium of voluntary associations' (Edwards 2008: 7). This was similar to Edmund Burke's 'little platoon' of social institutions that were 'the cornerstone of loyalty to nation and humankind' (1790: 68).

Notions of civil society took on a different form as the rise of the market economy led to an increasing differentiation of interests with 'communities of neighbourhoods being replaced by communities of strangers' (Edwards 2008: 7). Adam Smith in *The Wealth of Nations* (1776) saw the market as the core of civil society, 'where the invisible hand of self-interest would provide the wealth of nations, leading to economic progress and social prosperity' (Atkinson 2012: 19). The German philosopher, Georg Wilhelm Friedrich Hegel, built on the insights of Smith but argued that markets drive individuals towards self-interest and this inevitably produces inequality and social polarisation. For Hegel, civil society incorporated 'the spheres of economic relations and class formation as well as the judicial and administrative structure of the state' (Powell 2007: 480). However, because it was a deeply disjunctive system and prone to intractable conflicts, if left to its own devices, the role of the State was ultimately to intervene and provide for the greater good. This required 'constant surveillance by the state in order for the *civil* to remain' (Edwards 2008: 199).

The installation throughout Western Europe of broadly similar forms of the Keynesian social policy had major implications for civil society in the second half of the twentieth century. Within the post-war welfare settlement, the State was viewed as the sole guarantor of citizens' rights and increasingly took on the main responsibility for discharging a wider range of functions, in pursuit of 'third generation' social rights to employment and social provision' (Deakin 2001: 100). As Powell (2007) notes, social democratic thinkers shared a vision of a good society based upon, 'public-spirited railways, superb state schools that promoted equality of opportunity and an excellent, nationalized health service free on the basis of need' (2007: 16). An essential ingredient of the social democratic project was seeing rehabilitation as an obligation on the State to provide for those who fell through the welfare net and exposed themselves to crime and delinquency (Rotman 1990).

The liberal view of civil society as a protector of (civil) liberties and the social democratic view of the State as the protector of (social) rights played out after the Second World War in the development of the twentieth-century welfare state, enhanced by an appreciation of the problems associated with class-based inequalities. In his seminal essay on the concept of citizenship in Britain, T.H. Marshall (1950) formulated citizenship as having a legal, political and social dimension. Citizenship was conceptualised as a status 'bestowed on all those who are full members of the community and all those who possess the status should be seen as equal with respect to the rights and duties with which the status is endowed' (Behan 2014: 145). This is important because as Faulkner (2003) argues:

> the language of citizenship is a way of talking about people as human beings, in the context of their rights and legitimate expectations, and of their duties and responsibilities – to one another and to the state – in a liberal democratic society . . . It demands a sense of common 'belonging' and also in the sense that the majority recognize those groups as members of their own society and show them the same consideration and respect.
>
> *(Faulkner 2003: 288)*

However, from the 1980s onwards, much of the capitalist world has been dominated by a political credo of neoliberalism based on labour market deregulation, privatisation, low taxation and tight fiscal control. As a result, 'the interests of the public good became equated with those of the "free" market and notions of citizenship based on the social contract seceded to those based on consumer citizenship' (Corcoran 2014: 41). The primacy of the market once again became the dominant characteristic of a new global world order, where welfare was redefined as *dependency* and the very idea of society with its collective connotations was questioned.

Neoliberalism questioned both the scope and scale of the State, demanding it perform a residual role, 'to preserve an institutional framework that protects private property rights, free markets and free trade' (Powell 2007: 8). At the same time the scope and influence of the private sector expanded to the point where it has been suggested that we are witnessing the emergence of a *shadow state* of extremely powerful private providers (White 2013). Rather than increasing competition as intended, this can lead to the emergence of private sector monopolies that are not unlike the systems they are expected to replace. As we have discussed elsewhere in this book (see Chapter 5) this new orthodoxy has led to major changes in both the delivery and nature of local public services with an increased market for private sector providers. For present purposes, it is important to note that there has also been an increasing emphasis on individual choice and personalisation in the delivery of local services which, to a greater or lesser extent, have profoundly impacted on local communities and civic engagement. In criminal justice terms, citizenship has been recast as individual *responsibilisation* rather than ensuring the rights and resources upon which notions of citizenship rest.

## Contemporary visions of civil society

In the preceding section we provided a brief overview of the development of notions around civil society because in our view it has become something of a taken-for-granted term, yet one that has significantly shaped contemporary political discourses. As Faulkner and Burnett (2012) note, 'elites on both the political Left and Right argued the case for decentralising the welfare state and harnessing the potential of civil society to perform functions they have considered to be necessary or desirable but have not wished to perform themselves' (2012: 73). The motivations behind these appeals to civil society have been mixed, perhaps detracting from the credibility of the policies that they sought to pursue (Faulkner and Burnett 2012). To further complicate matters, strengthening the role of civil society has been seen as an important mechanism to assist successive governments in England and Wales to reduce public expenditure. Others have promoted a strong civil society as 'a mark of a strong and healthy society more generally, underpinned by a belief that it will exercise social control and encourage complaint behaviour' (Faulkner and Burnett 2012: 73). David Garland (2001) has described this process as a strategy of 'responsibilisation' in which government withdraws from its reliance on a direct approach to crime through the criminal justice process and promotes alongside it a network of less formal methods of crime control which depend on other organisations and influences beyond the State. In this respect the role of the State is one of *steering* the activities of others rather than *rowing* itself (Osborne and Gaebler 1992). Although there are differences in the ideological drivers and motivations behind the approaches taken, there are a number of common themes that have dominated thinking on both the political left and right in England and Wales to which we now turn our attention.

## Concerns about declining standards of morality and civility

The perception of a broken society, marked by family breakdown, economic dependency, addiction and anti-social behaviour has been an enduring leitmotif of political thinking since the 1980s in England and Wales, despite the absence of a convincing evidence base to support such claims. Appeals for the need to reverse national decline, initially highlighted by the Thatcher governments between 1979 and 1990, were not solely economic but were also moral in the sense that they were seen to require a revival of individualistic 'vigorous virtues' (Hayton 2012). Whilst generally acceding to the accepted orthodoxy of declining standards of morality and civility promoted by its predecessor, the New Labour government, elected in 1997, challenged what it saw as the excesses of Conservative individualism based on a culture of self-interest driven by market-based values. Community cohesion was seen as the means of restoring the moral balance within society by setting out duties and obligations as well as rights (Driver and Martell 1997).

Influenced by communitarian thinking, the then Home Secretary David Blunkett argued that 'civil renewal must form the centrepiece of the government's reform agenda for the coming years' (Blunkett quoted in Faulkner 2003: 292). In turn, the goal of civil renewal policies was to 'regenerate communities and the culture and lifeblood of mutual support in a highly complex 21st century globalised economy' (Blunkett, quoted in Davies 2012). The communitarian model, associated with thinkers such as Etzioni (1995), took issue with the libertarian model, arguing that human agency cannot simply be reduced to the notion of free individuals exercising choice but instead that we are social entities who 'are defined by a given set of relationships over which we have no choice' (Bottery 2000: 203). Communities are thus seen as a vital component of social life because they not only give us identity but also provide mutual support in our daily lives. This though is a reciprocal relationship. Communities themselves need our support and succour if they are to prosper because fragmented communities 'leave individuals alienated and bereft of the social context they need to develop as full human beings' (Driver and Martell 1997: 29).

The form of communitarianism adopted by New Labour challenged the neoliberal market model in three ways. First, it contended that community values like cooperation and collaboration were just as vital to a successful market system as competitive individualism. Second, it challenged the neoliberal assumption that general welfare is best left to the free play of private enterprise and endorsed collective action through the intermediate institutions of civil society supported by central government. Third, market individualism, it was argued, had eroded those institutions seen as vital to social cohesion and that in this way unrestrained market egoism had contributed to social fragmentation (Driver and Martell 1997: 33). Conversely, Labour's communitarians also challenged what they saw as a State-dominated approach to welfare that dominated social democratic thinking. This, they argued, was too universal, expensive and bureaucratic and had constrained the space for devolved ownership or individual choice. Moreover, in common with neoliberalism, they challenged what they saw as a rights-based culture which they claimed ignored duties and responsibilities and led to dependency on the welfare state. This, they argued, not only placed a huge fiscal burden on society, but 'further contributed to social fragmentation and a moral vacuum in society' (Driver and Martell 1997: 33). This attempt to harness supposed efficiency gains through market incentives with a focus on empowerment and innovation through Third Sector and service user involvement has been described as a form of *neo-communitarianism*, different from the individualistic discourse and focus on family and charitable welfare that has been characteristic of Conservative governments in England and Wales (Ehrenstein 2012).

The Labour governments between 1997 and 2010 produced a number of initiatives that were intended to tackle social inequality and enhance civil society. Their initiatives included the early years Sure Start programme; the New Deal for Communities, Action Zones for special action in health, education and employment; and the programme for 'active citizenship' and civil renewal. However, these seemingly progressive measures, aimed at supporting the mechanisms of civil society, were counter-balanced, certainly in criminal justice terms, by more authoritarian responses centred on legislation aimed at enforcing standards of behaviour in community life especially in relation to the perceived anti-social behaviour of young people. According to Millie (2010: 8) this form of 'state-enforced moral improvement' resulted in a 'labelling of minority populations as stigmatised "others" with their unwanted behaviour leading to censure'. As Faulkner and Burnett reflect:

> The search for 'quick wins', for immediately visible results and short-term political advantage diverted attention from long-term sustainable change. It was sometimes all too easy for the focus to slip away from situations and contexts and back to individuals who could be demonised and stigmatised through anti-social behaviour orders and naming and shaming.
>
> *(Faulkner and Burnett 2012: 72)*

Despite symbolising a shift in emphasis and political rhetoric the *social justice* agenda promoted further by the Coalition and the Conservative governments since 2010 continued to substantially draw on the Thatcherite ideological legacy, rather than representing a radical policy overhaul; its concern with declining standards of morality and civility was linked to a related critique of the bureaucracy and control of the New Labour era. Influenced by think-tanks such as Policy Exchange and the Centre for Social Justice, they criticised what they perceived to be the failed *Big State* of New Labour, promoting a form of *compassionate conservativism* that claimed to combine a strong sense of collective social morality with the Thatcherite desire for a smaller State. The expectation, or hope at least, was that communities, voluntary groups and families would fill the void created by the retreat from the State provision of core public services (Hayton 2012: 7). We will explore the implications of these ideas later but for now we turn our attention to one of the core elements of this thinking in terms of the promotion of community involvement through more active citizenry.

## Active citizens, empowered communities and democratic participation

The role of the individual within the community and their relationship with State institutions has been characterised by notions of active citizenship since the 1980s in England and Wales. As Corcoran (2017: 284) states, the 'neo-liberal version of public spirited citizenship is vested in claims that private and personalised interests are the fundamental driving forces of [the] common good'. Douglas Hurd, then Home Secretary, is attributed with launching a neoliberal form of active citizenship that entailed:

> involvement in charitable work and voluntary groups, for example, through neighbourhood watch and victim support schemes . . . There is a need for even closer partnership between the public, private and voluntary sectors. I have been having and will continue to have discussions with representatives of all three sectors in order to identify and publicise ways in which people can turn concern into effective voluntary action.
>
> *(Hurd 1989 cited in Bee and Pachi 2014: 104)*

According to Bee and Pachi (2014), Hurd's definition of active citizenship had three significant characteristics which subsequently shaped political discourses on community and civic engagement. First, it appealed to the perceived need to foster new values at the community level in order to meet the challenges of new and emerging social problems. Second, it attempted to foster a notion of active citizenship based on a renewed approach to local governance involving an enhanced role for civil society through voluntary action. Third, it stressed the reciprocal responsibilities to counter the dependency culture that was perceived to be characteristic of the welfare state. This form of active citizenship is entirely consistent with neo-liberal notions of active citizenship personified by the, 'dynamic individual who was self-reliant, responsible for his or own actions, and yet possessed a sense of civic virtue and pride both in country and local community' (Faulks 1998: 128). The Citizens Charter, launched in 1991, embodied the principles of active citizenship promoted by Conservative political discourse by promoting better access to public services, the need for public services to operate efficiently, and the guarantee of more choice for citizens based on market mechanisms. As Faulks (1998: 133) notes though, in promoting a consumerist culture, the Charter 'diverts the citizens' energies into complaints to the service provider rather than into an engagement with, or involvement in, governance'. Critics of the New Right style of active citizenship based on the preservation of individual liberty, pursued by the Thatcher and Major governments, argued that market-based policies were enhancing social divisions at the community level rather than promoting the social solidarity required to foster the actual exercise of active citizenship.

Active citizenship was also a central tenet of New Labour political discourse. New Labour emphasised participatory democracy and civic engagement to shape collective action at the local level in order to facilitate increased participation in the policy process. More specifically, it claimed to be a government 'determined to give people more control over the fight against crime' (HM Government 2010: 76), identifying 'a need for citizens to be active in helping to identify community safety priorities for their neighbourhood' (HM Government 2006: 23). In 2005 the government brought out a consultative green paper, entitled *Citizen Engagement and Public Services: Why Neighbourhoods Matter* (ODPM 2005) that aimed to reverse the alleged decline in civic engagement at the local level. It also promoted greater involvement by local groups in the shaping and delivery of local services. This was followed up by the 2006 White Paper, *Strong and Prosperous Communities*, which spoke of the need to empower citizens and communities through an expansion of neighbourhood governance arrangements (Atkinson 2012: 55).

However, this bottom-up approach initially favoured by New Labour, based on principles of participatory governance, eventually gave way to a less empowering approach to civic engagement centred on assimilationist principles following community disturbances in the North of England in 2001. Clashes between different ethnic groups in Northern England brought into question the basis of multi-culturalism and led to a series of policy actions by New Labour to counter a perceived separation between communities through a 'model of civic assimilation based on the idea of forging allegiance to core principles shared by all through the effective engagement of responsible "active citizens" located in "active communities"' (McGhee 2009: 49). As we have noted, this re-shaped notion of *strong community* demanded a strong adherence to common values and norms with sanctions imposed if necessary, especially in response to perceived anti-social behaviour. As we discuss later in this chapter, British Conservatives managed to turn the Third Way narrative around into a *Big State* narrative that basically served to deepen governance at the expense of solidarity. Jordan (2010: 19) asserts that 'because the Third Way model saw government as enforcing a contract with self-responsible individual citizens, the Conservatives could describe New Labour in the UK as creating an authoritarian "surveillance society" symbolised by identity cards, CCTV (closed-circuit television) cameras and unnecessary regulations'. The New Labour Third Way narrative was subsequently transformed into a moral discourse of social failure, represented by the so-called *broken society*.

In assessing the strategies deployed towards promoting active citizenship and engaging communities in criminal justice over the past 20 years, Weaver (2015) notes that policies have been primarily focused on improving public confidence in the criminal justice system and to increasing the visibility and enhancing the credibility of the system. The tone of policy documents has tended to be 'punitive, divisive and exclusionary in casting the offender as the object on which the system to seeks to operate and in focusing on empowering and including victims and communities as the primary beneficiaries of the justice system' (McCulloch and McNeill 2007). As Jacobs (2016: 24) points out, this 'can result in a situation in which laws and policies apply to large numbers of people who are excluded from the political process through which laws and policies are formulated'. Miller and Stuart (2017: 533) describe this as an 'alternate legal reality' in which the social, civic and economic participation for those who have offending histories is shaped by a complex web or laws, sanctions and regulatory penalties that are increasingly delivered by a range of actors within civil society who are outside of the formal criminal justice system. Thus, these authors through their analysis of the way in which those who offend are dealt with ironically become *supervisible* in that services are offered which reflect their status as an offender. In this sense these *carceral citizens* occupy a novel form of political membership (see also Chapter 4 for a fuller discussion).

## The collateral consequences of imprisonment

However we conceive of civil society, it seems that our approaches to punishment often push individuals to (or beyond) its margins. Yet, ironically, punishment often may have the effect of undermining the prospects of *active citizenship* and the development of the social capital required for desistance. At the point of incarceration, prisoners generally already lack social capital because of either their crime or background. Many prisoners come from neighbourhoods traditionally associated with imprisonment, low levels of education, high unemployment, social deprivation – and very low levels of political engagement. As such, they are substantively disenfranchised even before imprisonment exacerbates and formalises this excluded civic and political position. Being imprisoned is also likely to further reduce the social capital and civic engagement of an individual because imprisonment tends to weaken family and mainstream community bonds. As Halpern (2005: 119) contends, 'often little effort is made to rebuild these bonds or the communities affected whilst at the same time [they] may reinforce the individual's connections to alternative or criminal forms of social capital'.

In its modern form, the prison system is an institutionalised bureaucracy characterised by regimes and disciplinary structures based on rules, control mechanisms and formal and informal sanctions. Often, as Behan points out, 'these do not enhance the modes of communication and co-operation that are viewed as essential components of citizenship' (Behan 2014: 146). By failing to take account of individual agency, regimes of imprisonment tend ultimately to seek to create compliant rather than active citizens, undermining the sense of individual responsibility that they are trying to instil. Faulkner (2003) sums this up cogently in his observation that:

> the demands of security and personal safety (for both prisoners and staff), together with the pressures of overcrowding, always conspire to give the needs of the institution, and its ability to cope with pressure or disruption, priority over attempts to treat prisoners as citizens whose rights, expectations, duties and responsibilities they should be enabled to exercise.
>
> *(2003: 305)*

There are also collateral consequences of imprisonment that undermine and limit citizenship, even after completion of the sentence. Indeed, as Miller and Alexander (2016: 309) note, '[i]n the age of mass supervision, regimes of post-incarceration surveillance and ostensible social welfare provision serve to cement the legal exclusions of carceral citizenship'. The difficulties experienced in making the transition from *prisoner* to *member of the public* are well documented. Often individuals are faced with immediate practical challenges with housing, benefits, substance misuse and mental health and many lack records of employment of the kind that are helpful in seeking work. On release, they are likely to encounter a confusing plethora of faceless bureaucracies where institutional power is further exercised through rules which are 'uncertain, changing and indecipherable' (Carlton *et al.* forthcoming). Increasingly these functions are carried out by private actors under contractual arrangements with the State. As Muir (2014) observes, this can be viewed as part of a broader project of welfare reform in which 'the current regime of benefit sanctions is driving many people into abject destitution, with standardised and transactional approaches doing little to enable people either to find work or to live more independent lives' (Muir 2014: 283–285). Therefore, it could with some justification be argued that the reintegration of people back into the community – if it happens at all – is a process that continues long after an offender has completed their sentence and desisted from crime (Mercado 2016: 28).

Uggen argues that there currently exists a 'conceptual wall dividing "prisoner" and "citizen" in public consciousness' (Uggen in Behan 2014: xv). The challenge, therefore, as Antony Duff points out, is to:

> make the prison walls more porous, so that those in prison can maintain their connections with the ordinary civic world: can we find ways of welcoming them back into that world (perhaps by rituals of re-entry) so as to make clear that their exclusion was neither total nor permanent.
>
> *(Duff 2016: 20)*

In Behan's (2014) study of prisoners in the Irish Republic, there was a belief amongst those prisoners interviewed that their perspective mattered little to the world outside. This would appear to concur with Faulkner's contention that 'the public at large, are disposed to think of prisoners as people who have forfeited their right to citizenship and for whom the principle should be one of "lesser eligibility"' (2003: 305). This 'restricted or scrutinized form of citizenship' results in additional obstacles to ex-prisoner re-entry, including the attitude that, even after completing their sentence, a former prisoner is still to be regarded 'in terms of their risk defined past, rather than their self-defined present' (Buck 2014: 52). This in turn can deepen the sense of demoralisation and alienation felt by many people who have been in prison, the effects of which can last beyond release from prison, complicating efforts to reintegrate into community life. In Farrall *et al.*'s (2014) longitudinal study of criminal careers those identified as *desisters* were much more engaged and interested in political life and supportive of *local* (emphasis in original) government than those identified as *persisters*. They were also more likely to be registered to vote (70 per cent vs 39 per cent). Those who were still involved in criminality tended to be disconnected from their local communities and saw governance in terms of 'distant and uncaring bodies that did not permit any real participation in the political process' (2014: 252). This sense of continuing disenfranchisement (even after voting rights are restored) and resulting disengagement from the wider community has serious implications in terms of contemporary moves to devolve ownership and responsibility for delivery of public services to local communities.

## Decentralisation, devolution and choice

Localised control over the allocation and use of resources has been promoted as a means of instilling a stronger sense of local ownership and responsibility, providing greater capacity to take advantage of, and respond to, local circumstances and opportunities. This devolution of political power in the United Kingdom began under New Labour, most significantly in the form of devolved government to the Scottish Parliament and the Northern Irish and Welsh Assemblies and has subsequently been extended on a selective basis to some regions in England. Faulkner (2003: 293) contends that, under New Labour, moves to promote citizenship and social capital ultimately brought 'into sharp relief the Government's ambivalence over the balance between central control and devolution. Its instincts were ultimately more inclined towards greater central control.' Cooke and Muir (2012) similarly observe that the desire to enhance public sector performance under New Labour ultimately led to an increase in command and control management structures from the centre that in turn resulted in a proliferation of standardised processes that sapped professional creativity and local mobilisation. Ironically, as we have noted, for probation, the New Labour years resulted in increased centralisation with an attendant loss of local accountability. As Lockyer and Heys (2016) reflect, the central management and control of prisons and probation undermined the development and delivery of local responses to offending. Instead, the creation of the National Offender Management Service produced 'an unwieldy system of instructions and controls through which local leaders had to navigate and given the domination of prison service priorities achieved little in shifting funding from prisons to probation during this period' (Lockyer and Heys 2016: 18–19; see also Burke and Collett 2015: Ch. 3).

Nevertheless, devolution policies have continued to be popular with successive UK governments. The *localism* policies in England and Wales promoted by the (former) Coalition government were heralded as 'the strongest attempt yet to reconfigure citizen-state relations' (Hastings and Matthews 2015: 546). The guide accompanying the 2010 Localism Bill claimed that:

> the best contribution that central government can make is to devolve power, money and knowledge to those best placed to find the best solutions to local

needs: elected local representatives, frontline public service professionals, social enterprises, charities, coops, community groups, neighbourhoods and individuals.

*(HM Government 2010: 2)*

In criminal justice terms there have been attempts, partly driven by the search for cost effectiveness, to *unfreeze* the resources that are locked up in the prison system and ensure that local areas are incentivised to use them to prevent crime and develop community alternatives to custody. This form of *Justice Reinvestment* has been influenced by developments in the United States where, after years of being 'tough on crime' and imprisoning ever larger numbers of people, there has been a growing realisation (ironically led by right-wing Republican states) that large amounts of taxpayers' money is being spent on ineffective prison bureaucracies that do little to reduce reoffending (Allen 2015). Although there have been criticisms that in reality whatever money has been redirected has been used to reinforce other parts of the criminal justice system (such as policing) rather than local communities.

As Allen (2015: 1) points out, more than half of US states have introduced Justice Reinvestment laws or policies which, in the main, have sought to reduce the severity of sentences for non-violent offences, and to reduce breaches of parole and supervision, in order to avert unaffordable prison growth. The extent to which these measures have contributed to the stabilisation or reduction in prison numbers may be debatable but in some US states, for the first time in 38 years, both federal and state prison populations have fallen. Perhaps the most extensive example of devolved justice in England and Wales though has been the *Justice Reinvestment Pathfinder pilots* which were established by the Ministry of Justice in 2012. These initiatives sought to test the extent to which local partners could be financially incentivised to collaborate in reducing 'demand' on the prison system. The Ministry of Justice also devolved the youth secure remand budget to local authorities to incentivise them to invest in higher quality alternatives to custody. The results of these reforms were broadly positive: the numbers in youth secure remand fell and the pathfinders appeared to demonstrate substantial reductions in demand (Redgrave 2016: 9). However, it should be noted that evaluations were not conclusive as to the nature of causality (other changes to the sentencing framework may have been more significant). Indeed, there has been a reduction in youth crime amongst many jurisdictions suggesting that youth custody trends may be more likely the result of wider changes in young people's lives and interests. As such, in an evaluation of Justice Reinvestment projects in the UK and USA, Wong and Christmann concluded that we cannot yet 'unequivocally attribute benefits to JR through the way effectiveness is currently measured' (2016: 10).

In an attempt to boost civic engagement in respect of crime control, the Conservative/Liberal Democrat Coalition government also introduced directly elected local Police and Crime Commissioners (PCCs) in 2011. These, it was argued, would 'empower the public by giving them a voice and by strengthening accountability and transparency' (Home Office 2010: 8). However, such claims appear somewhat overstated given turnout in the first elections for the PCCs averaged only 15 per cent (BBC 2012). Hence, as Lister and Rowe conclude, 'claims that PCCs have ushered in an era of more democratically attuned or accountable policing should be met with caution' (2015: 373). According to Alcock (2012: 149) there is a fundamental contradiction in these developments in that although localised approaches are presented as being *bottom up*, in practice they have been imposed *top down* in that citizens and communities are constrained and regulated by central government and provision is primarily driven by market competition. There has been similar criticism of the devolution deals in England and Wales following the Cities and Local Government Devolution Act (2016); in practice, they too have been agreed and implemented between central and local elites without meaningful public consultation or involvement (Prosser *et al.* 2017: 253). As a result, many commentators have expressed concerns that contemporary forms of localism may serve only to further empower the already powerful in relation to public services.

By definition, decentralisation seeks to increase variety in service provision by allowing 'different communities to do different things in different ways to meet their different needs' (CLG 2010: 5). However, there are assumptions here both that citizens have equal access to the market and are free to choose better services and that the providers of public services will alter their products to meet variations in need. How appropriate is this in criminal justice contexts where services are mandated? As Weaver (2011: 1040) acknowledges, 'criminal justice services are not routinely associated with maximising choice, control and involvement for their service users or wider stakeholders in the way that perhaps adult social work and care services have developed', although there are increasing attempts to do so (Fox and Marsh 2016). Such approaches have been mainly applied to help service users shape service delivery. However, we would suggest that this needs to go further, promoting opportunities for those with criminal convictions to be able to exercise control alongside their fellow citizens, not only to shape the interventions they are subject to, but also positively influence the communities in which they reside. This will take strong political support and leadership because as Armstrong and Maruna comment:

> [i]f their hope is that ground-up, community-led responses to criminal offences and the rehabilitation of offenders will be more effective than government-led measures have proved to be, simply changing the method of rehabilitation delivery without changing the social and institutional message supporting these measures could limit their potential.
>
> *(Armstrong and Maruna 2016: 150)*

Whilst there are obvious merits in policies that seek to tailor services to meet local and individual needs and preferences, there are also inherent dangers in such an approach. As Miller and Stuart (2017: 534) note, politics may be local but 'carceral politics are hyper-local'. The authors highlight the fact that over half of released prisoners in Illinois return to just six neighbourhoods within the city of Chicago. Each of these neighbourhoods have levels of poverty, crime and unemployment that are three times the national average. Our guess is that similar trends would be evidenced elsewhere to a greater or lesser extent. Underfunding already disadvantaged communities is therefore unlikely to 'level the playing field between communities' (Hastings and Matthews 2015: 546). Davies and Pill (2012) highlight the danger that 'rolling back' the supportive infrastructure provided by the State could undermine rather than encourage social action and 'the strategic redistributive capacity of local state actors to negotiate between competing demands and promote equity' (in Hastings and Matthews 2015: 546).

With the increasing emphasis on individual choice, decisions around local services are seen as less and less predicated on the impact on the collective experience of the local community, but instead are viewed as a matter for individual preference. Individual control over resources, in most cases, aims to elevate the status of the individual from passive care recipient to consumer, but consumers are not necessarily empowered to shape services. In reality, many individuals may lack capabilities, capacities and opportunities to shape the services offered; and the 'choices' offered to them may be highly restricted. The choice agenda, as Atkinson argues, is unlikely to achieve a fairer redistribution of provision because 'some groups and individuals have an inbuilt advantage. The educated and the articulate, quick of mind and fleet of foot, can see their choices take preference over others' (Atkinson 2012: 120). Ultimately, then, whilst empowering individuals and increasing individual choice may have an intuitive appeal, the danger is that it can be used as a smokescreen for what is an abrogation of State responsibility towards the most marginalised in society. According to Avis (2016: 26), '[a]t best the new localism of Labour and the Coalition provides sites of contestation and at worst a technology of control that devolves accountability and responsibility'.

Moves towards greater justice devolution have been further complicated in England and Wales by the *Transforming Rehabilitation* reforms which have arguably led to increased centralisation of rehabilitative services in England and Wales. Throughout its hundred-year history probation has had some form of local accountability involving sentencers and local authority members amongst others. One of the most unfortunate aspects of the *Transforming Rehabilitation* reforms in England and Wales has been the destruction of local accountability. The former local Probation Trusts have been replaced with a centrally managed national civil service organisation delivered through a regional structure and centrally commissioned Community Rehabilitation Companies who are in the main run by companies with global concerns. These contracts are managed centrally by the Ministry of Justice and their geographic boundaries are not coterminous with those of many other aspects of the criminal justice system (such as the 43 police force areas or 11 prison service regions). This adds a further layer of complexity to the system of funding and services that are targeted at reducing offending. On another level, it has transformed the penal landscape into 'a new universe of contract, not custom, the driving down of costs by downsizing and outsourcing to the cheapest sources of supply, justified as promoting shareholder value' (Deakin 2001: 145). In rehabilitative terms, this can be located within broader attempts to re-engineer the institutions of civil society which we discuss in the next section.

## Marketisation, privatisation and the mixed economy of welfare

Under New Labour, it was believed that third sector organisations provided opportunities for participation in community life that would foster the trust and social capital necessary for civil renewal. As Ehrenstein notes:

> By strengthening the Third Sector, the New Labour government expected to create a higher degree of community and user involvement in public service reform, giving service users and community groups more opportunity to voice their opinion on policy issues, making sure that these 'voices' are being heard and included in government bodies' policy development.
>
> *(Ehrenstein 2012: 77)*

Consequently, successive New Labour governments sought to harness the third sector both as a provider of public services and as a channel for active citizenship (Fyfe 2005). Central to New Labour thinking was the promotion of a mixed economy of welfare services. During its three terms of office, it matched its political rhetoric with significant investment and capacity building programmes aimed at re-positioning the voluntary and community sectors. The Office for the Third Sector in the Cabinet Office was established and produced a framework agreement on relations between government and the third sector and how they would work together more closely (https://assets.publishing.service.gov.uk/government/uploads/system/uploads/attachment_data/file/61169/The_20Compact.pdf). The Ministry of Justice also published two papers, a *NOMS Third Sector Strategy* for improving policies and securing better public services through effective partnerships (Ministry of Justice 2008a), and a paper on *Working with the Third Sector to Reduce Reoffending* (Ministry of Justice 2008b) These initiatives suggested a new post-ideological political dynamic, in which the government was trying to forge a developmental model of social democracy, in partnership with civil society. Alongside this, 'traditional class politics' were 'replaced by a "business friendly" social democracy that sought to embrace the market as the driver of economic growth' (Powell 2007: 18). The Carter Report (2003), for example, promoted the private and voluntary sectors as catalysts of modernisation whose energy and innovation would create 'a new approach to . . . break[ing] down the silos of prison and probation and ensur[ing] a better focus on managing offenders'.

Voluntary organisations operating in civil society were thus intended to become active parties in the process of transformation of the sector rather than passive subjects of change. As we have noted, rather than simply supporting services provided by the State, voluntary and charitable organisations have been framed as alternative providers competing to improve service quality in a more diverse welfare mix, as well as being viewed as less bureaucratic, expensive and inflexible than statutory services. As a result, under New Labour, the diverse range of voluntary and community-based organisations that were rebranded as key constituents within civil society were recast as *the third sector* suggesting greater coherence and meaning in an attempt to gain policy traction and control. However, Deakin (2001) contends that the third sector label can be seen to have negative connotations in that it assumes the primacy of the first and second sectors, the State and the market. It also assumes that 'each is a self-contained area with distinct boundaries and that the status of this third sector rests on not possessing any characteristics of the first two' (2001: 9).

Despite the increased transfer of public funding and service provision to the third sector, the government (under New Labour) retained a high level of control as it assumed greater responsibility for the monitoring and regulation of the sector. According to Corcoran (2014), this has weakened the traditional campaigning role of the sector, 'eroding their autonomy and critical disposition towards institutionalized injustices' (2014: 40). Moreover, the competitive environment created by tendering has not always sat comfortably with emphasis on partnership working. According to Buckingham and Rees (2016: 942–943) the professional standards required of contracted third sector organisations have often left little room for volunteer involvement and the furtherance of the civil renewal agendas.

The policy aspiration of the *Big Society* pursued by the Conservative-led Coalition government in England and Wales led to a further linguistic change replacing *third sector* with *civil society* in official discourses. It presented a critique of New Labour's metropolitan worldview with its over-reliance on 'big state technocratic' centralism and promised an end to 'top-down targeting and micromanagement in public services' (Buckingham and Rees in Rees and Mullins 2016: 956). In the Green Paper *A Stronger Society: Voluntary Action in the 21st Century*, the Conservatives asserted that

> [t]he time has come for us to think of the voluntary as the first sector; not just in recognition of the historical origin of the public services and the institutions we rely on today – but as the first place we should look for answers that neither the state or the market can provide.
>
> *(Conservative Party 2008: 4, in Powell 2007: 12)*

This vision of a *Big Society* was presaged on the idea that 'we know instinctively that the state is often too inhuman, monolithic and clumsy to tackle our deepest social problems . . . we know that the best ideas come from the ground up, not the top down' (BBC 2010). Philip Blond's (2010) book *Red Tory* sought to reposition British Conservative politics away from neoliberalism and towards a *Big Society* ideal that combined economic equity with social conservatism in a new conservative narrative.

Powell describes Blond's conservatism as being 'based on the disaggregation of civil society from the state in a social project that would ultimately replace the welfare state with charity' (2007: 12). For those who are excluded from the consumer society, civil society – in the form of a rediscovery of charity – is seen as the solution to poverty. As Deakin (2001: 20) notes, '[p]artisans of a market economy have invoked voluntary action – usually in its guise as charity – to justify the consigning of the state to a marginal role in welfare'. However, even if one accepts the ideological assumptions underpinning this approach, there are real problems with this assertion both in terms of scale and metrics; charity accounts for little more than a small fraction of public expenditure with 40 per cent of voluntary sector funding coming from the State. As Powell (2007) notes:

> [g]iving appears to be primarily in the form of horizontal redistribution from people on relatively low incomes to people on very low incomes. This has more the characteristics of mutual aid (a form of utopian socialism) than of charity in its historically constructed form of the benevolence of the rich towards the poor.
>
> *(Powell 2007: 29)*

Even the Conservatives themselves have conceded that 'the most generous contributors to charity as a proportion of their income are not the richest groups but those below average income' (Conservative Party 2008: 15) This suggests that the tradition of mutual aid amongst the working class constitutes the most vibrant element in today's charity. It also implies that 'the traditional ethical construction of charity, as the rich helping the poor, may be little more than a myth' (Powell 2007: 130).

Ultimately, whilst the Coalition government's *Big Society* agenda was promoted as a means of releasing energy and innovation and of creating a new sense of social responsibility, in reality it could at best be viewed as an act of political window dressing, a public relations branding exercise, giving the illusion of a big new policy idea when in reality it was nothing of the sort. Recently there has been the adoption of an even more openly radical right-wing ideological agenda in England and Wales to reduce the scale and scope of the State. The third sector service delivery element of the *Big Society* agenda has been an early casualty of this shift. Whilst expectations of voluntary activity, particularly at the local level, have continued to increase, those third sector organisations that have remained in the market for providing publicly funded services have had to operate in increasingly marketised conditions, 'where the relinquishing of government control has been replaced not by greater autonomy, but rather by greater market discipline' (Buckingham and Rees in Rees and Mullins 2016: 1184). According to Rees and Mullins (2016: 204) the voluntary sector has in effect become a 'Trojan Horse' for privatisation and the widespread introduction of commercial practices and marketised approaches gives particular salience to these concerns. That is not to say that the sector has been merely a passive actor in these developments (Considine 2003).

In the context of England and Wales, successive policies attempting to reconfigure correctional services though market mechanisms from *contestability* (Carter

2003; see also Chapter 5) to the partial privatisation of probation under *Transforming Rehabilitation* appear at first glance even-handed in their support for both private and third sector providers to challenge traditional public sector models. Yet this belies the adoption of a subcontracting model in which predominantly private sector organisations act as managing agents of supply chains of (mixed sector) sub-contractors. According to Taylor *et al.* (2016), the environment determining the scale of financial risk facing potential providers is complex and determined by a number of inter-related issues such as the size of the contracts, the cost of bid-ding and the risks associated with taking on staff under protection of employment legislation (Transfer of Undertakings (Protection of Employment) TUPE) and the degree to which contracts are weighted to the financial reward of outcomes (in Rees and Mullins 2016: 3282). Unlike private sector companies, third sector organisations have less opportunity to raise the necessary capital by borrowing from banks or investors and have fewer cash reserves or assets which they could use to demonstrate their capacity to absorb risk. This is particularly pertinent in commissioning models based on *payment by results* as sufficient working capital and resources are needed to take on the risk of a contract in which payment is weighted towards the end of the contractual period. It is hardly surprising then that half of the privatised probation service contracts following *Transforming Rehabilitation* in England and Wales were subsequently awarded to just two preferred bidders – Interserve and Sodexo. Neither of these companies had an established record of delivering rehabilitative services and their expertise lay in the provision of a range of other services that have been outsourced through recent government contract-ing out activity. Despite making £10 million available to encourage the formation of staff mutuals, including those put together by Probation Trust staff, only one staff mutual was a successful partner in the bids, with private-sector-led partner-ships winning 20 out of the 21 contract package areas.

None of the charities who submitted bids to run the newly created Community Rehabilitation Companies (CRCs) were themselves successful although some became sub-contracted partners to the primary private provider. Those chari-ties who were unsuccessful in the bidding process complained that they found the process chaotic and much more complex than it needed to have been. They also felt that the specification offered limited scope to describe the quality of the bidders' proposed approaches. According to a report by the New Philanthropy Capital (2015) this exposed a tension within the *Transforming Rehabilitation* pro-cess between the policy rhetoric and stated commissioning intentions. Whilst the policy espoused the engagement of voluntary sector organisations, the procure-ment process sought to apply strict commercial terms. Decisions were seemingly 'made on the basis of the price and minimising risk rather than quality or any other aspect of the bids' (New Philanthropy Capital 2015: 2). There was also a structural bias encountered in the tendering process favouring the larger private corpora-tions as the insistence on a *parent company guarantee* to cover service failure was not easily achievable by charities or the third sector (New Philanthropy Capital 2015: 3). Ultimately, a report by Clinks (the umbrella body for the voluntary and community sector in criminal justice in England and Wales) concluded that voluntary sector involvement in *Transforming Rehabilitation* was undermined by funding cuts, a lack of transparency and a lack of clarity regarding what services would be funded by commissioners under the new arrangements (Clinks 2015). As Garven and Murray note there are broader concerns here in that:

> [a] clear role for community has been further blurred by politicians and policy makers who tend to regard communities and the organised third sector as a homogeneous horde, even though the latter includes sizeable, multi-million pound ventures themselves increasingly forced down competitive, at times predatory, business routes. In turn this has made vulnerable, and even displaced, smaller community organisations which have traditionally been in a strong position to reflect and respond to local need.
>
> *(Garven and Murray 2016: 4)*

As the selling of probation contracts following the *Transforming Rehabilitation* reforms demonstrates, the real winners in the outsourcing of public services are always likely to be large multi-national enterprises in a competitive environment shaped by neoliberal thinking around public sector delivery and the unrelenting drive towards privatisation and marketisation. Deakin contends that:

> the once-mighty state, Thomas Hobbes's Leviathan, has been cloned: in place of one potentially oppressive monster the state is often now a shoal of smaller creatures, swimming in a sea of business values and subject to all sorts of market disciplines.
>
> *(Deakin 2001: 16)*

Whilst we would generally concur with the sentiment in the above quotation, in reality the shoal of smaller creatures referred to has become 'dominated by a private "security-industrial complex" of global security organisations working in concordat with an increasingly centralised public sector' (Fitzgibbon and Lea 2014: 24). It would equally be a mistake to assume that the State has been shrunk in respect of every aspect of political life. As we outlined in Chapter 2, at the same time as there has been a general withdrawal from the provision of publicly funded welfare provision, the penal state has expanded ever further and 'governmental policy continues to be underpinned by parallel, contrary policies which are aimed at funding more community based intervention while *expanding* the prison estate' (Corcoran 2014: 43).

## Redistribution, recognition and structural inequality

> [T]thinking should be founded on a set of social values that sees those who are vulnerable, disadvantaged or troublesome, or who have committed offences or are at risk of committing offences, as members of society and

not as excluded or liable to be excluded from it. That is not to say that they should not have their liberty restricted if necessary by imprisonment or other penalties, but that communities should still regard them as 'their own people'; communities should accept responsibility towards them; and responsibility should be expected from them in return.

*(Faulkner and Burnett 2012: 86)*

If the last 30 years of neoliberal hegemony, culminating in the 2008 global credit crunch, has taught us anything, it is that community and societal well-being cannot come from the pursuit of individual self-interest and market solutions alone. Attempts to provide a third way between the market and the State or create a so-called *Big Society* based on charitable endeavour have failed to provide a credible alternative to the collectivist project of the welfare state. Postmodern society, defined by risk, polarisation, global markets, chronic change and fragmentation, and extremes of wealth and poverty provides little in the way of a solution to structural poverty. Certainly, the neoliberal vision for the role of charity is no solution to redressing these massive inequalities.

Furthermore, neoliberalism undermines civil society because it reduces societal relations to one of 'atomized individuals making individual choices in the marketplace' (Atkinson 2012: 32). It also 'weakens the bonds that hold democracy together, because of its association with the welfare reform agenda that is driven by the political objective of ending social justice as the basis of political community' (Powell 2007: 15). What is needed then is a new civic narrative that gives expression to social justice and the politics of equality. But what would such a narrative look like? For us a reimagined community and civic engagement agenda would be underpinned by a number of principles of which the following are indicative but not exhaustive:

1.  *It would adopt a collaborative whole-system approach that constructively engages with, and invests in, the community to support social integration.* However, we acknowledge that rehabilitation and reintegration occur within a judicial/legal framework which must be given legitimacy through national legislation and guidance. In this sense, we would agree with McNeill and Williams that:

    > [j]ustice must be dispensed on a national level to ensure that systems are delivered consistently and fairly and offer the same due process protections and levels of service to all citizens. Reintegration, however, must be local because people live and find (or fail to find) a sense of belonging in localities, and because needs and resources vary between communities.
    >
    > *(McNeill and Williams 2017: 12)*

2.  *It would require arrangements for the delivery of rehabilitative services through probation and other social services to be responsive to local concerns through effective engagement with the public and their elected representatives.* This would necessitate close

collaboration with a wide range of local stakeholders and community and voluntary sector organisations.

3. *It would require local services – specifically State-sponsored probation services – to develop open and responsive approaches to engagement that are underpinned by democratic accountability.* Such accountability would necessitate governance arrangements that engage key local participants in the strategic direction and management of resources at the local level. This is required for reasons of both effectiveness and legitimacy.

4. *It would necessitate rehabilitative services targeted where they have the most impact utilising a justice reinvestment approach.* Such an approach requires engagement beyond the criminal justice system and thus '[e]fforts should be made to more clearly articulate the responsibilities of the state (and all its arms), of civil society institutions and of all citizens in supporting reintegration' (McNeill and Williams 2017: 12). This should not be organised, as with the current arrangements in England and Wales, in ways that favour private multi-nationals or large, national quasi-commercial voluntary sector organisations. Rehabilitative services should be based on values that aspire to the common good rather than a means of providing profits for shareholders.

5. *It would require the redesign of probation services so that resources are invested in those local, grassroots community organisations that build collective efficacy and social cohesion – thus helping to create desistance supporting communities.* As we have argued throughout this book, the State's role is essentially one of redistributing resources to support reintegration; not for the State to dictate from above how communities will support the rehabilitative endeavour or indeed how individuals will conduct their personal journeys towards desistance. All the evidence supports the argument that the State must work with the agentic strengths of communities and individuals. This is why probation needs to re-create networks of local partnerships with community and voluntary organisations, local authorities and civil society more generally through which it can mediate and support reintegration.

6. *Service delivery would be built around service users, rather than service providers, and view individuals with offending histories as citizens with a contribution to make rather than cases to be managed.* A reimagined vision for community and civil society would therefore encourage service users to be seen as actual or potential contributors to their communities rather than risks, threats or liabilities to them. All too often public services have either neglected or been unwilling to consider how they can connect their users together to enable them to solve problems for themselves.

7. *Reimagining rehabilitation would be part of a broader project to tackle structural inequality and promote the availability of alternative opportunities.* Our contention is that this is not just about providing improved services for those who offend as desirable and necessary as this may be, but reimagining community life and civil society in a way that benefits *all* members of civil society. Such an approach:

> while condemning crime and harm to others, would appreciate the resentment felt by people in relative poverty, especially when they are aware of the extreme wealth of others, and understand the frustration of those who feel they do not have a stake in society.
>
> *(Faulkner and Burnett 2012: 85)*

Reimagining community and civil society therefore must involve a recognition that involvement in criminal activity can often be linked to underlying inequalities. Individuals on probation need to be treated with humanity and respect, and they need to be actively engaged in the process but they also very often need practical help with problems linked to social inequality (McNeill *et al.* 2017). As Corcoran (2014) contends, failing to tackle structural exclusion only further reinforces, 'the paradox of reintegration which simultaneously demands from "ex-offenders" that they demonstrate self-governance while denying them capacity to fulfil these imperatives' (2014: 44). Research has shown that high levels of criminal justice exposure occur in the same neighbourhoods where inadequate social conditions and inter-generational multi-deprivation have persisted (Executive Session on Community Corrections 2017: 6). Equally, as Halpern (2005: 132–133) has argued, concentrated disadvantage and inequality have been shown to correlate with lower *collective efficacy* (i.e. the extent to which neighbours trust one another and join together to enforce everyday norms of acceptable behaviour).

In the reality of everyday lives and how communities operate this inclusivity is incredibly difficult to achieve. Indeed, Fraser (1996) challenges Habermas's contention that participation in the public sphere represents the expression of a civic identity and freedom on the grounds that it fails to take into account the fact that many groups (including those who have offended) are often excluded from the public domain and struggle to get their voices heard. Often, they experience *non-recognition* (being rendered invisible); or *disrespect* (being routinely maligned or disparaged in stereotypical public cultural representations and/or in everyday life interactions). This inevitably raises the issue of democratisation in terms of who should count in matters of justice (Avis 2016: 3).

We would argue, following Fraser, that acknowledging the redistributive, recognitive and representative dimensions of social justice requires both structural and cultural shifts that prioritise not only equality in the distribution of particular goods but also egalitarian social relations; that is, relationships of equal power, esteem and standing between citizens in society. This means paying more attention to building solidaristic social institutions that bring people together for common purposes. As Malloch and Munro argue, '[r]eimagining a better world generally involves future aspirations for the good of all' (2016: 2). Whilst they contend that the distribution of justice plays a key role in this process they also warn that principles of justice become meaningless or even unjust if society is structurally unequal. Thus, visions of a just, crime-free society raise questions around material and social inequalities, private ownership and power relations.

When the problem of offending is viewed through the prism of citizenship and equality in all its forms (personal, social, political and economic) reducing reoffending must of necessity be reimagined as a matter of citizenship rather than one simply of individual behaviour. This is the argument that Miller and Stuart (2017: 544) put forward when they contend that:

> [t]heorizing mass incarceration and its community analogue mass supervision as a matter of citizenship rather than a problem of behaviour (of the accused or of the accuser) moves us toward a deeper understanding of the social arrangements that contribute to and shape social action in the carceral age.

A reimagined model of community and civic society would learn:

> from desistance research and attempt a more egalitarian economic model of social inclusion where individuals, companies and agencies join forces to provide a mutually supportive environment in which all parties cooperate to create viable economic structures that support the kind of society in which they want to live.
>
> *(Armstrong and Maruna 2016: 152)*

As such, reimagining community and civil society requires tackling inequality, promoting mutual respect and enabling us all to develop and express our better selves. At its best civil society 'enables people to act both individually and collectively to define and meet their needs and those of others' (Corry and Stoker 2017: 7). At worst the institutions of civil society are vulnerable to governments seeking to abdicate their responsibilities for ensuring that the fundamental rights of their citizens to the most basic of welfare provisions are protected.

On a structural level, one of the biggest challenges is the contemporary dominance of neoliberal thinking which promotes individualism and undermines a sense of connectedness. Recent reforms that promote the primacy of the market as the allocator of social goods have undermined connectedness and consequently undermined civil society. Charitable efforts and volunteering should not and in fact cannot step up where the State has stepped down or the market failed to deliver. It certainly shouldn't act as Corcoran points out 'as a buffer for state retrenchment from social welfare while facilitating ways of socialising communities and marginalised people to cope with the perpetual competitiveness and insecurities of market society and austerity programmes' (2017: 292).

Commercialisation and consumerism within contemporary society has, we believe, ultimately undermined the collective bonds of trust and mutuality upon which recognised notions of community and civil society need to be maintained and developed. As the opening quote to this chapter suggests, put so presciently by a *reformed* offender, reciprocity is not just the return of favours but the reinforcement of the very essence of civilised society.

## References

Akman, A. (2012) Beyond the objectivist conception of civil society: Social actors, civility and self-limitation, *Political Studies*, 60: 321–340.

Alcock, P. (2012) Pete Alcock replies to Sullivan, 'A Big Society needs an active state', *Policy & Politics*, 40(1): 149–150.

Allen, R. (2015) *Rehabilitation Devolution – How Localising Justice Can Reduce Crime and Imprisonment*, London: Transform Justice.

Armstrong, R. and Maruna, S. (2016) Examining Imprisonment through a Social Justice Lens, in Farrall, S., Goldson, B., Loader, I. and Dockley, A. (eds) *Justice and Penal Reform: Re-shaping the Penal Landscape*, Abingdon: Routledge.

Atkinson, H. (2012) *Local Democracy, Civic Engagement and Community: From New Labour to the Big Society*, Manchester: Manchester University Press.

Avis, J. (2016) *Social Justice, Transformation and Knowledge: Policy, Workplace Learning and Skills*, Abingdon: Routledge.

Barker, V. (2016) Civic Repair and Penal Reform: The Role of the State in Rebuilding Trust, in Farrall, S., Goldson, B., Loader, I. and Dockley, A. (eds) *Justice and Penal Reform: Re-shaping the penal landscape*, Abingdon: Routledge, 81–99.

Bauman, Z. (1998) *In Search of Politics*, Cambridge: Polity Press.

BBC (2010) Cameron and Clegg set out 'big society' policy ideas, http://news.bbc.co.uk/1/hi/uk_politics/8688860.stm (accessed 16 April 2018).

BBC (2012) PCC results: Breakdown, www.bbc.co.uk/news/uk-politics-20361626 (accessed 27 October 2017).

Beckett Wilson, H. (2014) Criminal justice? Using a social capital theory to evaluate probation-managed drug policy, *Probation Journal*, 61(1): 60–78.

Bee, C. and Pachi, D. (2014) Active citizenship in the UK: Assessing institutional political strategies and mechanisms of civic engagement, *Journal of Civil Society*, 10(1): 100–117.

Behan, C. (2014) *Citizen Convicts: Prisoners, Politics and the Vote*, Manchester: Manchester University Press.

Blond, P. (2010) *Red Tory*, London: Faber and Faber.

Bottery, M. (2000) *Education, Policy and Ethics*, London: Continuum.

Boyd, R. (2004) Michael Oakeshott on civility, civil society and civil association, *Political Studies*, 52: 603–622.

Buck, G. (2014) Civic re-engagements amongst former prisoners, *Prison Service Journal*, Issue 214: 52–57.

Buckingham, H. and Rees, J. (2016) The Context for Service Delivery: Third Sector, State and Market Relationships 1997–2015, in Rees, J. and Mullins, D. (eds) *The third sector delivering public services: Developments, innovations and challenges*, Bristol: Policy Press.

Burke, E. (1790) *Reflections on the Revolution in France and on the Proceedings in Certain Societies in London*, London: J. Dodsley.

Burke, L. and Collett, S. (2015) *Delivering Rehabilitation: The Politics, Governance and Control of Probation*, Abingdon: Routledge.

Carlton, B., Sim, J. and Tombs, S. (forthcoming) Deaths in Sites of State Confinement: A Continuum of Routine Violence and Terror, in Read, S., Santatzoglou, S. and Wrigley, A. (eds) *Loss, Dying and Bereavement in the Criminal Justice System*, London: Routledge, 54–64.

Carter, P. (2003) *Managing Offenders, Reducing Crime*, London: Strategy Unit.

CLG (Communities and Local Government) (2010) *Decentralisation and Localism Bill: An Essential Guide*, London: HM Government.

Clinks (2015) *Early Doors: The Voluntary Sector's Role in Transforming Rehabilitation*, London: Clinks, www.clinks.org/trackTR (accessed 29 February 2016).

Cooke, G. and Muir, R. (2012) (eds) *The Relational State: How Focusing on Relationships Could Revolutionise the Role of the State*, London: IPPR, www.ippr.org/publication/55/9888/the-relational-state-how-recognising-the-importance-of-human-relationships-could-revolutionise-the-role-of-the-state (accessed 16 April 2018)

Conservative Party (2008) *A Stronger Society: Voluntary Action in the 21st Century*, Green Paper No. 5, London: Conservative Party.

Considine, M. (2003) Governance and competition: The role of non-profit organisations in the delivery of public services, *Australian Journal of Political Science*, 38(1): 63–77.

Corcoran, M. (2014) How the public sphere was privatized and why civil society could reclaim it, *Prison Service Journal*, Issue 214: 39–44.

Corcoran, M. (2017) Resilient hearts: Making affective citizens for neoliberal times, *Justice, Power & Resilience*, 1(2): 283–299.

Corry, D. and Stoker, G. (2017) The 'shared society' needs a strong civic society, NPC, www.thinknpc.org/publications/the-shared-society-needs-a-strong-civil-society/ (accessed 16 April 2018).

Davies, J.S. (2012) Active citizenship: Navigating the Conservative heartlands of the New Labour project, *Policy & Politics*, 40(1): 3–19.

Davies, J.S. and Pill, M. (2012) Empowerment or abandonment? Prospects for neighbour-hood revitalization under the big society, *Public Money & Management*, 32(3): 193–200.

Deakin, N. (2001) *In Search of Civil Society*, Basingstoke: Palgrave.

Driver, S. and Martell, L. (1997) New Labour's communitarianisms, *Critical Social Policy*, 17(52): 27–46.

Duff, A. (2016) Punishment as civic engagement, *Scottish Justice Matters*, 4(1): 17–19.

Edwards, M. (2008) *Civil Society*, Cambridge: Polity.

Ehrenberg, J. (1999) *Civil Society: The Critical History of an Idea*, New York: New York University Press.

Ehrenstein, A. (2012) *Precarity and the Crisis of Social Care: Everyday Politics and Experiences of Work in Women's Voluntary Organisations*, Cardiff: PhD thesis, Cardiff University.

Etzioni, A. (1995) *The Spirit of Community, Rights, Responsibilities and the Communitarian Agenda*, London: Fontana Press.

Executive Session on Community Corrections (2017) *Towards an Approach to Community Corrections for the 21st Century*: Consensus Document of the Executive Session on Community Corrections, Program in Criminal Justice Policy and Management, Harvard Kennedy School.

Farrall, S. (2004) Social Capital and Offender Reintegration: Making Probation Desistance Focused, in Maruna, S. and Immarigeon, R. (eds) *After Crime and Punishment: Pathways to Offender Reintegration*, Cullompton: Willan.

Farrall, S., Goldson, B., Loader, I. and Dockley, A. (2016) Introduction: Re-shaping the Penal Landscape, in Farrall, S., Goldson, B., Loader, I. and Dockley, A. (eds) *Justice and Penal Reform: Re-shaping the penal landscape*, Abingdon: Routledge, 1–8.

Farrall, S., Hunter, B., Sharpe, G. and Calverley, A. (2014) *Criminal Careers in Transition: The Social Context of Desistance from Crime*, Oxford University Press: Oxford.

Faulkner, D. (2003) Taking citizenship seriously: Social capital and criminal justice in a changing world, *Criminal Justice*, 3(3): 287–315.

Faulkner, D. and Burnett, R. (2012) *Where Next for Criminal Justice?* Bristol: Policy Press.

Faulks, K. (1998) *Citizenship in Modern Britain*, Edinburgh: Edinburgh University press.

Fitzgibbon, W. and Lea, J. (2014) Defending probation: Beyond privatisation and security, *European Journal of Probation*, 6(1): 24–41.

Fox, C. and Marsh, C. (2016) Operationalising desistance through personalisation, *European Journal of Probation*, 8(3): 185–206.

Fraser, N. (1996) *Social Justice in the Age of Identity Politics: Redistribution, Recognition, and Participation*, The Tanner Lectures on Human Values Delivered at Stanford University 30 April–2 May (printed document).

Fyfe, N.R. (2005) Making space for 'neo-communitarianism'? The third sector, state and civil society in the UK, *Antipod*, 37(3): 536–557.

Garland, D. (2001) *The Culture of Control: Crime and Social Order in Contemporary Society*, Oxford: Oxford University Press.

Garven, F. and Murray, J. (2016) Hooray for community! *Scottish Justice Matters*, 4(2): 3–5.

Halpern, D. (2005) *Social Capital*, Cambridge: Polity Press.

Harding, J. (2000) A community justice dimension to effective probation practice, *Howard Journal of Criminal Justice*, 50(4): 369–373.

Hastings, A. and Matthews, P. (2015) Bourdieu and the Big Society: Empowering the powerful in public service provision? *Policy & Politics*, 43(4): 545–560.

Hayton, R. (2012) Fixing Broken Britain, in Heppell, T. and Seawright, D. (eds) *Cameron and the Conservatives: The Transition to Coalition Government*, London: Palgrave McMillan, 136–148.

HM Government (2006) *Improving Community Involvement in Community Safety*, London: HMSO.

HM Government (2010) *Decentralisation and the Localism Bill: An Essential Guide*, London: Department for Communities and Local Government.

Home Office (2010) *Policing in the 21st Century: Reconnecting Police and the People*, London: Home Office.

Jacobs, J. (2016) From Bad to Worse: Crime, Incarceration, and the Self-wounding of Society, in Farrall, S., Goldson, B., Loader, I. and Dockley, A. (eds) *Justice and Penal Reform: Re-shaping the penal landscape*, Abingdon: Routledge, 8–27

Jordan, B. (2010) *Why the Third Way Failed: Economics, Morality and the Origins of the 'Big Society'*, Bristol: The Policy press.

Laub, J., Sampson, R., Corbett Jnr, R. and Smith, J. (1995) The Public Policy Implications of a Life-course Perspective on Crime, in Barlow, H.D. (ed.) *Crime and Public Policy: Putting Theory to Work*, Crime and Society Series, Boulder, CO: Westview Press.

Lister, S. and Rowe, M. (2015) Electing police and crime commissioners in England and Wales: Prospecting for the democratisation of policing, *Policing and Society: An International Journal of Research and Policy*, 25(4): 358–377.

Lockyer, K. and Heys, R. (2016) *Local Commissioning, Local Solutions; Devolving Offender Management*, London: Reform.

Malloch, M. and Munro, B. (2013) *Crime, Critique and Utopia*, Basingstoke: Palgrave Macmillan.

Marshall, T.H. (1950) *Citizenship and Social Class and Other Essays*, Cambridge: Cambridge University Press.

McCulloch, T. and McNeill, F. (2007) Consumer society, commodification and offender management, *Criminology and Criminal Justice*, 7(3): 223–242.

McGhee, D. (2009) The paths to citizenship: A critical examination of immigration policy in Britain since 2001, *Patterns of Prejudice*, 43(1): 41–64.

McNeill, F. (2012) Four forms of 'offender' rehabilitation: Towards an interdisciplinary perspective, *Legal and Criminological Psychology*, 17(1): 18–36.

McNeill, F. and Williams, K. (2017) *The Future of Probation*, Paper for Sam Gyimah, Minister for Prisons and Probation, further to our meeting on 22nd November 2017.

McNeill, F., Owy Thomas, M. and Thorden-Edwards, K. (2017). Helping, holding, hurting: A conversation about supervision, *The Howard Journal of Criminal Justice*, 57(1): 1–13.

Mercado, S. (2016) Punishment beyond the gate, *Scottish Justice Matters*, 4(1): 27–29.

Miller, R.J. and Alexander, A. (2016). The price of carceral citizenship: Punishment, sur-veillance and social welfare policy in an age of carceral expansion, *Michigan Journal of Race and Law*, 21(2): 291–314.

Miller, R.J. and Stuart, F. (2017) Carceral citizenship: Race, rights and responsibility in the age of mass supervision, *Theoretical Criminology*, 21(4): 532–548.

Millie, M. (2010) Moral politics, moral decline and anti-social behaviour, *People Place and Policy Online*, 4 (1): 6–13.

Ministry of Justice (2008a) *NOMS Third Sector Strategy*, London: Ministry of Justice.

Ministry of Justice (2008b) *Working with the Third Sector to Reduce Reoffending*, London: Ministry of Justice.

Muir, R. (2014) The relational state: Beyond marketization and managerialism, *Juncture*, 20(4): 280–286.

New Philanthropy Capital (2015) *The Transforming Rehabilitation Tier 1 Tendering Process: The Voluntary Sector Perspective*, London: NPC, www.thinknpc.org/publications/transforming-rehabilitation-the-voluntary-sector-perspective/ (accessed 29 February 2016).

ODPM (2005) *Citizen Engagement and Public Services: Why Neighbourhoods Matter?* London: ODPM.

Okri, B. (2018) How to combat the populism that gave us Brexit: Active citizenship, *The Guardian*, 30 Jan 2018.

Osborne, D. and Gaebler, T. (1992) *Reinventing Government: How the Entrepreneurial Spirit is Transforming the Public Sector*, Reading: Addison-Wiley.

Perez-Diaz, V. (2014) Civil society: A multi-layered concept, *Current Sociological Review*, 62(6): 812–830.

Powell, F. (2007) *The Politics of Civil Society: Big Society and Small Government*, Bristol: The Policy Press.

Prosser, B., Renwick, A., Giovannini, A., Sandford, M., Flinders, M., Jennings, W., Smith, G., Spada, P., Stoker, G. and Ghose, K. (2017) Citizen participation and changing govern-ance: Cases of devolution in England, *Policy & Politics*, 45(2): 251–269.

Putnam, R. (1993) *Making Democracy Work: The Collapse and Revival of American Community*, New York: Simon & Schuster.

Putnam, R. (2000) *Bowling Alone: The Collapse and Revival of American Community*, New York: Simon & Schuster.

Raynor, P. and Robinson, G. (2009) Why help offenders? Arguments for rehabilitation as a penal strategy, *European Journal of Probation*, 1(1): 3–20.

Redgrave, H. (2016) *Examining the Case for Justice Devolution*, GovernUp.

Rees, J. and Mullins, D. (2016) *The Third Sector Delivering Public Services: Developments, Innovations and Challenges*, Bristol: Policy Press.

Rotman, E. (1990) *The Unpunishment: A New View of the Rehabilitation of Offenders*, Westport, CN: Greenwood press.

Senior, P. and Ward, D. with Burke, L., Knight, C., Teague, M., Chapman, T., Dominey, J., Phillips, J., Worrall, A. and Goodman, A. (2016) The essence of probation, *British Journal of Community Justice*, 14(1): 9–29.

Smith, A. (1776) *The Wealth of Nations*, Penguin Classics.

Snacken, S. (2016) Punishment, Legitimacy and the Role of the State: Reimagining More Moderate Penal Policies, in Farrall, S., Goldson, B., Loader, I. and Dockley, A. (eds) *Justice and Penal Reform: Re-shaping the penal landscape*, Abingdon: Routledge, 47–69.

Taylor, R., Damm, C. and Rees, J. (2016) Navigating a New Landscape: The Third Sector Delivering Employment Services, in Rees, J. and Mullins, D. (eds) *The Third Sector Delivering Public Services: Developments, Innovations and Challenges*, Bristol: Policy Press.

Uggen, C. (2014) Foreword, in Behan, C. *Citizen convicts: Prisoners, politics and the vote*, Manchester: Manchester University Press.

Weaver, B. (2011) Co-producing community justice: The transformative potential of personalisation for penal sanctions, *British Journal of Social Work*, 41(60): 1038–1057.

Weaver, B. (2015) *Offending and Desistance: The Importance of Social Relations*, International Series on Desistance and Rehabilitation, Abingdon: Routledge.

White, A. (2013) The shadow state: Probation chiefs voice doubts about outsourcing, 7 January 2013, www.newstatesman.com (accessed 21 January 2013).

Wong, K. and Christmann, K. (2016) Justice reinvestment: 'Motherhood and apple pie?' – Matching ambition to capacity and capability, *Federal Sentencing Reporter*, 29(1): 58–67.

# 7

# CONCLUSION

## Beyond the personal – reimagining something better, fairer and more effective?

[T]he question of 'rehabilitation' is today prominent less by its contentiousness than by its growing irrelevance.

*(Bauman 2000: 210)*

[T]he Humanitarian theory wants simply to abolish Justice and substitute Mercy for it. This means that you start being 'kind' to people before you have considered their rights, and then force upon them supposed kindnesses which they in fact had a right to refuse, and finally kindnesses which no-one but you will recognize as kindnesses and which the recipient will feel as abominable cruelties.

*(Lewis 1953: 230)*

[T]the ideal of rehabilitation is played-out through different disciplinary, welfare and security rhetorics, and yet with always the same effect – of malignantly returning poorer and already-disadvantaged lawbreakers to their place at the same time as benignly keeping richer and more powerful criminals in theirs.

*(Carlen 2013: 90)*

What the punishment paradigm has wrought 'in the real world' over the past decades is disquieting; doing more of the same would be an unpardonable mistake. It is time to take a new pathway – one that draws on Americans' long-standing cultural belief in offender reformation and on the emergent 'what works' scientific literature. We should reaffirm rehabilitation as corrections' guiding paradigm.

*(Cullen 2007: 728)*

It is future victims who are now 'rescued' by rehabilitative work, rather than the offenders themselves. The practice of rehabilitation is increasingly inscribed in a framework of risk rather than a framework of welfare.

*(Garland 1997: 6)*

In discussions of rehabilitation, people often seem to be talking at cross purposes, whether writing as its advocates, critics, practitioners, subjects or merely as observers. The quotes above – all from scholars whose work we deeply admire – seem almost to be talking about different things. Bauman and Garland offer sociological observations on the fate of rehabilitation in late-modern societies (see also Robinson 2008). The meat in this sociological sandwich includes C.S. Lewis's liberal critique of rehabilitation as an affront to individual rights and autonomy, Pat Carlen's radical critique of rehabilitation's role in the perpetuation of *social* injustice and inequality and Francis Cullen's staunch defence of rehabilitation's merits as a 'guiding paradigm' for evidence-based corrections and (by implication) for the production of a safer and more just society.

Rather than surrendering to confusion or pessimism about rehabilitation, in this book, we have pursued two related purposes: (1) to make the case for reimagining rehabilitation for the twenty-first century; and (2) to provide some of the resources necessary to do so. In one sense at least, the first of these aims has been much easier to achieve than the second. Even in the first few pages of the book's Introduction and later in more detail in several of the book's chapters, we have presented evidence about how the *rehabilitation revolution* in England and Wales has gone awry; delivering privatisation but, on current evidence, very little else. There are very few informed observers who would not concur that rehabilitation today in England and Wales stands in need of reimagining, at least in terms of penal *policy*. Both in practice and in research, commitment to the development of just and effective forms of rehabilitation endures, despite the privations, absurdities and paradoxes that privatisation has produced.

That said, recognising serious problems in relation to rehabilitation's current condition does not, in itself, make the case for reimagining it; indeed, it might support the case for its abandonment. However, this still begs the question of what we are trying to abandon when we do not have a common understanding of rehabilitation is? With that in mind, given the confusion around rehabilitation's multiple meanings and forms, in the latter part of the Introduction, we set out a model of rehabilitation that one of us has developed previously (McNeill 2014) and that we hoped together to develop more fully in this book. That model's insistence on recognising the interdependencies between four forms of rehabilitation – personal, legal/judicial, moral, and political and social – clarifies not just the meanings of rehabilitation but the conditions under which it might be legitimate, just and helpful in supporting desistance. In other words, in our view, it makes the case for rehabilitation's careful reconstruction, rather than for its consignment to the rubbish heap of penal history. Furthermore, we may challenge ourselves, as Cullen and Gilbert have reminded us (see Chapter 4), to ask why a State that abandons the attempt to offer rehabilitative resources to it citizens could or would punish individuals fairly and parsimoniously in its absence. For us, a criminal justice system that offers only punishment sinks almost automatically to the lowest common denominator whilst one that aspires to the rehabilitation of individuals offers the potential for a more engaged and humanistic civil society.

However, whilst McNeill's (2014) model may help to 'de-fankle' rehabilitation's complexities and to clarify the normative case for its reimagining, it falls far short of providing the detail required for that reimagining in terms of both policy and practice. This limitation pointed us towards this book's much more ambitious second aim: to explore *how* this model might be better articulated in an effort to reimagine rehabilitation, particularly within the community where it might be supported by probation (and parole) agencies. In the process, we have also been required to assess the cultural, social and political conditions within which such reimagining might or might not become possible. Indeed, even in setting out our commitments to engagement, social action and social change we make clear our insistence on recognising the fraught, fractured and fractious relationships between criminal justice and social justice. We argue that it is on those relationships that the fate of and prospects for rehabilitation ultimately hang. In this concluding chapter, then, we summarise our analysis of what constrains rehabilitation's reimagining, and of what, we insist on hoping, might be possible if we can connect criminal and social justice.

## Escaping dystopia?

In Chapter 2, we sought to provide some sociological context for the discussion of rehabilitation's different forms in the subsequent chapters. Our specific concern was to understand what social control may mean and how it may be experienced by both penal supervisors and supervisees. Our approach drew on the conceptual insights offered by the late Stan Cohen in his seminal work *Visions of Social Control*. Although published in 1985 and before the ubiquitous application of digital technology to our personal and professional lives, Cohen's classic remains both relevant to our understanding of current realities and capable of pointing us in the direction of a less coercive and more humanistic approach to the rehabilitation.

We held fast to Cohen's intellectual insistence that modern social institutions, including criminal justice, can aspire to both *doing good* and *doing justice*. Cohen argued that that *good* and *justice* are values that should underpin a *moral pragmatism* to social interventions that must go beyond achieving simply instrumental ends. Indeed, he showed how, through the pursuit of utilitarian policies within criminal justice, there had been a dystopian spread of social control in the decades before the publication of his 1985 book. More than 30 years later, we can now see evidence of much greater expansion of penal control across (many) European and American criminal justice jurisdictions, both in the forms of *mass supervision* and *mass incarceration*. There is also evidence that, in some jurisdictions, the depth, weight and tightness (Crewe 2011) of both supervision and imprisonment have increased; in certain circumstances and for some of its subjects, penal supervision can be understood not just as *panoptical* but also as *maloptical* (McNeill 2018).

What has changed since *Visions of Social Control* is the progressive application of technological hardware and software to the supervision both of penal subjects and of penal practitioners (via the spread and development of Information and Communication Technology in the working environment). We considered the implications, pitfalls and possibilities of these developments, being careful to distinguish the *technicism* implicit in certain approaches to penal supervision from the application of technologies to supervision in general. We briefly acknowledged the challenge that the grand theorists of technological determinism offer in relation to the deployment of technology within post-industrial societies. However, we also reasserted the importance and potential of human agency (of both supervisor and supervisee) in determining whether, how and in which of its forms rehabilitation might be achieved, even where technology also plays a role.

We also widened the notion of what is meant by *technologies* within current probation practice, considering how individuals experience the application of such technologies in variable ways; from the controlling to the supportive and helpful. Drawing on the work of several scholars (McGuire, Verbeek, Phillips and Nellis), we argued that whilst the technological environment can have a deleterious impact on the business of rehabilitation, it does so only if we forget the human and moral dimensions of technology and its implementation both in the workplace and in the penal sphere.

Before concluding, we used the introduction of tagging in England and Wales as a case study in the application of one technology. Then, by drawing on experience across a number of European jurisdictions, we suggested that both the application of electronic monitoring in general and its rehabilitative utility in particular reflect the policy and professional contexts of its deployment, rather than its intrinsic technological characteristics.

We concluded Chapter 2 by arguing for the reassertion of humanistic values and for the need to develop better understandings of the ways that technologies affect the lives of both workers, in their techno-bureaucratic organisations, and supervisees within their relationships, homes and communities. Such values and such understanding can help form the basis for using technologies to help rather than merely constrain those who have started their journey towards desistance.

## Finding a way to life after crime and punishment: Personal rehabilitation

Chapter 3 aimed to help us better understand those journeys and how they can be best supported. We began by considering the relationships between ideas of transformation, personal development and desistance, arguing that not everyone involved in criminal justice needs or wants personal transformation; that personal development is a near-universal human good; and that desistance is just one aspect of this wider process of personal development.

Picking up on the cultural trope of journeys of transformation and development, we offered a brief summary of the story of *The Odyssey*, using this throughout the chapter to illustrate how challenging change can be, even for heroic kings with (some of the) gods on their side. Comparing Odysseus's situation with that of most would-be desisters, we noted how their journeys typically start from highly inauspicious beginnings. The consequences of cumulative social disadvantage – the personally borne burdens of social injustice – mean that many subjects of supervision are ill-equipped for the path ahead. That path is intended – like rehabilitation itself – to lead to social reintegration but, as we noted, in many cases it is questionable whether society has ever provided for the integration of the marginalised and disenfranchised citizens who often find their way into the penal net.

Consequently, in Figure 3.1: 'Personal rehabilitation in context' (page 65), we suggested that rehabilitation must simultaneously support the personal journey towards social integration and the collective journey to social justice. Within those twin projects, desistance from crime (or more generally, living our lives in adherence to negotiated and shared values) is one part of our individual projects of personal development. Personal rehabilitation is just one part of supporting the process of desistance, and correctional rehabilitation (and its various interventions) plays an even narrower but still significant part in supporting that process, by helping people develop some of the motivation, attitudes and skills that they may need to avoid offending.

In seeking to clarify the intended destination of the desistance journey, we also drew on a recent paper by Kirkwood and McNeill (2015) and thereby on models of reintegration within the different spheres of criminal justice and migration. This allowed us to elaborate a vision of social integration founded on a person's legal status as a citizen; facilitated both by the sorts of skills and knowledge and the sense of safety and stability necessary in order to engage with others; enabled by the development of social capital; and both marked by and substantiated through access to decent work, housing, education and health. Hence, substantive social integration cannot be separated from the redistribution, recognition and representation that Nancy Fraser (2007) argues are central to social justice.

Using the work of Bottoms and Shapland (2011), we went on to elaborate the steps on or stages of the desistance journey, exploring why people travel, how they embark (and can be derailed, often by the very agencies intended to help them) and what enables them to keep going and to make it home. We explored the role of probation supervisors (and other criminal justice professionals) in supporting that journey as navigators, advocates or guides but, crucially, not as pilots. Having briefly reviewed the developing literature on how probation might best support desistance, we settled on McNeill et al.'s (2012) summary of eight principles:

1.  First, it is clear that desistance, for people who have been involved in persistent offending, is a complex process. Criminal justice supervision must be realistic about these difficulties and find ways to manage setbacks and difficulties constructively. It needs to be recognised that it may take considerable time for supervision and support to exercise a positive effect.
2.  Relatedly, since desistance is an inherently individualised and subjective process, approaches to supervision should accommodate and address issues of identity and diversity.
3.  Desistance research also suggests that the development and maintenance of hope may be a key task for supervisors (see Farrall et al. 2014).

4. Hope may feed the discovery of self-efficacy or agency which may also be important in desistance processes. Interventions are most likely to be effective where they encourage and respect self-determination; this means working *with* would-be desisters, not *on* them.

5. Desistance can only be properly understood within the context of human and social relationships; not just relationships between supervisors and supervisees (though these matter a great deal) but also between offenders and those who matter to them (Weaver 2015). Interventions based only on developing the capacities and skills of people who have offended (human capital) will not be enough.

6. It follows that supervision must address developing social capital, and with it the opportunities to apply newly acquired skills, or to practise newly forming identities (such as *worker* or *parent*).

7. Although a focus on risks and needs may be necessary, desisters also have strengths and resources that they can use to overcome obstacles to desistance – both personal strengths and resources, and strengths and resources in their social networks. Supporting and developing these capacities can be a useful dimension of supervision.

8. Finally, the language of practice should reflect this recognition of potential; striving to more clearly endorse, certify and reinforce positive potential and development, and should seek to avoid identifying people with the behaviours we want them to leave behind.

Crucially though, as is implicit in these principles and more clearly articulated in Chapter 3, we argued that supporting personal rehabilitation cannot and must not be separated from the other three forms. Whilst we can and should think about what personal and social resources a traveller needs in order to successfully complete such an arduous journey, the journey cannot be understood without a close examination of the terrain through which s/he must travel, and without consideration of how the climate and the weather may affect her or his prospects. These broader questions of terrain, climate and weather required us to turn our attention to other key players and agencies in processes of desistance and rehabilitation: in Chapter 4 courts and judges, in Chapter 5 probation supervisors and in Chapter 6 communities and civil society.

## Reimagining sentencing for legal rehabilitation

Our concern in Chapter 4 was to understand how the business of the courts (in sentencing and the management of sentences) might provide opportunities to support people to begin or sustain a journey towards a crime-free life. Our quest was to envisage the court process and the act of sentencing as contributing significantly to the first three stages in Bottoms and Shapland's *Seven-Step Desistance Process* discussed in the previous chapter. We argued that the values, beliefs and behaviours that form the court's response to the guilty defendant – as a member of our community, as a citizen, as a participating member of the polity rather than an individual defined by the bad things they have done – are critical not only to his or her personal rehabilitation but to building social justice.

In the book's Introduction, we had already introduced the work of the penal philosopher Anthony Duff. For us, the bridge between *the legal/judicial* and the wider *social* and *moral* aspects of rehabilitation is provided by his work; specifically, his normative theory of *punishment as the communication of censure*. But we added to his theory a concern with *ritual* as part of the sentencing process, drawing upon Maruna's work on *Reentry as a rite of passage*. Overall, we tried to consider judicial decision-making within a broad context of communication and dialogue, drawing on Duff's theory to propose the court as a crucible for active dialogue between those parties that have the potential to shape and deliver rehabilitation in social and moral terms.

We also considered the lessons that can be learnt from criminal justice legislation and specifically the much-debated 1991 Criminal Justice Act, contrasting the impact of that Act with that of current legislation and exploring the challenges that surround the search for consistency in sentencing via the use of comprehensive sentencing guidelines. We argued, based on our knowledge of the lived experience of individuals subject to supervision (and imprisonment), that the pursuit of a *thin* or formal conception of consistency ignores the future collateral consequences for the individual of the sentence, as well as failing to adequately reflect the difficult personal, social and material circumstances that may affect personal culpability. More broadly, we identified a number of measures that could immediately affect the levels of punishment meted out by the courts. This is critical because more parsimonious punishment will reduce the collateral consequences of conviction but also reduce the exclusion of individuals from our communities.

We also reviewed evidence and experience about problem-solving community courts, suggesting that the communication of censure and the democratic involvement of the community in the criminal justice system may be best developed within this sort of context. However, we noted that under recent government initiatives affecting both probation and the wider court system, it is becoming increasing difficult for the type of dialogue and communication we envisage to take place, undermining the potential of sentencing to support rehabilitation.

Supporting desistance would also require the courts (and the justice system more broadly) to reflect a political commitment to use imprisonment as a last resort. Additionally, it would demand that sentencers, in their individual decision-making, call upon a much more sophisticated and nuanced definition of culpability within more open problem-solving approaches to defendant and community engagement. Finally, it would require the delivery of probation services to the court based on quality assessments of individuals and effective supervision in the community that retains the confidence of the judiciary and magistracy.

Although we chose to concentrate on the sentencing process, we remain conscious that McNeill's (2014) conceptualisation of *legal* rehabilitation stressed the restoration of rights and status *after* punishment – ultimately as the requalification to full citizenship of the individual who has offended. However, our argument is that this process of formal requalification must be set in train in the court, even as the sentence is determined and also in how it is managed thereafter (for example, in the management of compliance). In this ongoing process, the formalities of legal or judicial rehabilitation do not stand apart from *moral* and *social* rehabilitation. Indeed, the sentencing process we have envisaged requires moral engagement with and respect for individual defendants (and we would add the victims and communities) throughout the process.

Justice – in the sense of reimagining legal or judicial rehabilitation – is ultimately about communication and dialogue. If individuals want to be restored to full citizenship, they must speak (however indirectly) to the victims and the communities they have harmed. However, if they must give an account of themselves, their actions and their future intentions as a citizen and member of the polity, then surely that must be heard by the court. The court will also have to speak and censure will be part of what the court communicates but often justice may require it to recognise the prior failings of the unjust State, and always, justice will require it to recognise the roles and responsibilities of the State and the community in rehabilitation and reintegration. Moreover, beyond the moment of sentencing, judges and magistrates (along with other criminal justice workers) must sustain a meaningful dialogue with those who have offended, not just to assist in the restorative process but also to support their desistance journeys. More broadly still, the wider polity must be continuously engaged in open and democratic dialogue about when, how and how much we punish and about how we rehabilitate.

## Reimagining probation practice for moral and political rehabilitation

Moving from sentencing in general to the implementation of probation sentences in particular, in Chapter 5 we explored how the dialogue required for moral and political rehabilitation might be best supported by probation staff. We began by acknowledging that desistance often involves a significant array of emotions and feelings. Individuals may need help in making choices and further support in dealing with the consequences; in this context, supervision involves considerable moral complexity. This chapter then sought to reimagine moral rehabilitation by analysing the values, skills and attributes required to support desistance journeys, focusing on the professional, organisational and occupational contexts that shape probation practice. We briefly reviewed some of the insights provided by Lipsky's famous work on *street-level bureaucracy* to help us to understand *punishment in practice*, making sense of how these professional, organisational and occupational cultures and structures influence rehabilitative work.

First, we outlined *professionalism from above*, as represented in central government policies and approaches that have sought to control local semi-autonomous probation services through performance targets and management to the marketisation of rehabilitative services. Second, we contrasted this approach with *professionalism from within* which speaks to a very different set of concerns focused on the relational and practice skills which practitioners themselves identify as being crucial in their work. We reviewed the increasing international evidence that these skills are associated with effectiveness in reducing reoffending, not just in their use with individual supervisees but also in their use within supportive staff groups.

Our analysis then switched to the politics of delivering rehabilitation and specifically the way in which organisational change has been experienced in England and Wales under the UK Government's *Transforming Rehabilitation* initiative. We charted the differentiated impact on staff and the means by which they adapt to the new arrangements of a National Probation Service and the privatised Community Rehabilitation Companies. We also considered how this has begun to impact upon broader occupational and professional cultures and, thereby, on the core values, skills and attributes that have been seen as central to probation over the years. Our concern is the lasting impact that the 'organizational bifurcation' (Burke and Collett 2016) brought about by the *Transforming Rehabilitation* reforms has had on what are now two separate organisational structures. Indeed, as we noted in Chapter 5, successive HMI Reports have highlighted the problems emerging from this fragmentation of service delivery. The most recent of these (HMI Probation 2018) uncovered a reluctance amongst some NPS staff to purchase services from the CRC. This was not limited to concerns over cost and quality but reflected a deeper 'enduring cultural dimension: professional probation staff do not see themselves as purchasers, and most do not want to be' (HM Inspectorate of Probation 2018: 13)

The penultimate section of the chapter was concerned with the legitimacy of rehabilitative practices and whether and to what extent the process of privatisation has impacted on this. We considered this question in relation to probation's external audiences (for example the courts) but also in relation to its internal audiences, since legitimacy with supervisees is vital to effective and ethical practice – and thus to rehabilitation. In the light of the burgeoning critique of *Transforming Rehabilitation* from official, academic and practitioner sources, we also discussed legitimacy in terms of the broader role of the private sector in corrections and the stages through which managerialisation, commodification and privatisation have re-shaped the penal system, in ways that, we would argue, undermine its public legitimacy.

We concluded by arguing that the recent organisational and occupational changes to probation in England and Wales seem inimical to those values and approaches that underpin effective practice. More than that, however, if rehabilitation is a dialogical moral undertaking, it is one that cannot be confined to supervisor and supervisee but must include the wider polity in addressing the harms done to those who offend as well as the harm done to individuals and communities. This kind of dialogue cannot and must not be instrumentalised, commodified and commercialised. Indeed, those processes make it impossible. It may be possible to 'manage offenders' through privatised systems and processes, but it is not possible to rehabilitate and reintegrate people through systems and processes; these challenges require a skilfully mediated engagement of citizens with citizens in communities, not of commissioners with contractors in markets.

## Reimagining community and civil society for social rehabilitation

In Chapter 6, we therefore turned to an examination of the crucial contribution that civil society could make to rehabilitation, exploring this through the lenses of citizenship, community and social capital. Our concern though was not solely limited to reducing individual reoffending alone, because we insist on seeing rehabilitation as an important component in the dispensation and development of justice that has both a social and moral dimension. These processes are *social* in the sense that rehabilitation seeks to promote the restoration or establishment of social bonds that will support the (re)integration of the individuals in communities, strengthening informal social control and collective efficacy. They are *moral* processes in that they involve what society ought, or ought not, to do, both in relation to those who have offended, and in relation to the pursuit of social justice.

More specifically, in addition to the individual's obligation to make good for offending, we argued that the community and the State must accept a duty to support rehabilitation. That duty rests on two principles. First, to the extent that the community and the State bear some complicity in permitting or exacerbating criminogenic social inequalities, they too must make good. Second, even under a retributivist approach to punishment, the polity has a duty to make sure that the punishment ends and that there is no punishment beyond the legal sanction. Both principles necessitate the engagement of the State and community in the rehabilitative project.

Yet, we also recognised that we write at a time when the State is seeking to devolve responsibility for rehabilitation to or through the market, and when probation has become increasingly remote from the communities it serves. Whilst communities should not and cannot be seen as panaceas for resolving social ills (especially where they have been impoverished and neglected by the State), they do have many resources, networks, groups and relationships that can support rehabilitation. The concept of *social capital* has been employed as a means of explaining how an environment of mutual trust, once created, helps to build up a bank of shared, relational resources that can support and sustain a whole variety of social goods. In fact, the evidence suggests that more equal societies with higher degrees of confidence in State authorities and higher levels of social trust have a propensity towards less crime, higher norm compliance and policing that is less brutal and more fair. Conversely, those societies with higher rates of incarceration and other forms of penal control tend to have lower levels of equality, reciprocity and trust.

Whilst ideas and practices of solidarity, democracy, trust and legitimacy are crucial in shaping practices of crime control and punishment, we also need to explore the reverse idea – namely that police, criminal justice and penal institutions can and should be civic agents, part of whose purpose is to contribute to the maintenance, repair and strengthening of social bonds, extending and deepening processes of democratic inclusion.

We therefore traced the development of ideas around civil society from the *agora* (public place) of Greek society to contemporary notions of the shadow state and of civil society. We identify a number of related themes that have dominated thinking in England and Wales around supposedly declining standards of morality and civility; the needs for active citizens, empowered communities, and democratic participation; the case for decentralisation, devolution and choice; and marketisation, privatisation and the mixed economy of welfare.

Here, we must revisit briefly the role of voluntary sector organisations. As we outlined in Chapter 6, the aspirations, in part, of the *Transforming Rehabilitation* reforms where that the CRCs would, through commissioning structures, involve the expertise of voluntary organisations and set up new supply chains. However, as we write, HMI Probation have released a thematic inspection of probation supply chains that highlights the fact that such provision is far less than anticipated 'and set to get thinner still' (HM Inspectorate of Probation 2018: 5) as the CRCs look to achieve further efficiencies to shore up their own precarious financial position. What this suggests is not just a *technical failure* in respect of the commissioning of services but the abject misunderstanding by the State of the moral and social dimensions to rehabilitation. Whether looking at voluntary endeavour through the lens of individual volunteering or the contribution of the organised VCS, it is the importance of moral engagement with individuals on their desistance journeys and the social engagement of community organisations – utilising the strengths of civil society – that are critical to rehabilitation. In this sense commissioning, as it is defined and used within the neoliberal technicalities of business design, is clearly at odds with these individuals and civic aspirations. Social and moral relationships *cannot be commissioned* but they *can be developed* over time.

We concluded that the manifest failures of the last 30 years of neoliberal hegemony show that community and societal well-being cannot come from the pursuit of individual self-interest and market solutions. Attempts to provide a third way between the market and the State or to create a so-called *Big Society* based on charitable endeavour have failed to provide a credible alternative to the collectivist project of the welfare state. We argued that a new civic narrative that gives expression to social justice and the politics of equality is required and for us a reimagined community and civic engagement agenda would:

- adopt collaborative *whole system* approaches that constructively engage with and invest in the communities to support social integration;
- deliver rehabilitation through probation and other social services that are responsive to local concerns through effective engagement with the public and their elected representatives;
- require local services delivered by open and responsive criminal justice organisations that are underpinned by democratic accountability;

- focus resources where they could have the most impact, utilising a *justice reinvestment* approach;
- require the redesign of probation services that would include the investment of resources in local grassroots community organisations crucial to social integration;
- be built around the people who use services, rather than the organisations that provide them, viewing people with convictions as citizens rather than merely as cases or risks to be managed.

Ultimately, we argued that reimagining rehabilitation must be part of a broader project to tackle structural inequality and promote social justice. Our contention is that this isn't just about providing improved services for people who have offended, as desirable and necessary as this may be. Rather it is about reimagining community life, civil society and the (welfare) State in a way that benefits all of us. Acknowledging the redistributive, recognitive and representative dimensions of social justice requires cultural, political and social change that not only prioritises the promotion of equality in the distribution of particular goods, but also egalitarian social relations; that is, relationships of equal power, esteem and standing between citizens in society. This means paying more attention to building social institutions that support solidarity, bringing people together for common purposes and in our common interests.

## Engagement, social action and social change

We have argued that public support for and engagement in rehabilitation is essentially a form of social action and, potentially, a driver of social change. Our overall approach has reflected an understanding of the complex nature of rehabilitation, exploring its four forms (legal, social, personal and moral). But first, and more broadly, we admit that we write from a normative perspective that reflects a number of specific themes. We hold that:

- working with those who have offended and been prosecuted is an inescapably moral and political activity. Worker and client will have moral and political views (whether implicit or explicit, cogent or chaotic) about the nature of crime, the culpability of the individual and the wider *causes* of crime and criminalisation;
- supervision involves the exercise of legally legitimated authority that allows one citizen to exercise highly unusual forms of power over another. Such work must therefore be conducted within a framework of professional ethics and standards and within a system of both criminal justice and legal rights and responsibilities;
- rehabilitation also takes place within the context of political processes that determine how and where resources should be spent on crime and justice,

who is and is not defined as an *offender* and how long and with what consequences they must carry such a label;

- crimes that are processed through the criminal justice system are mainly the crimes of the poor. This is not an accident; the power of criminal justice is often deployed (and restrained) so as to protect the interests of the powerful. Criminal in/justice is thus inescapably linked with social and economic in/justice. Any discussion of working with people who have offended must be located within a discussion of inequality in all its forms;

- a consequence of seeing crime and criminal justice in these ways is that, for us, rehabilitation can only be reimagined *as a dialogue* between citizens, and as being *in dialogue* with debates about social and political change. Our own analyses and prescriptions must and do reflect our moral and political principles (always also in dialogue with evidence) which are expressed not least in commitment to the minimisation of the use of incapacitating and repressive punishment in all its forms;

- reimagining rehabilitation requires, on the one hand, a highly strategic *national* focus on the rights and responsibilities of all the actors in the criminal justice system, reflecting the key role of the Criminal Courts and the implementation of national sentencing legislation and, on the other hand, the need to locate delivery mechanisms within *local* government and local communities;

- some people who have offended have highly complex needs that are nonetheless amenable to sophisticated and sometimes quite technical approaches to their rehabilitation. Nevertheless, reimagining rehabilitation requires the reassertion of the ability of individuals *themselves* to turn their lives around, with (and sometimes without) the active support and commitment of significant others, including criminal justice professionals;

- although professional status can be a source of power through which the interests of individual clients may sometimes be marginalised or diminished, professional roles and organisational and occupational cultures can also empower and support individuals in pursuit of their own legitimate goals;

- public engagement in and support for rehabilitative endeavour is a critically important but commonly neglected resource; one that must work alongside the skilled support of criminal justice professionals/agencies;

- technological approaches to punishing offenders do not, of necessity, need to be coercive and negatively experienced by the individual. Almost all approaches to supervision can be experienced as punishment and simultaneously as rehabilitative help. However, it must be of concern that certain approaches, particularly those employing new technologies have tended to be implemented in ways that prioritise constraint and control over change;

- the failure of rehabilitation to secure political support can lead to excessive levels of coercion in the community and increased levels of imprisonment;

- practical and utopian ideas can and must exist together.

## Final words: Finding our way home

Perhaps a little like desistance journeys, this book has taken us (and we hope you) on a long and winding road. As guides and navigators, we have attempted to provide a map at the outset – laying out the four inter-related forms of rehabilitation that we wanted to explore. That map was just a sketch of some of the main features of four over-lapping and interdependent territories – personal, legal/judicial, moral and social. The rest of the book has been exploratory and, as we have tried to travel deep into each territory, we have charted the terrain as we currently find it, however bleak and infertile it might be. We have also tried to point the way towards a better place; one with gentler and more fertile terrain, better weather and a climate in which human society can flourish. In this final chapter, we have tried to summarise both the lie of the land and what possibilities we can see over the horizon and how we might start to travel from here to there.

The challenge of reimagining is never an easy one; and when the subject of reimagining is as complex and contested as rehabilitation, the challenges multiply. However, as Albert Dzur, Ian Loader and Richard Sparks have argued in a series of important publications (Dzur *et al.* 2016; Loader 2010; Loader and Sparks 2010, 2012, forthcoming), we have no alternative but to confront these challenges. In a forthcoming paper, Loader and Sparks cite the pragmatist philosopher Roberto Mangabeira Unger's pithy observations on *unfreezing the present*:

> If I propose something distant, you may say: interesting, but Utopian. If I propose something close, you may answer: feasible but trivial. In contemporary efforts to think and talk programmatically, all proposals are made to seem either Utopian or trivial. We have lost confidence in our ability to imagine structural change in society, and fall back upon a surrogate standard: a proposal is realistic if it approaches what already exists. It is easy to be a realist if you accept everything.
>
> *(Unger 1998: 36)*

We would rather risk being accused of Utopianism than 'accept everything' as it is; indeed, politically and personally, we cannot accept things as they are, if we identify them as unjust. We have tried therefore both to offer critical assessments of the present and to express what Loader and Sparks would call 'reasonable hopes' for rehabilitation's future. It is always easier to critique than to construct but both tasks are necessary. The former without the latter seems cowardly; the latter without the former seems foolish. Doubtless *both* our critiques *and* our constructions have flaws – and we would welcome the efforts of others to identify and address those; even more so if those critics are prepared to risk offering constructions of their own. Ultimately, all that we hope for this book is that it offers some of the resources that we need to imagine rehabilitation as something better, fairer and more effective than it is today.

# References

Bauman, Z. (2000) Social issues of law and order, *British Journal of Criminology*, 40(2): 205–221.

Bottoms, A. and Shapland, J. (2011) Steps towards Desistance among Young Adult Recidivists, in Farrall, S., Hough, M., Maruna, S. and Sparks, R. (eds) *Escape Routes: Contemporary Perspectives on Life After Punishment*, London: Routledge, 43–80.

Burke, L. and Collett, S. (2016) Transforming rehabilitation: Organizational bifurcation and the end of probation as we knew it? *Probation Journal*, 63(2): 120–135.

Carlen, P. (2013) Penal Imaginaries: Against Rehabilitation; For Reparative Justice, in Carrington, K., Ball, M., O'Brien, E. and Tauri, J.M. *Crime, Justice and Social Democracy*, London: Palgrave, 89–104.

Cohen, S. (1985) *Visions of Social Control: Crime, Punishment and Classification*, Cambridge: Polity Press.

Crewe, B. (2011) Depth, weight, tightness: Revisiting the pains of imprisonment, *Punishment and Society*, 13(5): 509–529.

Cullen, F. (2007) Make rehabilitation corrections' guiding paradigm, *Criminology and Public Policy*, 6(4): 717–728.

Dzur, A., Loader, I. and Sparks, R. (eds) (2016) *Democratic Theory and Mass Incarceration*, Oxford: Oxford University Press.

Farrall, S., Hunter, B., Sharpe, G. and Calverley, A. (2014) *Criminal Careers in Transition: The Social Context of Desistance from Crime*, Oxford: Oxford University Press.

Fraser, N. (2007) Reframing Justice in a Globalizing World, in Lovell, T. (ed.) *Misrecognition, Social Inequality and Social Justice. Nancy Fraser and Pierre Bourdieu*, London and New York: Routledge, 17–35.

Garland, D. (1997) Probation and the Reconfiguration of Crime Control, in Burnett, R. (ed) *The Probation Service: Responding to Change, Proceedings of the Probation Studies Unit First Colloquium*, Probation Studies Unit Report No. 3, Oxford: University of Oxford Centre for Criminological Research.

HM Inspectorate of Probation (2018) *Probation Supply Chains: A Thematic Inspection by HM Inspectorate of Probation April 2018*, Manchester: HMIP.

Kirkwood, S. and McNeill, F. (2015) Integration and reintegration: Comparing pathways to citizenship through asylum and criminal justice, *Criminology & Criminal Justice*, 15(5): 511–526.

Lewis, C.S. (1953) The humanitarian theory of punishment, *Res Judicatae*, 6(230): 224–230.

Loader, I. (2010) For penal moderation: Towards a new public philosophy of punishment, *Theoretical Criminology*, 14(3): 349–367.

Loader, I. and Sparks, R. (2010) *Public Criminology?* London: Routledge.

Loader, I. and Sparks, R. (2012) *Beyond Lamentation: Towards a Democratic Egalitarian Politics of Crime and Justice*, Edinburgh School of Law Research Paper No. 2012/23, Edinburgh: University of Edinburgh.

Loader, I. and Sparks, R. (forthcoming) *Reasonable Hopes: Social Theory, Critique and Reconstruction in Contemporary Criminology*.

McNeill, F. (2014) Punishment as Rehabilitation, in Bruinsma, G. and Weisburd, D. (eds) *Encyclopedia of Criminology and Criminal Justice*, DOI 10.1007/978-1-4614-5690-2, New York: Springer Science and Business Media, 4195–4206.

McNeill, F. (2018) Mass supervision, misrecognition and the 'Malopticon', *Punishment and Society*, first published 29 January, 2018, https://doi.org/10.1177/1462474518755137.

McNeill, F., Farrall, S., Lightowler, C. and Maruna, S. (2012) Re-examining 'evidence-based practice' in community corrections: Beyond 'a confined view' of what works, *Justice Research and Policy*, 14(1): 35–60.

Robinson, G. (2008) Late-modern rehabilitation: The evolution of a penal strategy, *Punishment and Society*, 10(4): 429–445.

Unger, R. (1998) *Democracy Realized: The Progressive Alternative*, London: Verso.

Weaver, B. (2015) *Offending and Desistance: The Importance of Social Relations*, London: Routledge.

# INDEX

Note: page numbers in italic type refer to Figures; those in bold type refer to Tables.